Rethinking Social Work

Rethinking Social Work

Towards critical practice

LONGMAN

An imprint of
Addison Wesley Longman

Jim Ife

Addison Wesley Longman Australia Pty Limited
95 Coventry Street
South Melbourne 3205 Australia

Offices in Sydney, Brisbane and Perth, and associated companies
throughout the world.

Designed by Designpoint
Set in 10/12 pt Trump Mediaeval
Printed in Malaysia through Addison Wesley Longman China Ltd, PP

National Library of Australia
Cataloguing-in-Publication data

Ife, J. W. (James William), 1946– .
    Rethinking social work: towards critical practice.

    Bibliography.
    Includes index.
    ISBN 0 582 80694 1.

    1. Social service – Australia – Philosophy. 2. Social
    work education – Australia. 3. Social service –
    Political aspects – Australia. I. Title.

361.301

Contents

Acknowledgements

My own 'rethinking' of social work, which is reflected in this book, has been a difficult but exciting personal journey, and there are many who have helped me along the way. Most of them cannot be named here, partly because there are so many, and partly because it is impossible to remember all the influences on my thinking over the past twenty years during which many of these ideas were formulated. I am particularly indebted to many past and present students—with whom I have discussed these ideas both formally in seminars or supervision and informally in a variety of settings—who have contributed many things to this book. Colleagues at the University of Western Australia and at Curtin University, as well as other academic colleagues throughout Australia and overseas, have remained an important source of support and inspiration, and I am also indebted to my many friends in the social work profession and in various community change organisations. The people who commented favourably on my previous book have helped to convince me that I might indeed have something useful to say, and that writing books is worthwhile.

Stuart Rees has had a particular influence on this book. The first version of Chapter 2, from which the rest of the book eventually developed, was drafted immediately after hearing his paper at the 1994 conference of the Australian

Association for Social Work and Welfare Education, and was directly influenced by his vision. He also helped to convince Longman Australia (now Addison Wesley Longman) that the project was worthwhile, and read through the final draft making many helpful comments and suggestions. Stuart's vigorous campaigning against economic rationalism and managerialism, and in favour of an assertive and empowering social work based on a humanist vision, was a constant source of inspiration while this book was being written.

Heather D'Cruz, Lucy Fiske and Angela Perkins provided invaluable help in undertaking library research to support the writing of this book, and also read through drafts and provided many helpful comments. Tina Fernandes, Anne Markiewicz, Sonia Tascon, Jo Worswick and Susan Young also read a draft of the manuscript, and their many suggestions have made this a much better book than it otherwise might have been.

At Addison Wesley Longman, it was largely due to Sandra Rigby's initial enthusiasm for the project that the book was eventually written. After Sandra left the company, the publisher's role was taken over by Ron Harper, and then seen through to conclusion by Peter van Vliet. All three have been very helpful and supportive in the process. Carmen Riordan has again proved to be an extremely helpful, supportive and co-operative editor.

Finally, my very special thanks to Gwynneth, Julia and Bronwyn, for their continued love and support.

JIM IFE

Introduction

This book was written out of a sense of outrage at the increasingly uncaring and oppressive environment in which social workers are required to work, a sense of concern for new graduates trying to find their way in this hostile environment as they seek to implement their idealism and vision of social justice, and a sense of solidarity with those who are struggling to formulate some sort of critical or alternative social work practice. It was also written out of a personal commitment to social work, a vision of social justice, and a belief that social workers have both the capacity and the obligation to work towards an alternative system, in the interests of a better world, and coincidentally in the interests of their own professional survival. Although the book attempts to maintain an analytic and conceptual perspective, and is in that sense an academic work, it is far from dispassionate, and is certainly neither value-free nor politically neutral; indeed it is written from a conviction that such neutrality is impossible in social work, because of the essentially ideological nature of all social work theory and practice.

Economic rationalism, also known as neo-conservatism, the new right, Thatcherism, Reaganomics and other less complimentary terms, has increasingly dominated the practice environment of social workers. It attacks and undermines the fundamental value base of social work as well as the social democratic values that have represented social work's ideological mainstream. It also attacks and undermines the structures within which social work has located itself, by its attempts to dismantle the welfare state as a significant location for the meeting of human need. Economic rationalism has been embraced by both major political parties in Australia, and indeed has become increasingly uncontested in political discourse throughout the Western world. The globalisation of the economy and the power of trans-national capital have meant that any political party aspiring to office has had to incorporate the policies of economic rationalism or face the wrath of 'the market', which has the power to ruin economies and nations overnight.

Social work has always been a contradictory and perplexing profession, having to balance the competing demands of a society that wants both to help and to control the disadvantaged, usually at the same time. Social workers are expected to fill both roles, supplying some form of 'caring control' or 'controlling care'. It has long been accepted that these contradictions are part of social work, and that social workers will inevitably struggle in their attempts to make difficult moral decisions on behalf of a society which may subscribe to a rhetoric of justice, equality, democracy and freedom, but which in reality is unjust, unequal, coercive and oppressive.

Living with contradictions and having to make difficult moral choices is nothing new for social workers, but the political context of economic rationalism and the organisational context of managerialism have made the job much more difficult, and have forced social workers to make major reassessments of where they stand, and of the nature of the social work task. The political nature of social work practice can no longer be set aside (if it ever could be), and for increasing numbers of social workers the context of their practice requires a more overt, sophisticated and informed political response. The aim of this book is to clarify the nature of some of the choices facing social work, and to outline some possible directions for a critical or alternative form of practice. Social workers, because of their contradictory location within the modern welfare state, and because of their insistence on linking the personal and the political, are in a key position to undertake critical practice aimed at articulating a critique of the oppressive nature of economic rationalism and managerialism, and establishing an alternative.

Chapter 1 examines a number of assumptions inherent in the way social workers have constructed their professional identity, and shows how these do not fit well with the changing political and organisational context of practice. This is followed by a brief canvassing of some possible future scenarios, to provide a backdrop for the subsequent exploration. Chapter 2 presents a framework for understanding the competing discourses of human services, and uses this framework to identify some of the issues and dilemmas facing social workers as they attempt to relocate their practice in a changing environment. In Chapter 3, this framework is then reconstructed, and related to conceptualisations of postmodernism and feminism, each of which is shown to be important, though not of itself sufficient, as a basis for a critical or alternative social work. In Chapter 4 a similar conclusion is reached in relation to a humanist ideal; the centrality of a humanist vision is fundamental to social work, but it needs to be set alongside an adequate structural analysis of humanism. The chapter concludes with a humanist vision based on a universal discourse of human rights linked to a relativist discourse of needs. Chapter 5 outlines a version of critical theory as a framework for understanding social work theory and practice, drawing on the discussion of previous chapters. This is followed in Chapter 6 by a consideration of the relationship between policy and practice, and the ways in which social workers might more effectively participate in the policy arena. Finally in Chapter 7 some of the implications and possibilities of a critical social work are outlined.

Rethinking Social Work is located in the Australian context, and has been written primarily for social workers and students in Australia who are seeking creative responses to the political and organisational dilemmas of practice. There are, however, significant parallels in other Western nations, as many of the challenges facing Australian social work do not have a specifically Australian origin, but are the consequence of transnational forces. In the era of globalisation, the experiences of social workers who are working in the decaying welfare states of Western democracies are depressingly similar. They are the consequence of the same processes, and many of the issues raised in this book will no doubt resonate with the experience of social workers in other contexts.

Setting the context

A disillusioned profession

The context of social work practice has changed significantly in the last decade, and social work, as conceptualised, taught and practised, has not been able to keep up with that change. This is, at least in part, because the changes in the political, economic and ideological environment are seen by many social workers to be fundamentally contradictory to the values of the profession; it is not easy to adapt to a changing environment if that means compromising the very values that make up the foundation of social work practice. Social workers find themselves in an unfriendly, if not downright hostile, practice environment, which is problematic for someone who genuinely believes that the role of social work is to make the world a better place, and to further the cause of social justice by seeking to empower the disadvantaged. It can be a rude shock to discover not only that this is an unfashionable value position, but that government policy, management practice and powerful media all serve to obstruct, rather than to facilitate, social workers in seeking to achieve that worthy goal.

Social work's strong value position, and its insistence on locating itself within a social and political analysis, has led social workers to be less than fully accommodating to the demands of the new managerialism, specified competencies, privatisation and economic rationalism. Some other professions, especially within the health field, have been more ready to adopt new procedures, and to redefine their existing practice to fit the prevailing ideology. As a result, many social workers fear that their ideological scruples may leave them 'out in the cold' as they see 'valuable ground' surrendered to nurses, occupational therapists, health workers, psychologists and others.

This fear of losing territory is not the only problem facing social workers trying to come to terms with the reality of practice in the 1990s. There is a widespread concern among social workers that present structures of human service delivery are not adequately meeting the needs of their clients, because of declining resources and because of the way that service delivery is defined within an increasingly managerial paradigm (Bates and Linder-Pelz 1990). Far from furthering the aims of empowerment and social justice, many service structures are seen by social workers as disempowering, and as reinforcing processes of disadvantage. Policy and management decisions often do not facilitate effective social work practice; rather they militate against it.

It is not only the clients who are disadvantaged by the economic, social and political orthodoxies of the day, but social workers as well. For many, social work has ceased to be professionally rewarding, and has become a simple matter of survival. Many social workers report increasing levels of stress; burn-out is not uncommon; and morale in many social agencies seems to be extremely low (Rees and Rodley 1995). Anxieties about the increased possibility of litigation, or appeals against their decisions, do not make social workers any more comfortable, given the increasing trend for aggrieved consumers to pursue redress through the legal system, and social workers fear becoming the scapegoats of the inadequacies of public welfare. Public and media perceptions, frequently blaming social workers for the inadequacies of the system, do not help the self-image of social work.

This book seeks to locate contemporary social work within its social, organisational and political context, in order to

2

understand why social work has reached this point of crisis. Far from advocating that social work should adapt to these changes, it provides a framework not only for analysis, but for the development of an alternative form of social work practice that can confront these issues in a more effective and positive way. It is written in the belief that social work has much to contribute in developing human services that more effectively meet the aims of empowerment and social justice, and it seeks to provide social workers with a basis from which to engage the dominant order and to influence both the policy discourse and practice reality.

The professional tradition

Social work has never been a single entity, and all generalisations about it, including those in the previous paragraphs, run the risk of over-simplification. Modern social work had several historical origins: the 'scientific charity' of the Charity Organisation Society; the need for social control and regulation of the poor in order to maintain political and social stability, the social development ideals of the settlement houses, the peace movement of Jane Addams; the 'enlightened socialism' and social administration of the British Fabians; and so on (Woodroofe 1962). These different and conflicting origins, together with a variety of influences such as Freudian psychotherapy, behaviourism, Marxism, empiricism, feminism, postmodernism and many others, mean that social work has always been a complex and pluralist occupation, whose essential nature has been strongly contested. To this can be added the different constructions of social work in different countries; despite some attempts to develop universally applicable models of social work practice, social work has, for good reasons, developed differently in different places. Australian, British, American, Canadian and New Zealand social work are all different from each other in several important respects, and the differences become greater still with countries where there is more cultural and language variation.

Despite this diversity, in the Australian context one can still make some generalisations about a 'mainstream' construction of social work, reflecting an educational and practice orthodoxy that developed up to the early 1980s, and represents

3

the assumptions on which many social workers, and social work educators, still base their practice. This mainstream construction has always had its critics (e.g., the radical social work movement of the 1970s), but it is summarised here as representing a common heritage of contemporary social work.

For the purposes of the following discussion, this heritage incorporates six characteristics: social work is seen as providing *services*, it is located primarily within the context of the *welfare state*, it is seen as a *profession*, it a *generalist* occupation, it is a *secular* occupation, and it involves the integration of *knowledge, skills and values*.

Services

While social work roles can be described in a variety of ways, a social worker is generally understood as providing *services* for people. Often this is in the context of a wider category of services, such as 'health services' or 'services for the aged', while at other times the service involved is more specific, an example being 'counselling services'. This locates social work within a broader category of 'human services' or 'social services', but for present purposes it is the notion of *service* that is important. The idea of service originated with the notion of the servant, and in this context providing a service means to do what another requests or requires. Here the master/mistress has the power to determine what the servant will do, and the provider of service must do the will of the person to whom the service is given. Thus the power is largely if not exclusively with the recipient rather than the provider of the service. This assumption of power is still present in the notion of 'service industries', which are there to meet the expressed needs and demands of the consumer.

The modern discourse of social work and social policy, however, has significantly changed the idea of service. Like many other ideas, it has become commodified, in that a service is now understood as something that can be traded, measured, provided, and frequently quantified and priced (Dingwall Eekelaar and Murray 1995). Talking about a service in the same way as one might talk about a physical entity completely changes its meaning and significance, and in consequence the 'giving of service' becomes essentially a technical exercise. The power relationship in service provision is also changed—indeed reversed. Providing services in a professional relationship defines the professional (or giver of service) as the expert who really knows what is required, rather than as the servant who is there to do the master's or mistress' bidding. The person receiving the service becomes the passive recipient in a process that is essentially controlled by the professional expert (Illich et al. 1977). The servant, through the commodification and professionalisation of service, has become the master, and ironically often has a qualification called a 'master's degree' to prove the point.

One of the assumptions behind the provision of 'social services', by people like social workers, is that it is an effective way to deal with, or 'solve', social problems. This is consistent with the liberal reformist view of social problems (Taylor-Gooby and Dale 1985), and is an assumption behind a good deal of state intervention in people's lives. It is also an assumption behind social work—the provision of social work 'services' becomes the preferred way to deal with social problems from unemployment, poverty and juvenile crime, through to mental illness, intellectual disability and domestic violence (Graycar 1990; Mullaly 1993). If there is a perceived problem the conventional policy response is to set up services for those involved (whether victims, perpetrators or relatives). This view of social problems, however, has for some time been under challenge, both in academic circles and in the popular media. Critics from the left point to the ineffectiveness of the social services in counteracting structural disadvantage (George and Wilding 1984; Gough 1979), while those on the right criticise the 'welfare mentality' and dependency created by the increasing public provision of human services. No longer can social workers accept that most of the population think the services they provide are automatically a 'good thing' and are worthy of support. From being relatively uncontroversial and highly valued, the notion of social work services is becoming increasingly problematic, and so the legitimacy of the social workers who provide those services is increasingly questioned.

The welfare state

The conventional heritage of social work, in the Australian context, is that its services are largely provided through the structures of the welfare state. Social work education has been strongly influenced by British writers in the Fabian tradition such as Richard Titmuss (1968, 1974), T. H. Marshall (1965), R. H. Tawney (1954) and David Donnison (1991)—strong advocates of the welfare state as the mechanism for a civilised society to meet the needs of its citizens, as a matter of right, and to bring about a fairer and more just society through the provision of a wide range of programs and services for all. The emphasis is on an institutional approach to welfare, with a strong package of universal programs and benefits, supplemented where necessary with selective targeted programs for the most disadvantaged. The corresponding higher levels of taxation and government spending were seen not as an impediment to prosperity, but as the cost of a decent, civilised society where human well-being was valued above all. This view found its Australian counterpart in the writings of, among others, Hugh Stretton (1987) and H. C. Coombs (1981, 1990), and in the policies and programs of the Whitlam government of 1972 to 1975.

These ideals have been very influential in social work. Generations of social work students have been exposed to the inspiring writings of Titmuss and others, and have come to share this vision of a strong welfare state. Social workers have reacted to the dismantling of the welfare state by seeking to defend it and to fight the 'cuts' in public programs. Social work itself is largely practised within the structures of the welfare state, with most social workers employed either directly within government agencies or in non-government agencies that are largely supported by government funding programs. In either case, social workers are part of the welfare state, and have come to define their roles predominantly within welfare state structures.

This has effectively linked social work's future with that of the welfare state. If the welfare state survives and expands, then social work can be expected to do likewise, but if the welfare state withers and dies, social work may well share this fate unless it is able to establish some kind of alternative location. This issue will be explored later, but for the present it is sufficient to note that the future of the welfare state looks far from healthy. The 'crisis in the welfare state' has been a recurring theme in social policy writing for the last decade or more (Mishra 1984; Pierson 1991; Saunders 1994; Bryson 1992), and the Fabian vision of Titmuss and the others appears increasingly to be a historical phenomenon rather than something that catches the imagination of many contemporary Australians. The welfare state has been under sustained attack from both the right and the left, and does not appear to represent the dominant ideology of today. Governments of varying political persuasions are intent on privatisation, corporatisation, reducing government activity, dismantling universal programs and targeting government programs only to the most disadvantaged or 'needy'. There have been attempts by some academics and commentators to defend the welfare state against these trends (Donnison 1991; Stretton 1987), or to repackage the idea within the context of definitions of 'citizenship' (Beilharz, Considine and Watts 1992), but while such attempts are both interesting and valuable, they have so far failed to catch the imagination of policy makers, the media or the Australian public. Like the idea of service, then, the location of social work within the welfare state is no longer straightforward, but has become increasingly problematic.

A profession

Social work in Australia, more than in most other countries, has operated from a model of professionalism. Although there has been a significant anti-professional critique, which reached its peak in the 1970s, social workers' self-definition as professionals has been strong. The Australian Association of Social Workers (AASW) has seen its role as maintaining and improving professional practice standards, safeguarding professional ethics, ensuring the quality of social work education programs and preventing those who do not meet its standards from practising or being employed as 'social workers'. The Association has no legal authority for this activity, as social work is not a legally registered profession, despite the strenuous efforts of the AASW to achieve formal registration. However its de facto authority to control the practice of social work and the education of social workers is strong, and employers have conventionally accepted eligibility for membership of the AASW as a criterion for employment of social workers.

This approach by the AASW has led to criticism of social workers as being elitist, as being removed from the disadvantaged in whose interests they claim to work, and as excluding and marginalising many people who are doing important and effective work that in most other countries would be unambiguously identified as social work. It has also, in some cases, led to a concentration on what might be called the trappings of professionalism: conferences, training courses, the pursuit of qualifications, and a concern with status (Tesoriero and Verity 1993). On the other hand, few would wish to argue with the social work profession's concern for the maintenance of high ethical standards and its seeking to ensure and safeguard the highest possible quality of service to clients. There is, however, an issue about how these ethical and practice standards are defined, and whether they represent a practice which is really in the best interests of the disadvantaged. The whole question of professionalism in social work remains to some extent problematic, despite the undoubted increase in the acceptance of social workers as professionals.

Whether or not social work can legitimately classify itself as a profession, or whether indeed it is desirable that it should do so, is not the major issue for this discussion, though it will be returned to in later chapters. The important issue for present purposes is that this has been a major component of Australian social work's self-definition, that it is part of the socialisation of every social worker, and that it is an important aspect of how most social workers perceive themselves and what they do. It may also be a perception that is preventing social work from responding effectively to its current crisis.

Generalism

One of the most important aspects of social work has been its insistence on a generalist rather than a specialist approach to practice. The pressures to specialise have been strong, and many social workers in fact do specialise in particular aspects of social work, either by field (e.g., a specialist in child welfare) or by method (e.g., a family therapist). However the definition of social work remains broad, and this is reflected in social work education programs which aim to provide a broad generic education rather than training in defined areas of specialisation. The assumption has been that a social worker is equipped to begin practice in any field of social work, and that specialised knowledge and skills will be developed in the course of one's career. Social workers therefore can, and frequently do, change their fields of practice and their primary methods of work, according to interest, opportunity or circumstance. This is in contrast to, for example, the medical profession, where specialist training normally leads to a lifetime of practice within a narrow field of specialisation, and 'general practice' is itself increasingly seen as something of a specialist activity.

Social work's insistence on a generalist perspective stems in part from its attachment to holistic principles (Germain 1991). Understanding the individual in her/his social environment, which is perhaps the essence of social work, requires awareness of a multiplicity of interrelated factors: psychological, biological, social, cultural, economic, political, organisational and spiritual. Social workers have to deal with complex systems, and readily perceive the necessity for a wide-ranging holistic perspective. Narrow specialisation sits uncomfortably with this world view, and social work by its very nature has tended to value the holistic and to mistrust the narrow confines of specialist practice, though there are of course some social workers who have chosen to become 'experts' in a narrowly defined field, and have gained career rewards as a result. The holistic generalist view of social work, however, is not compatible with trends in policy and management, where jobs are being defined in more specific and confined terms, and where generalist social workers often cannot readily articulate their roles in terms of specified and measurable competencies. In this world, the specialist is always likely to win, and the generalist will find it increasingly difficult to gain employment.

Secular

Social work has been conceptualised largely as a secular occupation. Within conventional social work discourse there is little room for, or acknowledgement of, spirituality, the sacred, religion, and other aspects of human experience that are outside the rational, secular scientific paradigm (Sanzenbach 1989). Social work education programs pay little if any attention to such issues, despite the fact that for many people spirituality is a critically important component of the human condition. Even social workers employed in church agencies often define their work in secular terms. For example, it is usually not necessary for a worker in such an agency to hold personally the actual beliefs espoused by the church concerned, but merely to support their value underpinnings, 'to operate within a

Christian framework' or some other vague wording, and to agree not to undermine the faith of those who do believe (though this is not always the case, especially in some more conservative Christian agencies that are more explicit in their requirements). This is only possible if social work is seen as essentially a secular activity, rather than as a practice which takes account of and is concerned with spiritual matters. Social, psychological and (to some extent) physical functioning are all legitimate matters for social work assessment and intervention, but one rarely hears any social work discussion of 'spiritual functioning'.

For Aboriginal people, like indigenous people in other countries, spirituality is a fundamental aspect of all life, and for social work to deny or marginalise spirituality is to deny or marginalise Australia's indigenous population. Similarly, organised religion is critically important for many Australians, and such people can be marginalised by the primarily secular understandings of social work. Many other people, while rejecting organised religion, would claim that a sense of the spiritual or the sacred is an important part of their lives.

The reasons for social work's ignoring of the sacred and the spiritual lie in its striving for scientific or professional status, its location as a discipline within mainstream university discourse, and its foundations in the 'Western world view', which is strongly influenced by the secular heritage of the Enlightenment (Imre 1990). There is little room in such a paradigm for anything other than the scientific and the observable, and phenomena that do not lend themselves to 'scientific study' and 'rational analysis' are readily discounted. Social work's emphasis on being non-judgemental has perhaps also led to a mistrust by some social workers of religiously based world views which may be regarded as highly judgemental (for example, in terms of the role of women in Islam, and the effect of Christian missionaries' evangelical zeal on Aboriginal culture and communities).

This is not to say there are no social workers who are concerned with mystery, magic, spirituality, religion or the sacred (Sanzenbach 1989). Some forms of therapy have seen these as important, as have some forms of community work (especially if undertaken with indigenous communities). Some social workers have operated from a specifically religious perspective, and some will openly admit the importance of some of these phenomena that seem to be outside the realm of rational scientific inquiry. Religiously based agencies have always been important in the history of social work, and have been significant locations for social work practice. The fact remains, however, that such a perspective has by and large occupied a deviant or marginal position within mainstream social work education, research, writing and practice.

Knowledge, skills and values

The final characteristic of social work that will be considered is its insistence on the importance of knowledge, skills *and* values as the basis for practice. Few professions or occupations pay as much attention to their value base as social work, and social work has consistently defined itself not in value-neutral terms, but as operating from a clear and explicit value position. While this value base may be defined using different words ('social justice', 'the worth of the individual', 'commitment to the disadvantaged', etc.), it is important to emphasise that social work has consistently been defined as a *normative* activity. It does not simply do what political leaders and managers tell it to do, but rather it works towards a better society, defined in its own terms. It is thus more than a technical activity, and is out of place in an environment of increasing bureaucratic and managerial control, where 'accountability' is defined as accountability to management rather than accountability to the community or to the consumer. The current environment of practice does not readily allow for the kind of dissent, creativity and seeking of alternatives that are a natural consequence of social work's primary commitment to a value position. 'Their's not to make reply, their's not to reason why' is hardly a creed for social workers, whose value base frequently requires them both to attempt to reason why and also to make vocal and assertive reply wherever possible.

Emphasising both knowledge and skills, as well as values, also has implications for the nature of social work practice. If knowledge is as important as skills, then understanding is as important as competencies. Social workers regard themselves as thinkers as well as doers, and as people who have to make judgements on the basis of knowledge and experience before acting accordingly (the professional judgement). This again is in conflict with a practice environment where managers set outcome goals and firm guidelines as to how these are to be achieved, seeking as much as possible to remove discretionary judgements from social workers. Social workers are increasingly having to operate in an environment of regulation, practice manuals and administrative directions, which serve to limit their effective capacity to make discretionary professional judgements. This may be a comfortable environment for some, but it is in conflict with the conception of social work as a relatively autonomous profession making judgements on the basis of professional expertise rather than bureaucratic regulation.

The linking and affirming of knowledge, skills and values, then, causes some problems for social workers in the current organisational, political and managerial context of practice. It has been an important component of contemporary social work's self-definition, but like the other characteristics described above, it now appears somewhat problematic, as social workers find themselves pressured to conform to the competency agenda and the new managerialism.

The practice context

The construction of social work that has been briefly outlined, while one with which most social workers would be comfortable, is becoming increasingly out of step with the reality of the contemporary practice context. It is still largely present in the curricula of schools of social work and in the agenda of the professional association, but it is not providing social workers with a practice base that is readily accepted in the organisational, social and political environment. This leads one to ask whether social work indeed has a future, and if so what that future might be. The remaining chapters of this book outline a perspective within which those questions might be answered. For the present, however, the discussion will focus on the hostile environment within which social workers are seeking to practice, or in some cases, simply to survive. Four interrelated characteristics of this environment will be considered: *economic rationalism, managerialism, rationality,* and *competencies.*

Economic rationalism

The term 'economic rationalism' seems to be largely an Australian label, though the phenomenon it describes has permeated most of the English-speaking Western world; elsewhere it is known as 'the new right', 'neo-conservatism', 'Thatcherism', 'Reaganomics', or sometimes other more derogatory terms. It has become the accepted wisdom of governments and oppositions of whatever nominal political persuasion, only it is sometimes clothed in different rhetoric to suit the needs of different political constituencies. In the Australian context it has been enthusiastically embraced by both Liberal and Labor governments, though the latter have perhaps not always adopted economic rationalism in its most extreme form.

The essence of economic rationalism is that good policy is policy which makes good economic sense, and if the economy is 'healthy' all will benefit (Saunders 1994). The only effective way to measure human well-being is in terms of wealth, as people are able to use money to purchase whatever it is that will give them the greatest satisfaction. This is preferable to the state, or anyone else, deciding what is best for people and imposing it on them. Hence all other policy must be secondary to economic policy (Benn 1991), which should aim to maximise individual economic freedom and to minimise regulation, taxation and restrictive social legislation. The market, subject to the laws of supply and demand, provides the best form of regulation because it represents individuals' own wishes through their spending choices. It also allows maximum freedom to the individual. Hence market activity should be maximised, and should as far as possible be allowed to operate free from regulation. From this perspective, government spending is an impediment to economic health. It interferes with and undermines the market, and the required taxation reduces the incentive for potential wealth creators to invest and to take risks. Government spending, especially on welfare, is seen as a disincentive to working hard and to making profits. Hence levels of wages, the provision of human services, cultural activity, recreation and everything else should be determined through the market; people's free choices will determine the level of supply, and the market price. Competition in the market will ensure that prices are kept to a minimum, and that services are efficient and meet the needs of the consumer (Saunders 1994).

To achieve these ends, social and economic policies have sought to establish the primacy of the market, and to wind back the familiar forms of welfare state expenditure that have provided the context for social work practice. One way in which this has been achieved is through privatisation, where government enterprises, from airlines to prisons, have been sold or contracted to the private sector, to be operated on a profit basis (Rees, Rodley and Stilwell 1993). Another way is by encouraging competition, allowing (and indeed encouraging) the private sector to compete directly with government activity, thereby subjecting public services to the discipline of the market. 'Marketisation' is a term for another policy direction, which is to create quasi-markets, or internal markets, by allowing government agencies to compete with each other as well as with the private sector. Under such programs social workers have found a role as brokers of services, helping consumers to 'purchase' the services they need using an allocated budget of public funds. Voucher systems, where a consumer is given a voucher with which to purchase the service from the preferred provider, is another form of marketisation. A final way in which governments have sought to move to a more market-based approach is through 'corporatisation', where the public sector is required to look and act as much as possible like the private sector, in the belief that this will make it more efficient. Hence public enterprises are encouraged to become entrepreneurial, to earn money in the market place, to adopt similar structures and employment practices to those of the private sector, and to be concerned with 'corporate image', 'customer focus', 'quality management', 'business plans', 'mission statements' and whatever else may be flavour of the month in the world of corporate management. Movement of employees between the public and private sectors, often on a short-term contract basis, is encouraged, and governments make extensive use of private consultants rather than the expertise of their own staff.

Quality of life is equated with the economically defined 'standard of living', and for the overall standard of living to improve, according to economic rationalism, productivity must increase. Hence wage rises should only be granted in return for increased productivity, not on grounds of need or social equity. Indeed wages should be set by market mechanisms, rather than any other considerations. Trade unions are thus regarded as interfering with the operation of the market, and are therefore seen as acting counter to the national interest.

The belief in the market extends beyond national boundaries, and hence free trade is a strong plank of the economic rationalist platform (Brecher and Costello 1994). Removing trade barriers, through agreements such as GATT and APEC, is therefore seen as likely to bring significant benefits to the economy (and indeed to other economies), and hence will be to the benefit of all.

In such a policy environment, public services of the type social workers are used to providing are not highly valued. They are seen as reducing incentive and as a drain on the economy, and hence as adversely affecting people's well-being and quality of life. They are also seen as an intrusion on people's fundamental freedom and individuality. For social workers, who may have thought that their work was actually about improving well-being and quality of life, and who have prided themselves on their commitment to the worth of the individual, it is indeed a cruel irony to be cast as villains or as 'wimps' (Franklin 1989) rather than as the heroes in the struggle for a fair and just society. Yet that is the consequence of the economic rationalist position.

The power of economic rationalism among policy makers in Australia was clearly demonstrated in Pusey's landmark study of the attitudes and backgrounds of senior Canberra public servants (Pusey 1991). Pusey found that Canberra's most senior bureaucrats were strongly influenced by economic rationalist world views, and did not allow for the legitimacy of an alternative viewpoint. He contrasts the contemporary public service with the public service of earlier times, when public sector was seen as a life-long career rather than a job much like any other in the private sector; when public servants came from backgrounds that meant they were more in touch with the culture and values of the majority of Australians; and where economic considerations were seen as secondary to social concerns and human welfare. More recently, however, economic rationalist values have been enthusiastically embraced, and the self-defined role of senior public servants has changed from one of 'public service' to one of 'public sector management'.

It must not be thought that economic rationalism is without its critics, or that its economic and social position is unassailable. Indeed, a powerful critique can be made of economic rationalism (Horne 1992; Rees, Rodley and Stilwell 1993; Saunders 1994; Brecher and Costello 1994; Ekins and Max-Neef

15

1992), demonstrating that it has its own fundamental contradictions, and that it is by its very nature unable to deliver the good life claimed by its advocates (for any more than a minority of the population, at least). One lesson that can surely be learned from the history of 200 years of capitalism is that, despite capitalism's many successes, it is singularly incapable of meeting human need and of providing adequately for the many disadvantaged victims of the competitive market place. The advocates of economic rationalism seem blind to this history, and to the fact that the modern welfare state developed specifically because of the inadequacy of the market to provide for the needs of the majority of the population. Further critique of economic rationalism, however, will have to wait until later chapters, as the aim of the present chapter is simply to set the context of contemporary social work.

Managerialism

Another important aspect of the environment of contemporary social work is the so-called 'new managerialism' (Rees and Rodley 1995). This can be summarised as a belief that good management is able to solve the problems of human service organisations, and will make them more effective and efficient. Management is seen as a generic skill that can be applied in all circumstances; as essentially the same whatever the nature of the organisation that is being managed. Hence someone who has shown an ability to manage a manufacturing plant or an insurance company has the necessary skills to manage a public sector organisation. Similarly, within the public sector, managerial skills are interchangeable across departments, so someone with a good management record in a department of fisheries or transport should readily be able to manage a welfare department, a prison or a hospital.

This has effectively changed career opportunities for social workers. Prior to the 1980s social workers interested in management could expect to move into senior positions in the welfare bureaucracy, as it was assumed that human service professionals would know best how to manage human service departments. This is no longer the case, and social workers who are interested in management are increasingly having to gain management qualifications, rather than to rely on their social work qualifications and experience. This not only provides a block on the career paths of the ambitious, but it also affects the way social workers in senior positions think about their role and their professional identity; those social workers who occupy management positions are less likely to define themselves as social workers and to identify with the values of the social work profession. Instead they are given an alternative professional identity: that of manager.

The philosophy of management does not only apply at the most senior levels of human service organisations. Middle management positions (from where social workers involved in service delivery are often supervised), are also increasingly being defined as management jobs, which are thus appropriately filled by 'professional' managers rather than by experienced social work practitioners or by others with relevant substantive expertise or experience. Hence social workers in their day-to-day work are having to come to terms with managerialism, and are held accountable to managers who may know little if anything about social work practice, and who are not necessarily committed to social work values, although in some agencies there is also allowance for a professional supervisor who is distinct from the line manager. Further, many social work jobs have now been redefined as 'case managers', reflecting the apparently complete conquest of the human services by the management ethos. 'Management', with its connotations of power, top-down control and authority, is hardly compatible with the kind of social work described above where ideas of empowerment, self-determination and value-based practice are seen as being of central importance.

The trend towards managerialism has seen social workers devalued in terms of their traditional role as human service professionals. They are evidently losing much of their professional autonomy, and are not able to operate as the creative, innovative and empowering professionals that the conventional social work self-definition has emphasised. This loss of status, seniority, autonomy and respect is most noticeable in public welfare within the large state welfare bureaucracies (Hough 1994, 1995; Markiewicz 1994), but is evident to some degree in many other social work settings.

This trend has also been the cause of significant value conflicts and dilemmas for social workers. Instead of being accountable to social work supervisors, social workers are finding themselves accountable to managers who do not always hold the same value position as social workers. Managers, because of their training and socialisation, are likely to value efficiency and effectiveness almost at all costs, while social workers will tend to place a higher value on human well-being, social justice and human rights.

The dominance of the managerial approach manifests itself in another important way that affects social workers. When things are not working, or there are problems, the inevitable managerial response is either to bring in yet more managers or to institute an organisational restructure, in the belief that problems are best solved through organisational change. Hence social workers find themselves working in an almost constantly changing environment of restructuring and organisational 'development', with the corresponding problems of uncertainty, insecurity and low morale.

Modernist rationality

A third important aspect of the environment in which social workers practise in the 1990s is the assumption of modernist rationality. This is closely related to the discussion of economic rationalism, but in the previous discussion the primacy of economics was identified as the determinant of rational decision-making. Here, the focus is on the notion of rationality itself, whether economic or otherwise.

The assumption of modernist rationality means that the organisational and policy context of social work is seen as being determined by logical analysis on the basis of objective data. There is little room for values or ethics in the analysis; rather it is a utilitarian system where careful and reasonable calculations are made about the best way to proceed. Such a system leads to often simplistic cause/effect reasoning, and prediction in terms of measured 'need', projected scenarios and measurable outcomes. This fits closely with the managerial approach, and rational models of planning and policy development including cost/benefit analysis and business plans. Because such a rational perspective can easily be reduced to an essentially technical exercise, this reinforces the technical nature of policy develop-ment and service delivery, which does not always fit with the norms of social work practice. It leads to a basically empirical approach, involving measurement and data collection as being the most acceptable way to arrive at the 'truth' or to establish a 'fact' or 'reality'. In such an environment, many of the important values of social justice and empowerment can readily be marginalised.

The modernist rational approach also results in a quest for uniformity. It naturally leads one to assume that there is 'one best answer' to any problem, whether it be how to reduce juvenile crime, how to define and prevent child abuse, how to organise and deliver health care, what is a minimum 'poverty line' below which incomes should not be allowed to fall, what constitutes the 'best' form of care for the aged, and so on. Hence one develops policies that seek to find this one best answer, and then to impose it on the entire population. This readily down-plays or ignores the importance of diversity: cultural, regional, class, and so on. A valuing of diversity might suggest that there is not a single answer to any of these problems, but rather that one should be adopting a pluralist or postmodernist position that allows more than one such answer to emerge, at different places and in different circumstances. Such a position is perhaps more in keeping with a social work perspective, which tends to emphasise culture and difference, but this has not stopped some social workers from enthusiastically em-bracing the rational model, seeking empirical and 'scientific' solutions, and advocating single (and often simplistic) policies or programs to be applied to all. One example, among many, is the set of child protection guidelines developed for use in Western Australia, which were expected to apply throughout the state, including remote Aboriginal communities in the Kimberleys, Vietnamese families in Perth, farming com-munities, mining communities, alternative communities in the south-west, and so on. There was little acknowledgement of the massive differences in cultural definitions of the family, child care, the place of children, 'adequate' parenting, and so on, and no suggestion that there should perhaps be community involvement in establishing community-based definitions of what constituted adequate care and protection and what constituted abuse. The centrally prepared, rational document was seen as the answer for all, and was imposed on all communities in a naive belief that this was somehow equitable, and that variation meant inequity. Such a program can only be justified under a model of centrally planned rationality.

This example indicates another aspect of the rational model, namely that it is generally associated with centralised, top-down planning, rather than bottom-up participatory approaches. Wisdom resides at the top, or the centre, and is communicated outwards or downwards; it is only information that flows in the reverse direction. It therefore fits well with the managerial perspective discussed above.

The rational modernist approach is so entrenched in Western thought that it is seldom questioned in the world of policy and management, though at an intellectual level it can be, and has been, subjected to substantial critique. It is worth emphasising that it is the legacy of the Enlightenment, and has only been part of the Western intellectual mainstream for the past 200 years or so. Indeed many writers in the postmodernist, green or new paradigm traditions have suggested that the Enlightenment world view, while responsible for much of the 'progress' of the Western world over the last two centuries, has also led to many of the problems Western society seems unable to handle, such as environmental degradation, third world poverty, social inequality, the loss of human community, and the loss of spiritual values (Capra 1982; Ornstein and Ehrlich 1989; Henderson 1991). Other paradigms, as advocated by such writers, would allow for very different forms of organisation and decision-making.

Social work has had something of an ambivalent relationship to the rational model. Some schools within social work, particularly those influenced by positivist social science, have enthusiastically embraced the scientific rational paradigm (Bloom and Fischer 1982). There has always, however, been a contrary tradition in social work, which has emphasised the qualitative, and has allowed room for intuition, practice wisdom, phenomenology, grounded theory, and so on. Such a practice perspective has not always been legitimised in course curricula, accreditation guidelines or recommended text books, but it has remained part of the lived experience and practice wisdom of social workers in their day-to-day work as they try to make sense of the dilemmas and contradictions of their own and their clients' experiences. This is a very important debate, which will be revisited in greater detail in later chapters.

Competencies

The organisation, appointment practices, accreditation and education programs of human service occupations have been significantly affected since the early 1990s by a concern with competencies. The competency movement arose, in part, in order to break down professional monopolies and to make it easier for people with overseas qualifications to practise in Australia. It was also seen as a way of allowing for career development by delineating paths through which people could upgrade their qualifications and skills. The basis of the competency movement is that occupations should be defined according to the competencies required to perform them, rather than through the formal qualifications required of the worker concerned. Hence training courses are obliged to specify those competencies people will acquire by undertaking the program. Jobs are advertised and filled in terms of required competencies rather than in terms of qualifications or professional affiliations. It is perhaps not much of an exaggeration to say that no longer do employers employ a person, but instead they employ a batch of competencies, and this suggests, importantly, that the human element of the job is devalued.

The competency movement has led to jobs that were previously regarded as exclusively for social workers being thrown open to others who can demonstrate the specified competencies. Similarly, it has opened up for social workers the possibility of applying for jobs from which they might previously have been excluded. Thus there are now fewer jobs designated 'social worker', with positions instead being characterised in terms of their specific function, for example, 'rehabilitation counsellor', 'youth outreach worker', 'child protection worker', 'disability services case manager', 'community liaison officer', and so on, open to anyone who can demonstrate the specified competencies. Social workers thus have more jobs for which they might apply, but face greater competition to secure them.

Of more concern than this widening market is a perceived threat to the very identity and future of social work. One of the consequences of social work being a generalist profession is that social workers are able to do many different things at a basic level of competence. However most of the things social workers can do, *if taken in isolation*, may be seen to be done better by someone with more specific training in that particular skill: someone with specific counselling training will be seen as a 'better' counsellor than a social worker; someone with specific research training will be a 'better' researcher; someone with small group training will be a 'better' group worker;

someone with a specific community work qualification will be a 'better' community worker; someone with a diploma in youth work will be 'better' able to work with youth; and so on. The strength of social work is its generic, holistic perspective, which relates these areas to each other; indeed from a social work perspective the narrowly trained counsellor, youth worker, community worker or whatever will not be the 'best' person to do those jobs, because they will not be able to locate them in a broader context and act accordingly, or to deal with the many 'problems' of a single client or family. A specialist child protection worker, for example, may not be able to appreciate the impact of cultural background, the consequences of institutional racism, or changes to a family system in the patterns of child care and abuse, and may not be able even to recognise, let alone deal with, a pattern of elder abuse or of addiction in the same family context. This generic view, however, is at odds with the rationalist managerial paradigm, which seeks to define, to specify and to fragment, and which is inherent in the competency-based approach.

An emphasis on competencies will inevitably emphasise the technical aspects of a social work role, as it is what a social worker *is able to do* that counts as most important. This is at odds with social work's self-definition as a blend of knowledge, skills and values, with each being critically important. A discourse of competencies will highlight the skills component, may make some allowance for the knowledge component, but will not readily accommodate the values component, though it should be noted that the AASW definitions of social work competencies do seek to incorporate values in the construction of 'competency'. Nevertheless it remains true that the competency approach, in the hands of managers and employers, can readily reduce social work to a mere technology and can undervalue what social workers have traditionally seen as one of the critically important aspects of their professional identity.

The competencies approach can also lead to increasing the power of managers and decreasing the power and professional autonomy of social workers. Under the competency-based system, a manager is effectively saying 'I am employing this person to perform tasks A, B and C', instead of saying 'I am employing this person to perform the role of a professional social worker'. The difference is critically important in determining the way the manager will view the work of the social worker, the nature and direction of accountability, and issues of professional autonomy. Competencies are very much part of the modernist rational paradigm, and social workers under this system readily become seen as cogs in the machine, to be controlled and regulated.

If this is the case, one might well ask whether there is a need for extended professional education for social workers? Social workers would not need to study the social and political context of their work, and should not be encouraged to ask questions and to seek creative alternatives (unless of course these are specified competencies, but they would be unlikely to appear in public sector job criteria in the present environment). The human service competencies 'required' by rational managers within the economic rationalist framework can surely be provided more inexpensively than through extended professional training in a tertiary institution, and hence the competency approach represents a significant threat to the future of social work, at least in the form in which it has been taught in Australian universities.

In search of a critique

The above description of the contemporary context of social work practice has been presented largely without critique. This is not because there is no critique available, but rather because the aim of the remainder of this book is to develop a framework within which such a critique can be derived and, more importantly, articulated.

The organisational and political context of social work has changed significantly during the 1980s and 1990s, and this has resulted in the familiar, conventional and comfortable con-structions of social work practice seeming out-of-place and somewhat irrelevant to the organisational and political imperatives facing social workers. The ideal of the welfare state, the Fabian vision of socialism, the idea of strong public services, a society committed to collectivist values of social justice, and the idea of professionalised human services being delivered by relatively autonomous professionals are all in retreat, and do not have the legitimacy they once enjoyed (Tesoriero and Verity 1993). The only alternatives that seem to present themselves and to enjoy popular currency are unattractive to many social workers, and seem to be contradictory to the characteristic social work values of social justice, caring and sharing, empowerment and self-determination. Many of the ideological and organisational foundations of social work practice, as traditionally understood, seem to be crumbling, and it is not clear whether what will take their place will be able to support the social work profession in anything like its present form.

The hostile context has posed some serious dilemmas for social workers. Should they try to adapt and join the 'new order'? Indeed, many have sought to do so, by becoming entrepreneurial, by entering and supporting private practice, by taking MBA degrees, by trying, with varying levels of enthusiasm, to define social work in terms of specified competencies, by concentrating on therapy at the expense of a concern for social justice, and by generally attempting to make social work fit more comfortably within the system. This, it might be argued, is necessary for the survival of the profession, and is essential if a social work perspective is to be retained in policy and practice debates. It is fine to be concerned for principles, but if this means no jobs for social workers and no future for social work, ideological purity will have been self-defeating. From this position, the responsible path is to join, and to seek to influence, the new order.

Alternatively, it can be suggested that for social work to embark on such a course is to negate the very nature of social work itself: its commitment to the disadvantaged, its base in social justice, its concern for empowerment, and so on. It would appear that social workers who have sought to join and influence the new order have had only limited success in the former aim and almost none in the latter. If indeed the environment is fundamentally hostile to social work values, it is important for social work to be articulating a strong critique, and seeking to demonstrate and establish alternative forms of human service delivery. Far from joining the new order, social workers should be at the forefront of the opposition to it.

One of the reasons why social workers find themselves in this dilemma, and find the current practice environment particularly disillusioning, is that they have not been able to articulate an effective and valid critique in a way that can be taken up by those who control the practice and policy discourse, and which will make sense outside the rarefied world of the university. Positivism, economic rationalism, managerialism, the rational model, the competency approach and the rest can all be subjected to a powerful critique, and this has been done in universities and academic publications. The critique, however, has not filtered through to the managers, politicians, journalists, media editors, front-line workers and others who collectively define the policy and management discourse within which social workers have to practice. The 'new order' thus remains largely unchallenged *in the arenas that matter*. Hence social workers seeking to develop and implement a critical alternative have little foundation or support for their work.

Future scenarios

Before proceeding further to develop an alternative critical perspective on social work, it is important to consider possible future changes to the context of social work practice. One of the greatest mistakes that can be made in locating social work within the current political, economic and organisational context is to assume that the context itself will not change. A historical perspective is required in order to realise that the contemporary context is the result of many dynamic processes, and that these processes will continue, will interact, and will inevitably produce a future that will be different from the present. Indeed, if one takes seriously the criticisms of those who have emphasised the ecological limits to the ever-increasing growth on which the economic system is based, the one thing of which we can be certain is that the future will not be like the present, because the current political, economic and social order is so blatantly unsustainable in anything other than the very short term.

Assumptions that the existing order is more or less perma-nent, and that present trends will continue into the foreseeable future, have proven to be seriously mistaken. In social policy, the optimistic founders of the welfare state assumed, up to the early 1970s, that they were establishing something that would be long-lasting, and that they were shaping the future welfare of many generations. Typical of such optimism is Wilensky and Lebeaux's statement, 'The "welfare state" will become the "welfare society", and both will be more reality than epithet' (Wilensky and Lebeaux 1965, p. 147). Such writers did not seriously consider the possibility that within only two decades there would be a general consensus that the welfare state was 'in crisis', and that its future would be, to say the least, equivocal.

The same is true of the current advocates of economic rationalism. It is seen as a regime that will be permanent, and many policy writers do not take seriously the possibility that it too might be a transitory historical phenomenon. Yet there is no strong reason why economic rationalism should have a longer life span than post-war consensus welfare state policies; it is just as fraught with contradictions, and it too is likely to be seen, in retrospect, as a passing phase.

This is a critically important point when considering the future of social work. It is easy to accept the assumption of historical stability and continuity, and yet this can blind one to the likelihood, or indeed inevitability, of significant historical change. Social workers who were educated in the optimistic days of the 1960s and 1970s are still practising, but in a very different environment from that assumed by their university teachers and by those who wrote their text-books. It is surely only reasonable to expect that today's graduates will similarly have to practise in a very different environment well before the end of their professional careers. This emphasises the importance of social work not simply seeking to adapt to the present, but also trying to anticipate the future, and to educate students to be adaptable, flexible, and able to see possibilities beyond the constraints of the present practice context. This is an important part of the empowerment of social workers and students; to assume the present context to be enduring and inevitable is to disempower oneself and others, and denies the possibility of social workers being active in formulating alternatives and instigating change. In the present ideological climate, it leads to disillusionment and low morale.

It is therefore necessary to discuss the context of social work practice not as a static, permanent phenomenon, but as a dynamic, changing system. To attempt to predict the future is, of course, highly problematic, given the complexity of the social, economic and political forces that are in constant interaction. Social work itself will reflect this complexity, and is likely to react to future conditions in characteristically divergent and contradictory ways. History has a habit of proving predictions to be totally wrong, and of showing that apparently stable sets of circumstances can alter quite rapidly (a prime example being the rapid and largely unpredicted decline in the power of communist states and the end of the 'cold war'). However, on the assumption that whatever the future holds, it is unlikely simply to be an extension of the present, it is worth considering a number of feasible future scenarios for social work and the context within which it is located. This will facilitate a consideration of a more proactive social work that will be relevant not simply to the present, but to the practice environment over the next two or three decades—that is, within the careers of contemporary social work students. The scenarios are not mutually exclusive; indeed it is likely that several or all of them will be experienced at different times in the future.

More of the same

The first scenario, which seems likely to hold within the next few years, is that the current trends of economic rationalism, the market and 'new managerialism' will continue. The strength of transnational capital is such that the emerging global economic order seems likely to strengthen. Certainly the current policy directions of many governments can only support such a trend, given the relative lack of economic sovereignty of nations in the 'new world order', and the likely economic and political consequences for governments who may seek a more independent direction. The ownership of global media by the same interests only entrenches the capacity to control, and weakens the possibility of serious critical alternatives entering the public arena. Although there are significant voices of opposition, they do not have the capacity to be heard or the legitimacy to be taken seriously by more than a small minority.

The prospect of more of the same means increasing privatisation, reduction in public welfare programs, further erosion of welfare state services, increasing acceptance of managerialism, and more expectation that people are responsible for meeting their own needs through the private market. This does not promise to be a conducive environment for creative social work practice, or for the furthering of the values of social work, unless forms of practice such as private practice and management are adopted by more social workers as has occurred in the USA. But if these trends do continue, social workers are going to have to develop strategies for survival in a hostile environment in the short term, and it is unrealistic to pretend otherwise or to hope that suddenly it will all go away.

Such survival strategies must be both at the personal and at the institutional level. Individual workers will obviously be concerned for their own survival, their mental health, their job security, their capacity to provide a reasonable service to their clients, and so on. This leads to a number of strategies, some of which involve accommodation with the dictates of economic rationalism, and some of which involve game-playing; doing much the same as one has always done but using different language to describe it, creative completion of statistics forms and time sheets, imaginative 'rule-bending', and so on. Another strategy is simply to 'keep one's head down' and go on doing the job hoping that the managers have more important people to notice.

At the institutional level, such survival strategies are important not merely for the survival and sanity of individual workers, but in order to keep alive both the institution of social work and the social justice ideals for which it stands. In a time of rapid social change it is surely more important than ever that the values of social work, and social work itself as an occupation committed to social justice, not only survive but are strengthened in order to make a contribution to a future world. If indeed social workers have something important to offer (as most social workers understandably believe), then the survival of the institution of social work also becomes an important imperative at this time. This requires strong leadership by the professional association, and social workers taking leadership roles in a variety of political and community activities, demonstrating the value and the importance of a social work perspective and a social work contribution.

These survival strategies, whether at individual or institutional level, are at best short-term measures, and will not suffice if indeed we are entering a lengthy period of economic rationalism and managerialism. If, however, other scenarios are possible, and the days of current economic and political orthodoxies are numbered, these survival strategies are vital to give social workers breathing space. For this reason it is important to examine the feasibility of alternative scenarios, and social work's place in them.

Uncertainty and instability

Another scenario suggests that with the contradictions of economic rationalism becoming increasingly significant, the future will be one of increasing uncertainty and instability. The certainty and predictability of the post-war period, and of the modernist rationalist paradigm, do not adequately reflect the reality of policy making and service delivery in social welfare. It has become increasingly clear that social and economic problems, because of their fundamental structural causes, cannot be adequately solved within the constraints of what is conventionally regarded as politically and economically feasible. Hence the response of governments is to make yet more cosmetic changes, such as organisational restructure and renaming, in an increasingly futile attempt to be seen to be doing something effective. The general ineffectiveness of government programs, which at best only ameliorate the worst aspects of social problems without attacking the underlying causes, only serves to reinforce the problematic and contradictory nature of the social issues with which governments claim to deal.

In such a climate, instability is likely to increase. As an example one can consider the area of crime. The increasing inequality of society (an inevitable consequence of economic rationalism) and the consequent denial of opportunities for many to participate in the 'good life' as defined within the popular culture, will inevitably contribute to increasing levels of criminal offending. As the gap between the advantaged and the disadvantaged widens, and as the relentless message of advertising defines an ideal world of material possessions and affluence that is denied to increasing numbers of the population, crime (along with other 'problem' behaviour such as addiction, mental illness and suicide) will continue to rise. This will result in increasingly strenuous attempts to 'do something' about it; at times this may lean towards the punitive, with tougher action demanded of the courts, and at other times it may lean towards the therapeutic, with counselling, group therapy, recreation programs, and so on. As long as there is no attempt to deal with the underlying structural issues, such policy 'initiatives' are bound to fail, and governments are likely either to lurch from one extreme to the other with increasing frequency, or to pursue one direction (more likely the punitive, for reasons that will be discussed below) with even more fervour.

As will be argued in subsequent chapters, the traditional social policy dichotomy of 'the market versus the state' has become transformed into a contest between managerial and market discourses of service provision. This suggests that the current conservative context is not one of monolithic consensus, but rather that we might expect a degree of conflict between the essentially 'bottom-up' advocates of the free market and the 'top-down' rationality of managerialism. This is likely to be a continual source of tension and instability for social workers.

At a wider level of analysis, it can be suggested that Western societies are entering a period when uncertainty and instability will be the rule rather than the exception. The very rapid rate of technological change, with its inevitable social consequences, suggests a future where change at all levels of society becomes the norm, and to predict the directions of such change is impossible, given the many interacting variables involved. Changing knowledge and changing discourses mean that the one thing of which one can be reasonably certain is that the future is one of uncertainty and change.

Many critics would argue that Western society (and indeed global society, given the effects of globalisation) is entering a period of crisis. This crisis has several manifestations:

- ecological crisis, as the limits to growth and industrialisation in a finite world become evident;
- economic crisis, as the global economy develops to the point where nobody will be able to control it, and where those who claim to be able to do so will probably not understand it;
- political crisis, as politicians find it increasingly difficult to govern and to solve issues within the parameters they have set for themselves;
- social crisis, as patterns of community and extended family, which have sustained the human race throughout its history, break down in the name of economic progress;
- cultural crisis, as those specific cultural factors that give people a sense of identity and belonging are submerged in a bland Americanised global consumer culture; and
- spiritual crisis, as the rational secular world view devalues mystery, spirituality, religious values and beliefs, emotion, and anything else that cannot be measured or counted.

If such a view of the immediate future is correct, the context of social work practice will be more changeable, unpredictable and unstable than ever, and the capacity to cope with change, uncertainty and crisis will be the most important attribute of a social worker. Those who will have to deal with the human costs of this instability will have to work at the 'front line' of crisis and change, and their effectiveness and creativity could have a significant impact in helping to create an alternative future, as will be discussed in later chapters.

Control

Increasing instability and uncertainty are in turn likely to lead to a scenario of increased control by those who will seek to hold on to their power in a turbulent environment. This increased control may happen in either the public or the private sector, or both.

In the public sector, governments are likely to find it increasingly difficult to deliver on promises of peace, prosperity, security and economic growth, and to solve or even control social problems such as crime, delinquency, mental illness, drug abuse, poverty, unemployment (or underemployment), etc. This will be even more the case as long as conventional wisdom maintains that government expenditure must be continually reduced. In such an environment, voter dissatisfaction with governments could increase, and the temptation to resort to coercive measures to stay in power becomes stronger. The form of increased government repression and coercion may vary according to circumstances, and it is important to emphasise that overt coercion, through the use of police, military and security forces, is only one way in which it might be achieved. Increasing powers of censorship (formal or informal), coercive practices in government bureaucracies, and limitations on freedom of speech, freedom of assembly, and freedom of association (e.g., the right to form a trade union) can all be achieved without the overt use of military or police power. Such a scenario may not be as far removed from the present as some may think, given the growing alarm in the labour movement about increasingly coercive employment practices, and the apparent readiness of some governments to erode rights such as freedom of association, particularly in the case of trade unions.

This increased control in the government sector may be matched by increasing control in the private sector, often achieved (as in the public sector) under the guise of the new managerialism (Rees and Rodley 1995). Coercion and control are more readily practised in the private sector, because of the relative lack of public accountability and regulation. Indeed, one of the consequences of privatisation is that it removes activity from public scrutiny and allows many things to be hidden under the excuse of commercial confidentiality. This creates a climate where coercive and repressive practices can be more readily instituted, and more readily concealed. For this reason, those concerned with the possible increase in state control and repression should also be concerned with similar trends in the private sector, where public accountability is harder to maintain.

The power of large private sector operators is already substantial and frightening. The large international consulting firms, which operate clearly in the interests of trans-national capital and which embrace economic rationalist ideology, provide advice to many governments and non-government organisations and have assumed the role of international purveyors of wisdom in how to run almost anything. If their advice is not heeded, the consequences for governments and agencies can be serious in terms of 'investor confidence' and other such economic rationalist indicators. Private sector operators have often been as ruthless as repressive governments in stamping out criticism and dissent, whether from within or without, an example being the way in which environmental protest groups have been pressured and threatened with crippling legal action by those with vested interests in mining, logging, pollution, nuclear power, and other environmentally disastrous forms of so-called development.

For social workers, such a scenario has serious implications. It would certainly make it harder for social workers to advocate and act for social justice and human rights, and social workers in countries like Australia would need to learn some lessons from social workers in other countries where the cost of speaking out is much higher (PAHRA 1995). Australian social workers have enjoyed a relatively high degree of freedom to present opposing views, but the price of such freedom is likely to increase, and there are signs that this is already the case (Hough 1994).

It also suggests that many social work clients themselves will be victims of state or private sector repression; again, this is to some extent already the case, but seems likely to increase. The role of social workers, in terms of advocacy for their clients and seeking redress for social injustice, would therefore become much more risky in terms of the worker's own job, livelihood, reputation, and even personal security. It remains to be seen how many social workers will be able to maintain a social justice value commitment and orientation to their work under such circumstances.

Another possible outcome of such a scenario is that social workers may be encouraged to become more closely identified with the instruments of state or private sector repression. The argument that social work is a form of social control has, of course, been used by Marxists for many years (Bailey and Brake 1975; Corrigan and Leonard 1978). However the pressure to become overtly identified with, and implicated in, the exercise of state and private sector power could well increase. There is a real temptation for social workers to ensure the survival of social work by linking it more closely to the forces of power and control, thus divorcing it from notions of liberation and empowerment, and to feel comfortable in a more authoritarian professional role as part of the coercive state. Certainly this would be more likely to lead to job security, career advancement, and social work being 'recognised' as having an important role to play. This would be accompanied by an increasing acceptance of social workers making 'appropriate use of authority' to represent the best interests of society (as defined by managers and politicians), and the control of new managerialism would help to entrench such an approach to practice.

Social workers therefore need to revisit the familiar debate about social control versus empowerment and liberation. The rewards from social control are likely to increase, as will the costs of empowerment and social action. In such an environment it may not be possible for social workers to continue to live with the present degree of ambiguity about these conflicting roles; some social workers have been content to adopt social control roles in the workplace while at the same time supporting empowerment and liberation as 'ideas which inform our practice' in a rather vague sense, and supporting the moderately reformist position of the professional association. This has been reinforced by feelings of loyalty to one's employer, which is to some extent supported by the AASW Code of Ethics, and it is likely that such loyalty will be more stringently enforced by employers in future within the scenario of increased control, for example, through workplace agreements. The political choices confronting social workers are therefore likely to be starker, and to require a more definite commitment either to the politics of liberation or to the politics of control.

The decline of the welfare state

An important future scenario, as suggested earlier in this chapter, is the continuing decline of the Western welfare state. The contradictions of the welfare state have been well documented, and it is becoming increasingly clear that the crisis of the welfare state, in Western nations such as Australia, is likely to deepen rather than be satisfactorily resolved. There appears to be little political or popular support for the large welfare state, and it is certainly opposed by the dominant regime of economic rationalism. The steady erosion of virtually all public services, including health, education, public housing, public transport and the personal social services, in the name of the market, is likely to continue at least in the short term. Even if the headlong rush towards privatisation and reductions in public expenditure is slowed or halted, it is not easy to see a groundswell of support for it being actually reversed, and the welfare state effectively re-established.

The crisis in the welfare state has been discussed and predicted for some time, so it should hardly be surprising for social workers to find themselves caught up in it. The problem for social workers, however, has been that they have persisted in defining their role as being located within the structures of the welfare state, and have been reluctant to seek roles in other structures except for the traditional social work roles in the non-government (non-profit) welfare sector. The reluctance of social workers to seek jobs elsewhere has resulted in many jobs that social workers are well-equipped to do being filled largely by people with other qualifications, and not being seen either by employers or by social workers themselves as legitimate social work jobs. Such jobs include youth work, community work, many jobs involved in working with the aged, housing, rehabilitation, working in electoral offices, working with ethnic communities, local government welfare and community development, working with refugees, working for activist organisations (unions, environmental groups, human rights and development groups), cultural development (community arts, theatre, etc.), and working with self-help groups. While there are some social workers involved in all of these settings, social workers have largely failed to develop a significant presence in them, and have not laid claim to them in the way that they have to the traditional practice areas of child welfare and hospital social work. This is despite the fact that social work values, knowledge and skills are clearly relevant to all these areas. This has left social workers in danger of being redefined as being primarily child protection and public welfare workers, thereby omitting them from consideration for the kind of jobs that may develop in the post-welfare state era.

It is therefore important for social workers to come to terms more explicitly with the decline of the welfare state, and the need to re-position social work in other sorts of human service structures. If the mainstream of social work remains wedded to the structures of the welfare state, the future of social work will be as uncertain as that of the welfare state itself. Unless social workers are able to be more imaginative and creative in their definitions of their own roles, and are able to move beyond the welfare state, the only alternative for survival is to move to join the managerial and market orthodoxies of economic rationalism, as some social workers have already done. The remainder of this chapter, and indeed of this book, rejects such an outcome, and therefore seeks to develop creative and alternative directions for the formulation and definition of social work theory and practice.

Creating alternatives

The above scenarios are not particularly conducive to the values of social work as outlined earlier in the chapter. A more optimistic scenario, however, sees opportunities in the instability and contradictions that are characteristic of both the present and the immediate future context of social work practice. Significant change is more likely to develop in times of instability than in times of stability, and the very idea of crisis implies opportunities to do things differently. Indeed, a situation of crisis implies that things cannot go on in the same way, and that change is inevitable.

This scenario suggests that, perhaps paradoxically, there may now be more opportunities for social workers, and others committed to social justice, to bring about effective change than was the case in times of relative certainty and stability. If the system is indeed approaching a point of crisis, changes that may have earlier seemed naive, impractical or impossible suddenly become real possibilities. The emergence of a new order, from the ruins of the old, may indeed be a realistic option during the next two decades.

If this is the case, there are significant possibilities for creative social work practice. The opportunity is there for social workers to have an impact on the development of alternative structures, which may develop both from within the existing system and also from outside it. This will be taken up in later chapters, but at this stage it is important to outline how such a scenario might develop.

One way of conceptualising such a change is to use the insights of postmodernist and poststructuralist critics of the idea of a single dominant order (see Chapter 3). If indeed a single imposed reality is being replaced by multiple realities, and discourse is constantly redefining the nature of power and of all social relationships, it is not necessary to think of effective change as something that must take place within the existing structures of apparent power and control, such as the parliament, senior management and the corporate boardroom. It becomes possible to play a part in the redefinition of power, justice and social reality wherever one happens to be practising; indeed the very act of 'practice' plays a role in such redefinition. The capacity for change, therefore, is within the reach of all social workers, whatever their location.

From this perspective, the structures of the welfare state, or of non-government and private sector welfare organisations, are possible locations for creative change, and social workers employed in them need not feel totally disempowered. New realities and structures can emerge from within existing ones, and indeed this process is constantly occurring. For social workers to deny this is to disempower themselves, and to ignore what is for many social workers the most likely immediate arena for creative and alternative practice.

Alternatives can also be developed from outside existing structures, and this too is an important arena for social work initiatives. If the existing system is approaching a point of crisis, the possibility of system collapse must be considered, and in this case it is important that there be alternatives which have been established and shown to be workable, even if at present they only operate in a marginal position. This suggests that it is important for social workers to support people and groups who are developing counter-institutions or alternative structures, even if these seem to be naive and unrealistic. It is from such experimentation that genuine alternatives may develop in a future when circumstances will be very different (Ife 1995). As an example, we can consider the possibility of global economic collapse. Given the global nature of the economy, and the apparent incapacity of economists and politicians to control economies under all circumstances, this is not a particularly remote scenario. If this were to eventuate, the experiments that have been made with alternative economic and currency schemes, such as LETS schemes (Dobson 1993; Dauncey 1988), become critically important in helping communities come up with new ways of exchanging goods and services. Even if the global economy does not collapse, it seems likely that numbers of communities, and indeed nations, will feel that this economy has failed them, and will seek alternatives; in such circumstances, the LETS experiment is of obvious relevance. Encouraging imaginative alternatives (of which LETS is just one), and helping to make them workable, can therefore be a very important role for community-based social workers, even if they seem to be at present of only marginal relevance to mainstream society.

A further way in which alternatives can develop is by external pressure, and again there is potential for social workers to be involved in working for change. This involves engaging with the political process, either through the conventional modes of policy debate and political pressure, or through participation in the so-called 'new politics' of social movements. Social movements, such as the women's movement, the peace movement, the environment movement, and many more, are in the forefront of social and political change, both in bringing pressure to bear on existing politicians and decision-makers, and in articulating an alternative vision. The potential for social workers to participate in such social movements, whether in a paid or a voluntary capacity, is significant.

These themes will be taken up in more detail in later chapters, which will seek to outline some approaches to alternative social work practice. For present purposes, the important point is that this scenario, unlike the others, identifies a potential for practice that is not simply reactive and survival-oriented, but that identifies social workers as being able to play a major role in seeking to implement the social justice values of the social work profession.

As pointed out earlier in the chapter, attempting to predict the future is fraught with difficulties, and any attempt to be too specific is likely to be proved to be ludicrously wrong. However the scenarios identified above do represent likely future practice contexts for social workers, and it seems probable that the future will contain elements of all of them. The social work response to these scenarios must inevitably be, to some degree, reactive. Social workers will need to try to preserve their jobs, their profession and the ideals it stands for, their work places and their services to their clients. This involves some degree of accommodation to the existing order, and a capacity to play the game in order to survive. It is also important, however, that the social work response be more than this, and that it seek to create alternatives for future development both of social services and of broader social structures. The tension between the two is difficult to maintain, yet it is essential to do so if social work is both to survive and to remain true to its vision and values. This is the challenge for social work practitioners in the contemporary context.

This chapter has simply set the context for exploring the issues and dilemmas of contemporary social work. The aim of the chapters that follow is to establish an alternative critique, and to consider ways in which it can be more effectively articulated by social workers. The aim is also to develop an approach to policy and practice that will enable social workers to work from within an alternative paradigm. The discussion is based on the belief that simply seeking to join and adapt to the economic rationalist managerial order will be in the interests neither of the social work profession nor of the people in whose interests social workers claim to act. It is not only possible for social workers to articulate an alternative vision and to practise from within an alternative paradigm; from the value base of social work it is their clear responsibility to do so.

CHAPTER

Competing discourses of human services

In order to make sense of the issues and dilemmas discussed in Chapter 1, this chapter will outline a framework for analysis within which the changes affecting contemporary social work can be understood. It relates directly to the experience of social workers, and represents a way of understanding the competing discourses of social work and of human services. This framework represents a convenient starting point in the search for an approach to social work that can provide a genuinely critical or alternative practice.

The analysis will be undertaken in terms of competing discourses in the human services. The importance of discourse as the location in which power is defined and redefined has been a central theme of Foucault's work (Foucault 1972, 1973, 1975; Flynn 1994), and it provides a useful way of understanding the contested field of human service provision, and of enabling social workers to develop ways in which they can seek to alter the discourse and have an impact on working towards change. Such possibilities for change will be specifically discussed in later chapters, but in the meantime it is important to consider the varying discourses, or 'regimes of practices' to use Foucault's terminolgy, which operate in the contemporary context of social work. These discourses construct the boundaries of practice, suggest what is to count as good practice, and, most importantly, define and legitimise relationships of power between the various actors (e.g., social workers, managers and clients). The existence of several competing discourses is one reason for the confusion and fragmentation of the contemporary social work experience.

A conventional form of social policy or social work analysis is to describe the issues facing social workers and the welfare state in terms of differing ideological positions, or more crudely, the 'left' versus the 'right'. Using a model such as that of George and Wilding (1985), Taylor-Gooby and Dale (1985) or Mishra (1981), the issues facing social workers can be understood in terms of competing ideologies of welfare, for example, collectivism versus anti-collectivism, capitalism versus socialism, or the various sub-categories and variants of conventional ideological discourse, such as 'democratic socialism', 'liberal reformism', 'Fabian socialism', 'neo-Marxism', 'corporatism' and so on. Such an approach analyses the key questions in terms of a conflict between different ideas, values, world views or belief systems.

In these terms, the current crisis facing social work is seen as resulting from the decline in legitimacy of the conventional Fabian foundations of social work theory and practice, or a 'shift to the right' in political values. While such an ideological analysis is very important, and helps to identify the value base of social work and the contested values of the current environment, it has not proved adequate in helping to frame an alternative contemporary practice. It has tended to result in pleas for the resurrection and reaffirmation of some apparently tired political ideas—usually some variation of socialism—which do not fit comfortably with contemporary political discourse. It has also not always led to adequate alternative formulations of practice. For example much of the older 'radical' or Marxist social work literature (e.g., Bailey and Brake 1975; Corrigan and Leonard 1978) can be criticised as being stronger on analysis than it is on prescriptions of what a 'radical' social worker should actually do. There have been sound, indeed devastating, critiques of 'the new right', 'economic rationalism', 'neo-conservatism' and the rest (Frost and Stein 1989), but relatively few writers have been able to develop from this analysis a viable and genuinely alternative conception of radical practice.

For this reason, the starting point for the development of an alternative form of social work will not be this traditional ideological debate, nor will it be an argument about the need for a structural analysis, which underpins much of that debate and has been at the core of many attempts to develop a radical social work. This is not to say that ideology is not important— indeed it is critical—and similarly it is not to deny the importance of a structural analysis, whether based on class, gender, race, or some other form of structural disadvantage. These forms of analysis remain of critical importance, and they will inform much of the discussion of later chapters. Similarly, the debates of structuralism versus poststructuralism, and modernism versus postmodernism, while they are central themes of much of the later exploration, are not the starting point for analysis. I have chosen instead to begin with a model of competing discourses of the human services, which has proved to be one that social workers and students have found directly reflects many of the dilemmas of policy and practice, and helps to make sense of the current practice environment. This model, however, is simply a first step in the development of an alternative approach to social work. It is a convenient starting point, rather than necessarily being an answer in itself.

The framework in summary

The framework starts from a position that is directly related to the reality of social work practice in the managerial and economic rationalist environment of the 1990s. It incorporates two dimensions of analysis: a power dimension, *hierarchic/anarchist*; and a knowledge dimension, *positivist/humanist*. It must immediately be noted that power and knowledge cannot be regarded as independent, and their portrayal below as apparently independent dimensions for analysis will be further discussed in Chapter 3, where the framework will be refined in the light of further theoretical discussion. For present purposes, however, using the two dimensions provides a convenient framework for locating social work practice and its dilemmas. It is a framework not unlike those used by Burrell and Morgan (1979) and David Howe (1987) in their discussions of organisational theory and social work theory respectively, but in this instance is applied to the currently competing discourses of human services.

The power dimension: hierarchic/anarchist

The *hierarchic/anarchist* dimension can also be described in more accessible terms as 'top-down/bottom up', and represents a fundamental dichotomy in thinking about human services. The hierarchic, or top-down, approach assumes that wisdom lies at the top of an organisation, that policy should be made at senior levels, and that workers at lower levels of the organisation have a primary role of implementing, rather than shaping, policies (Rees 1991; Wilding 1982). This assumption lies behind conventional bureaucratic organisations, and is commonly accepted by many social workers and others within the human services. Every time a worker talks of aspiring to attain promotion or seniority in order to influence policies and programs 'for the better', that worker is tacitly adopting the hierarchical perspective. It is incorporated in the assumptions of managerialism; the role of managers is to 'manage', and it is with senior management that most of the power is located. The conventional wisdom that policy is made 'from above', and that the role of front-line workers is to pass information 'up' to policy makers so that they can make 'better' policy, is also a result of the hierarchic position. The hierarchic approach can be seen in organisational charts, lines of accountability, ideas of supervision, the perceived desirability of promotion, selection of staff to attend important conferences, and in salary differentials. Basically it can be summarised as 'those at the top know best'. Accountability, therefore, is largely *upward* to those in authority, rather than *downward* to the client or *outward* to the community.

Inherent in the hierarchic position is also a view of worker/client interactions. The client or consumer is implicitly seen as being in a less powerful position than the worker, and as not being as knowledgeable or skilled as the worker in dealing with the client's problems. Top-down assumptions of welfare organisations lead to top-down assumptions of service delivery; in the hierarchical order, the front-line social worker is inferior to senior management, but superior to the consumer of services, in terms of knowledge, wisdom, insight and skills. It is a carefully ordered hierarchical world, in which everyone is supposed to know their place and to act accordingly.

By contrast, the *anarchist* or bottom-up position takes the opposite view. Anarchists argue that the imposition of order and structure, however well-intentioned, denies people's freedom and stifles people's capacity to live and act creatively; it is in the absence of imposed structures that people are able to exercise true freedom, realise their full potential, and form meaningful associations (Ward 1988; Marshall 1992a). This perspective values knowledge, wisdom and action 'from below' rather than 'from above'. In an organisational context, it identifies the activities of front-line workers as being the most important in the organisation—after all, they are the people who are actually delivering the service. Wisdom is seen as much more likely to reside with those 'at the coal-face' with first-hand experience of the problems and issues. As one moves further up the organisational chart one becomes more removed from the reality of human service work, and hence more irrelevant and out of touch. The activities of managers and supervisors are likely to obstruct rather than facilitate useful work, and front-line workers have to find ways to subvert the system or to by-pass the regulations in order to provide an appropriate service. Indeed, as Lipsky (1980) has pointed out, this is often simply a survival tactic for a human service worker, who has to try to make sense of a bewildering and frequently contradictory set of policies and regulations that bear little relation to the reality of the consumer. This view is frequently espoused by social workers and other human service workers, every time they complain that management 'doesn't know what they are doing' or that policies from above are out of touch with the real needs of real people— a not uncommon feeling in the world of social work practice. From this view, the more important 'policy' is not a grand design from above, but rather the totality of front-line worker behaviour. A police force, for example, may have an official policy of racial equality, but if many of its officers in their day-to day work behave according to racist assumptions, its policy *in actual fact* will be very different; from the anarchist perspective, the racist policy 'from below' is the 'real' policy, and the official pronouncements of non-racism from senior officers, despite being impressively recorded in regulations and cited in glossy annual reports, are merely an exercise in public relations.

The anarchist approach to organisations also has its counterpart in actual practice. The view that wisdom may, and indeed should, come 'from below' leads to a position where the consumer or the community is seen as 'knowing best', and where the wisdom of those most affected by social inequality is both legitimised and valued. The understanding of account-ability is therefore that accountability *downward* to the client or *outward* to the community is more significant than account-ability *upward* to management. Such an approach leads much more naturally to developmental and empowerment models of practice (Rees 1991), such as that pioneered by the Brother-hood of St Laurence in Fitzroy (Liffman 1978), which pervade much of the community development literature (Ife 1995). Social workers seeking to work on the basis of an empower-ment model of practice must adopt, at least to some extent, a 'bottom-up' or anarchist perspective. It is a very powerful approach, but one that is directly contradictory to many of the assumptions behind the structures of the welfare state.

It is important to note that contemporary social work discourse incorporates elements of both the hierarchic and the anarchist positions, even though there is an obvious contradiction between them. The need to identify the two conflicting views, and locate social work more clearly in relation to them, forms the first component of the analytical model developed in this chapter.

The knowledge dimension: positivist/humanist

The other dimension of the model proposed in this chapter is the *positivist/humanist* dimension. The positivist paradigm of social science can be briefly summarised as assuming that the task of the social sciences is like that of the conven-tionally understood physical sciences, namely, to discover the universal laws by which society works, through careful measurement, hypothesis-testing, and prediction (Fay 1975; Thompson 1995; Payne 1991). This leads to studying the social world as if it consists of objectively measurable facts or entities—phenomena such as need, alienation, justice, poverty, crime and dependency are 'operationalised' so that they can be quantified and measured. They therefore take on the characteristics of objects that exist in their own right, and can be studied and measured objectively by a detached observer in a value-free way. The skill of a social scientist is in empirical measurement, rather than in interpretation and subjective understanding. Social and behavioural phenomena are seen as obeying universally valid laws, and an understanding of these laws is seen as enhancing the ability to bring about desired change, whether to an individual, a group, a community or a society.

Positivism assumes a particular form of rationality, and indeed seeks to appropriate the very idea of rationality by denying that any other paradigm can be regarded as 'rational'. It forms the basis of economic rationalism, as discussed in Chapter 1, as well as other forms of rationality; 'rational decision-making', planning, and most common understandings of what it means to be 'rational' are characteristically positivist.

This paradigm has been reflected in the social work literature concerned with empirical measurement (e.g., Gibbs 1991), and especially in the single system design approach, which seeks to apply the model of empirical research to interaction between social worker and client. Perhaps the ultimate expression of this perspective in social work is in *Evaluating Practice: Guidelines for the Accountable Professional* (Bloom and Fischer 1982). The authors categorically state 'if a problem exists, it can be measured' (p. 34); indeed from their perspective 'anything that exists can be measured' (p. 35), and they then argue that not only can any problem be measured, but that it must be if social work is to be effective, scientific and accountable. The remainder of the book is taken up with ways of using empirical measurement in social work practice. In one of the most extraordinary and revealing statements in social work literature, they acknowledge and then dismiss any questioning of this view; 'There are, of course, a number of philosophical implications in these arguments, and we'd prefer not to become embroiled in them' (p. 34). While other writers might not be as extreme or forthright as Bloom and Fischer, the empirical positivist tradition has been influential in social work, and can be seen in the many quantitative studies reported in social work journals, and in the contents of a number of social work research and management texts. It can also be seen in the traditional social work definitions of its 'body of knowledge'. In summary, the positivist position deals with social and behavioural issues as if they represent objectively measurable 'facts', which behave predictably according to certain understandable laws. The social worker becomes a skilled technician, who, understanding the 'laws', can 'intervene' appropriately to bring about change.

By contrast, the humanist position insists that the alternative anti-positivist view is worth more than Bloom's and Fischer's single sentence in a book of nearly 500 pages, and that it is essential for social workers to become 'embroiled' in the 'philosophical implications' that Bloom and Fischer prefer to avoid. From this perspective empirical measurement is not everything, and indeed frequently diverts attention from the most significant aspects of human life, suffering, oppression, and social work help. Operationalisation can be seen as simple reductionism, where a concept like need, alienation, dependency or depression is stripped of most of its significant meaning in an attempt to develop some form of measuring instrument. Understanding can come from a variety of sources, of which empirical measurement is only one, and often the least important. Using interpretive sociology, ethnomethodology, collaborative enquiry, participatory action research, or a number of other qualitative measures, social scientists can come to a much richer understanding of the human condition without necessarily having to 'measure' anything, often through 'unscientific' or 'irrational' methods.

This approach emphasises the importance of the person and her/his humanity, and therefore in this chapter has been labelled 'humanist', although the term 'humanism' is perhaps misleading, and can imply an identification with the rationalist Enlightenment world view (Carroll 1993; see also Chapter 4). It rejects as arrogant the positivist notion of social workers as skilled technicians 'intervening' to make things better, and instead emphasises a practice based on the centrality of human values and the need to understand another's unique subjective reality in order to communicate effectively and to join in another's struggle to define and meet her/his needs. It values intuition, practice wisdom, and insights from a broad range of human experience including art, music, spirituality, nature, and other fields that cannot readily, or at all, be measured with the reliability and validity of the positivist. It reflects the social work of some of the earlier writers in the psychoanalytic tradition, as well as many more recent humanist writers such as Nicholas Ragg (1977), Ruth Wilkes (1981), Hugh England (1986) and in Australia Stuart Rees (1994, 1995) and Janet McIntyre (1995). The humanist perspective values uncertainty and difference, it treats individual people as unique, rather than seeking to categorise people for the sake of generalisation. Human values dominate over scientific rationality and utilitarian principles.

Putting the dimensions together: the four discourses of human services

The above summaries are simply meant to identify the two dimensions of the analytical model that forms the basis of this chapter. Each of them clearly covers much more complex and contested terrain, which will be discussed in more detail in later chapters.

These power and knowledge dimensions can be used as the axes of a simple two-dimensional grid, and the resultant model is illustrated in Figure 2.1. This shows the two axes identifying four discourses of human service delivery, the *managerial* discourse (hierarchic positivist), the *market* discourse (anarchist positivist), the *professional* discourse (hierarchic humanist) and the *community* discourse (anarchist humanist).

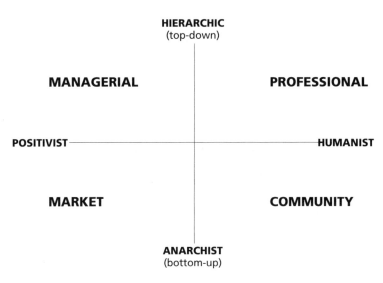

Figure 2.1 Competing discourses of human services

Combining the hierarchic or top-down approach with the positivist paradigm produces the *managerial* discourse of human service delivery, in the top left quadrant. Wisdom and expertise are seen as located at senior levels of the organisation (whether in the public or the private sector), with classical bureaucratic understandings of accountability and decision-making, together with an apparently 'scientific' approach that seeks to develop the ideal machinery with which to provide human services. The emphasis is on measurable outcomes, effectiveness, the efficient use of resources, rational planning, optimising the cost-benefit ratio, and so on, rather than on meeting the felt or expressed needs of human beings with their own particular problems, anxieties, perplexities and aspirations. Workers have only instrumental value in such an organisation; they are there in order to achieve certain ends, but are not valued in themselves, and can be readily dispensed with or replaced should the need arise. Such instrumentalism is a characteristic of the positivist paradigm.

In the lower left quadrant is the *market* discourse of human service delivery, which combines the positivist paradigm with an anarchist, 'from below' perspective. In its ideal form, the market as championed by economic rationalism requires this approach, in that it is the decisions of individual actors, buying and selling goods and services, that are the essence of market transactions. In practice, much of the activity which takes place in the name of the market is more 'top-down', as a result of monopolies and large-scale corporate interests, and this will be the subject of further discussion in later chapters. However, the anarchist assumption remains a strong one in market rhetoric, which is concerned with absence of restraint, deregulation, and allowing people maximum freedom to make market choices for themselves, instead of taking what is provided for them by those in authority. The Thatcherite critique of the 'nanny state', for example, drew heavily on anarchist themes. The market approach is also characteristically positivist, in that the market, and the famous 'invisible hand', are seen as operating according to certain rules. Humanist values are subordinated to the values of the market, and the common way to analyse the market is to see it as some kind of complex machine that needs to be understood and carefully tended by expert technicians, otherwise known as economists.

The hierarchic and humanist perspectives combine to create the *professional* discourse of human services in the top right quadrant. This is characteristically top-down, in that it relies on the skill and expertise of the professional who 'knows best' and who is responsible for delivering a quality service. It can be characterised as humanist because the individual 'client' is the major focus of attention; service is carefully tailored to meet that person's unique needs and there is not necessarily any generalisation or universalising of the person's problem. Humanist values are prominent in the overt value and ethical bases of professionals in the human services, and the person is seen as more important than the 'system' or the economy.

Finally, in the lower right quadrant, the *community* discourse combines the humanist position with an anarchist or 'from below' perspective. Here the empiricism and gener-alisations of positivism are rejected in favour of the humanist position, and this is coupled with a rejection of hierarchy and an affirmation of 'bottom-up' development. It is the basis of a good deal of community-based work, community development models, and empowerment-focused practice. Both the value and the wisdom of ordinary people are emphasised in this approach to human services.

Characteristics of the four discourses

Variation in language highlights the significant differences between these discourses, and a consideration of five aspects of human services will serve to identify and highlight the important elements of each.

The nature of welfare

Each of the four discourses implies a very different view of the nature of welfare. For the *managerial* discourse, welfare is essen-tially a *product*. The rational hierarchy designs and produces welfare, which is then made available to the consumer of that product. This is perhaps most clearly seen in the attempts to develop a 'production of welfare' approach to social policy decision-making (Knapp 1984), a classic form of the positivist-hierarchic approach. Some analogies used in the managerial discourse include the 'one stop' approach, the welfare agency likened to a travel agency providing a number of pre-packaged options (Hough 1994), and the very idea of a 'welfare industry' or a 'social and community services industry'. Such labels iden-tify welfare as being concerned with making a product, and hence they associate with welfare practice those characteristics that go with industry. Once this assumption is made, the way is open for cost-benefit analysis, measures of efficiency, outcome measures, and other elements which have their origins in the world of commercial production but which have been increasingly appropriated in the public service sector (Jones and May 1992). The *market* discourse sees welfare as essentially a *commodity*, to be purchased in some form of market place, and thus similar to other 'goods and services' traded in market transactions. Marxist analysis (Marx 1954) has emphasised the importance of commodification, and in the capitalist environment of the market discourse it is only natural that welfare should be defined in commodity terms. Because commodities must be valued, measured and traded, positivism is an essential component of the market discourse of welfare; anything that could not be so measured and defined could not be traded and analysed from the market perspective.

The *professional* discourse of human service delivery is most compatible with an understanding of welfare as *service*. The human service practitioner supplies a professional service to the client, and the idea of services is very significant in the discourse of the professions, though, as was noted in Chapter 1, this can involve a perversion of the original meaning of the word 'service'. In the context of professionalism, the 'service' is provided to the client, is tailored to that client's individual needs (unlike the generalised 'product' of the managerial mode), and is not readily measurable or able to be traded within the mechanisms of the market.

The *community* discourse, by contrast, emphasises welfare as social activity, or *participation* in a community context. In contrast to the other three discourses, it is more of a process than an outcome. It is 'people helping people', and is grounded in the relationships and transactions that occur between people within the context of human community. While this can involve some degree of market-like exchange, this occurs not from the positivism of the market discourse but from transactions between individuals as part of community interaction.

The recipient of welfare

Following directly from the above discussion one can identify four distinct constructions of the recipient of welfare services, characteristic of each of the four discourses. The *managerial* discourse of human services identifies the recipient as the *consumer*, a role that is necessarily implied by the idea of welfare as product, discussed above. Consistent with the top-down nature of the managerial discourse, the consumer is characteristically passive, and has no say in the actual design and delivery of the product, though of course can often choose whether or not to accept it. The word 'consumer' has become very common in human services discourse, but it commonly has connotations of relative powerlessness—the consumer can 'take it or leave it', but the 'product' is designed and packaged by others. The product is intended for consumption, but with a top-down view of what the consumers need or want, and what is likely to be in their best interests.

In the *market* discourse, by contrast, the welfare recipient is more likely to be seen as a *customer* than as a consumer. The 'customer' is more active, autonomous and powerful than the 'consumer', as customer decisions are seen as determining what will be provided and how this will be done. Customer choice is one of the primary forces driving the mechanisms of the market, and from this perspective the market discourse can be seen as empowering the recipient, and as therefore preferable to the managerial discourse. Indeed this argument is frequently used by advocates of economic rationalism as part of their advocacy of the rule of market forces. The word 'customer' has developed a strong currency, with 'customer focus' being one of the catch-cries of those advocating the latest version of public sector 'reform'.

In the *professional* discourse, the service recipient is defined in the traditional social work terminology of the *client*. The professional relationship is seen as one between professional and client, and this has various connotations of contractual agreement, confidentiality, ethical standards, and so on. Importantly, it is an individual and private relationship, not one with the more public connotations of 'consumer' or 'customer'. This has significant implications for accountability. The professional is supposedly 'employed' or engaged by the client, and therefore the client controls the relationship, though 'professional expertise' means that in reality the professional maintains a major degree of control and authority. This ambiguity in the professional/client relationship has been a significant area of conflict and contradiction for social workers in attempting to come to terms with the power dimensions of social work practice.

Finally, in the *community* discourse the recipient is re-garded as *citizen*, with an independent, autonomous role in a democratic context. This involves the recipient as part of the process, having a major role in terms of both policy and practice. It also involves a much more visible, and potentially collective, role for the recipient. The very notion of citizenship implies participation in civil society, which contrasts with the essentially private and individualised roles of consumer, customer or client.

The social work role

Just as the recipient is seen differently in the four human service discourses, so the role of a social worker engaged in direct service is seen very differently in each. The *managerial* discourse requires a social worker who will participate in the structures and processes of management, and hence the term *case manager* has become popular (Bamford 1990). The social worker becomes someone who 'manages' cases, with all the technocratic and power implications which that term conveys. Helping people with problems becomes a matter of 'manage-ment', and the managerial model in this way has invaded the realm of human service practice. Social work is technical, controlling, and dedicated to the achievement of measurable results using available resources in the most efficient way. There seems little room in such a model for a feeling of common humanity with another, for personal growth, for empowerment, for empathy, or for self fulfilment, unless these are seen in strictly instrumental terms.

In the *market* discourse, a social worker, like other human service workers, plays two possible roles. One is that of *broker* (Bamford 1990), assisting the 'customer' to purchase the most appropriate service, at the lowest possible price, from the range of both government and non-government programs on offer. Here the social worker provides expertise and guidance in order for the customer to make a properly informed market choice, and this is a model that now operates extensively in the area of home and community care for those defined as dependent. The other role for the social worker is that of *entrepreneur*, where the social worker her/himself is operating in the market place, either alone or in partnership, and is seeking to create a market and to provide a program people will pay for. This involves risk-taking, marketing, tendering, and so on. The increasing tendency towards privatisation, and the contracting out of public services, has encouraged many social work agencies and individuals to adopt this particular approach to social work practice, whether at the level of individual service, at the level of consultancy, or at the level of program management and administration.

The *professional* discourse requires the direct service worker to work as a *service professional*, providing professional services in the way familiar to most social workers, under the assumptions outlined in Chapter 1. This role represents most aspects of 'conventional' social work. Given their education and socialisation, it is the social work role with which practitioners are likely to feel the most comfortable.

In the *community* discourse, the worker takes the role of the *community worker* or *enabler*. Human services become the responsibility of the community, and are generated out of community level activity. The social worker enables and encourages such activity to occur, rather than being the person who necessarily provides the service her/himself. This role is familiar to many social workers, especially those working in community development: helping a community to establish and operate a women's refuge, a child care centre, facilities for youth, adequate aged care programs, and so on. It is the community that provides the energy, resources and initiative, and the social worker's responsibility is to stimulate, encourage, assist, and generally to help it all happen.

Accountability

The nature of social work accountability is also understood differently in these four discourses of human service delivery. In the *managerial* discourse, social workers are seen as largely accountable to their organisational superiors, namely *managers* and *supervisors*, through normal bureaucratic channels. The very nature of the organisational arrangement requires that social workers 'do as they are told', following policies, procedures and regulations laid down 'from above'. In traditional public service structures accountability is ultimately to 'the people' through the legislature, but this is achieved through bureaucratic structures that are accountable to their respective ministers, and so the reality for the front-line social worker is accountability upward. In a similar way, a private sector organisation is accountable to its owners or shareholders, but again this is normally achieved through a hierarchical form of organisation.

In the *market* discourse, accountability is achieved by *customer choice*, and the discipline of the market is expected to provide an accountability mechanism; if a worker or agency is not providing a service that is wanted, at a price people are prepared to pay, that worker or agency will rapidly go out of business. Hence a worker is seen as being accountable to the customer, who is able to choose to go elsewhere.

Such a form of accountability to the recipient is also inherent in the *professional* discourse, through the idea of the *client* who is seen as engaging the professional's services. However, in the case of professions such as social work, the client does not often have the power of the 'customer' in the market discourse, and the professional relationship is inevitably unequal and potentially disempowering. Hence the formal organisation of a profession takes on an accountability role through the establishment and policing of a *code of ethics*, through the accepted *professional association* (such as the Australian Association of Social Workers).

In the *community* discourse, a worker is held to be account-able through a process of *democratic decision-making* at community level. Rather than an individual or a bureaucracy, the community engages the social worker, and so the social worker is accountable to whatever community-based structures may be in place, such as a community management committee or collective.

Policy

The four discourses of human service delivery imply different social policy agendas, in order to facilitate 'better' programs and services. In the case of the *management* discourse, what is needed is seen to be *better management*. The response to any organisational problem, from a management perspective, is defined in management terms (Jones and May 1992). It is the quality of the management, and of the managers, that is critical in setting goals and standards, and in achieving effective results. Resources are invested in the recruitment and the continuing training of managers, and the refining of management techniques is seen as having high priority. The latest management tool (total quality management, strategic planning, business process re-engineering, management by objectives, development of a corporate culture, or whatever) is enthusiastically launched on managers and employees with the implicit promise that it will solve everyone's problems, and yet more training packages are designed in order to help the organisation to function better. This has led to increasing proportions of available energy and resources going into organisational development and maintenance, with the result that resources available to those who are actually doing the front-line work of the organisation are severely depleted.

In the *market* discourse, the clear policy thrust is to allow more *competition, privatisation* and *deregulation,* so that the conditions necessary for the market to operate effectively can be created and sustained (Rees, Rodley and Stilwell 1993). This involves reducing direct government activity, allowing the private sector to operate where possible, creating internal markets, contracting out, tendering, and so on. Such policies are based on the assumption that the inadequacies of the market are due to the regulatory constraints under which it has to operate, and that market forces will bring about the most desirable results.

The *professional* discourse incorporates a policy direction which emphasises the importance of both the quality and available quantity of human service professionals. The way to solve social problems is seen as being to provide skilled professional services for those affected, in sufficient quantity to meet identified needs. Hence the emphasis is on standards of *professional training,* the adequate *certification* of professional workers, and the *employment of more workers.* Such recommendations are frequently made by bodies such as the Australian Association of Social Workers.

Finally, in the *community* discourse, desirable policy directions will include *decentralisation,* the *facilitation* of community-based processes and structures through the provision of resources and expertise, and allowing space for community-based initiatives to develop. The community discourse assumes that there is a viable community structure in which human services can be based, yet in contemporary society community structures have been significantly weakened as a result of the processes of industrialisation and modernisation. Hence a policy of encouraging *community development* is a necessary corollary of the community discourse.

The four discourses of community service, as identified in Figure 2.1, thus have significantly different characteristics, and different implications for social workers. These are summarised in Figure 2.2.

HIERARCHIC
(top-down)

MANAGERIAL
welfare as *product*
for the *consumer*
worker as *case manager*
accountable to
management

PROFESSIONAL
welfare as *service*
for the *client*
worker as *professional*
accountable to *client*
and profession

POSITIVIST ——————————————————————— **HUMANIST**

MARKET
welfare as *commodity*
for the *customer*
worker as *broker* or
entrepreneur
accountable through
customer choice

COMMUNITY
welfare as *participation*
for the *citizen*
worker as *community*
enabler
accountable through
democratic decision-making

ANARCHIST
(bottom-up)

Figure 2.2 Competing discourses of human services (expanded)

Locating social work

Although social work can be practised within any of the four discourses, as discussed above, the conventional construction of social work is largely located within the professional, or hierarchic/humanist, discourse. This is the discourse in which traditional social work has been most comfortable, with its emphasis on professional expertise, individualised service, and its combination of humanist values and 'top-down' intervention. It reflects many of the assumptions behind the approach to conventional social work identified in Chapter 1, which represents the educational background and professional socialisation of most social workers. The traditional social work concerns with professional standards, adherence to a code of ethics, the value of the individual and professional models of practice all fit easily within this view.

Social work has, however, never been exclusively located within the professional discourse represented by the upper right quadrant of Figure 2.2. Throughout the history of social work, going back to its origins in the Settlement House movement (Farris, Murillo and Hale 1971; Woodroofe 1962), there have been social workers who have seen themselves reflecting the community discourse, represented by the lower right quadrant. These have included community workers (Ife 1995), the so-called 'radical social work' movement (Mullaly 1993), and social workers who have located their practice within the struggles of social movements such as the women's movement (Marchant and Wearing 1986), the peace movement, the environment movement (Ife 1991) and the trade union movement (Jones 1983). Such social workers have often been perceived as being in a minority within the profession, and many indeed have discarded the label of 'professional'. They have, however, exerted an important influence on social work, in that they have prevented social workers from feeling too comfortable in a 'professional' role, they have reminded social workers of the importance of an analysis of power, and they have held out hope for a more radical alternative. This influence has been very important in preventing social work from becoming too complacent, and in maintaining a 'critical edge' to social work theory and practice.

Until relatively recently, most social workers have been somewhat uncomfortable with the discourses represented by the left hand side of Figure 2.2. Social workers have generally found it difficult to come to terms with the demands of the management discourse (Jones and May 1992), which has served to deny social workers what they see as their legitimate professional autonomy, which has denied the legitimacy to which practitioners have become accustomed, and which represents values of control and expediency that are contradictory to the assumed values of social work.

Before the era of 'new managerialism' it used to be assumed that social workers often made good managers of welfare organisations, and that their expertise was important in such a role. Indeed, management and administration were, and still are, seen by many authors as legitimate forms of social work practice (Donovan and Jackson 1991). In this regard social workers have been unusual; medical practitioners who become managers do not necessarily see themselves as 'practising' medicine, and the same can be said of lawyers and other professionals. Certainly their professional training and value base will lead them to act in certain ways in their management roles, but this does not imply that they are actually practising their profession by doing so. Social workers, however, have clung to the notion that in undertaking management and administrative tasks they are actually practising social work. This has meant that the appropriation of management functions by professional managers has been seen as an assault on the social work profession. By taking this stand social workers have assisted in the reification of 'management', a process that is at the heart of modern managerialism, rather than trying to demonstrate the inadequacies of the entire management paradigm.

The market discourse also presents problems for social workers, and many have felt uncomfortable about practising from that perspective. This is because of the perception that the market does not adequately meet the needs of the disadvantaged, that it exacerbates social and economic inequalities, and that it does not further the ends of social justice. As a result of their education in the welfare state ideals of Titmuss (1968, 1974) and the evils of privatisation, many social workers are understandably mistrustful of the assumption that market forces provide the best answers and will work to the benefit of all. Many of their clients, indeed, are the victims of the market, and it is hard to see how the market can be the solution as well as the problem. In addition, the accepted values of social work do not fit easily with the demands of practice in the market place, where it pays to be aggressive and competitive, and where one has to be able to sell oneself. Social workers tend to be more at home with co-operation, consensus and a certain self-effacing modesty—characteristics that will not help them to compete in the market.

While most social workers are undoubtedly more comfortable locating their practice in the right hand quadrants, and particularly in the top-right quadrant of the 'professional' discourse, that is not the location of most of the contemporary policy debates or organisational contexts that set the framework for their practice. These are firmly located on the left hand side of Figure 2.2, in the managerial and market discourses. The technocratic demands of the 'new managerialism' and the insistence on the sanctity of 'market forces' have become major parameters within which most of the social policy debate takes place. Even the conventional social policy discourse of 'the market versus the state' is located firmly on the left-hand side of Figure 2.2, as the 'state' has come to be seen very much in managerial terms. If the only legitimate alternative to the oppressive structures of the state is the 'free' market, and the only alternative to the inadequacies of the market is the managerial state, then social workers and their values are left well and truly out of the debate, and become irrelevant to what are seen as the major issues. Most proposed policy changes regarding the delivery of human services currently represent either the managerial or the market discourses, or some combination of the two (for example, through controlled 'internal markets' in health care, and in tendering processes for non-government agencies).

It is ironic that public policy and organisational structures have moved significantly towards the left (positivist) side of Figure 2.2 at the same time that the weight of academic social science discourse has moved in the opposite direction. This has happened through the emergence of the critique of positivism, critical theory, poststructuralism and post-modernism, which have served to strengthen a more humanist position in social work departments in Australian universities. In the 1970s and early 1980s it was not uncommon to hear social work academics advocating a more empirical and scientific approach to practice, and lamenting the lack of such empirical rigour and research competence in the field. By contrast, in the mid 1990s, social work departments in universities are often much more interested in qualitative research or participatory action research. Empiricism is seen as suspect, and the 'meta narratives' of positivism are denounced from the standpoint of post-modernism. This is happening at the very time that social workers in the field are being asked to measure everything, to specify their concrete competencies, to be concerned for efficiency and effectiveness measured in empirical outcome terms, to justify their practice on the basis of hard research evidence, and to work in a system that demands generalisation. From the luxury of academic analysis, this is a practice world based on demonstrably false assumptions. Yet academic social work has largely failed to provide practitioners with the means to translate this analysis into the public agenda, partly because the analysis has been undertaken using language that is not readily accessible to workers, politicians, managers or bureaucrats. One of the aims of this book is to suggest ways in which this problem can be rectified.

This emphasises the critical importance of the horizontal (positivist—humanist) axis of the model in Figure 2.2. In terms of the most immediate needs for social work adequately to contextualise itself, social workers need to come to terms with the issues raised by the horizontal dimension, either by learning to work effectively in the managerial and market discourses, or through the more difficult agenda of seeking to influence the policy and organisational agenda so that the humanist ideals, inherent in social work, are reaffirmed and legitimised. The latter is the approach advocated in later chapters of this book.

This emphasis on the horizontal axis is not to deny the importance of the vertical axis. The top-down/bottom-up debate is also critically important, as it has been, and remains, a source of significant debate and division both inside and outside social work. It is therefore necessary to consider both dimensions, though it will be argued in Chapter 3 that the two axes of Figure 2.2 are in reality not independent.

The four discourses also provide a framework for an analysis of social work education. It can be argued that social work education, influenced by the accreditation guidelines of the professional association, remains firmly located within the top right quadrant, with the major 'alternatives' to the dominant discourse being from the community-based, social action and 'radical social work' formulations of the lower right quadrant. On graduation, however, students are increasingly being expected to practise in the left-hand quadrants—managerial and market—for which they are ill prepared.

The analysis of the subsequent chapters is based on a rejection of the economic rationalism, managerialism and blind faith in market forces so characteristic of the managerial and market discourses. By contrast it contends that the legitimate location for social work practice is the community-based, humanist/anarchist discourse, as this reflects both the value base of social work and the most effective contribution social workers will be able to make towards social justice in an increasingly unstable and unpredictable world. Such an approach is not without its risks, and is in many ways problematic in the current context. This book demonstrates ways, both through analysis and action, that social workers can begin to articulate such an alternative, and to have some impact on the policy and organisational context in which they are required to practise. The remainder of this chapter, however, will explore further the four discourses of human services, and consider the implications of each for contemporary social work.

The four discourses of human services: contradictions and possibilities

Management-based social work

The managerial discourse, representing a hierarchic and positivist position, is dominant in contemporary human services (Rees and Rodley 1995). Within the public sector, managerialism is in many instances replacing the older style of professional human services, as is seen in the appointment of specialist managers to senior positions, rather than people with appropriate professional qualifications (e.g., teachers in an education department, health professionals in a health department, or social workers in a welfare department). It is assumed that management is content-free and hence that management skills in one area can readily be translated to another, and that management is essentially the same process, whether it is applied to education, fisheries, roads, prisons, hospitals or water supply (McKnight 1977). Thus an appointment is made to a 'Senior Executive Service' rather than to a substantive position, and postgraduate qualifications in management or economics (rather than, for example, in social policy) are seen as the 'right' courses to take for an ambitious public servant (Pusey 1991). This has the effect of devaluing the substantive knowledge and skills associated with a particular field or profession. Knowledge of health, housing, education or social welfare is not regarded as of great importance for those who are actually managing the agencies that provide these services, and the wisdom and experience of those who have worked in the field is devalued in favour of management expertise. This arises naturally from the positivist tradition of management, emphasising its universal applicability rather than the importance of different contexts for the location of action.

The impact of the managerial model, however, extends well beyond the employment of senior managers. The management approach inevitably defines problems as being resolvable through managerial solutions, and hence the characteristic response to a perceived problem is usually in management terms (Buchanan 1995). It can represent an attempt to impose an imagined certainty (reflected in impressive organisational charts and process diagrams) on the uncertain and contradictory world of human services. Most commonly this results in an organisational restructure, and since the mid 1980s public sector organisations seem to live in a state of almost perpetual reorganisation. Other typical management solutions to problems are to appoint more managers, to provide more management training, or to introduce new mechanisms of accountability. If, for example, there is a perceived 'drug problem', a typical response will be for the government to announce an organisational shake-up of the relevant department, perhaps combining it with another department, splitting one department into two, or removing responsibility for some programs from one department to another (e.g., from Health to Education). This would be accompanied by new forms to be filled out by front-line workers to provide more information on drug problems, on the kind of 'interventions' used by workers, and on the costs involved. In the current ideological context where any increase in public expenditure is seen as irresponsible, there would also be an attempt to make the service more 'efficient' and 'targeted', by seeking to eliminate waste, to ration services to those most 'in need', and so on. This requires more accurate measurement of inputs and outcomes, and more stringent monitoring of worker activity. This in turn implies more things to be measured, counted, timed or recorded by workers, and thus an increased administrative load (Solondz 1995). It also means that professional discretion must be circumscribed, in order to prevent inefficiencies and meet targets. There will be an increase in upward accountability of workers to management, most likely accompanied by decreased accountability 'downward' to the client or 'outward' to the community.

Some of these changes may indeed be worthwhile; few would argue, for example, with an attempt to make a service more efficient, though exactly what should count as efficiency remains controversial. The point of the above discussion is that the conventional management approach only seeks solutions in certain directions, and is therefore limiting in its capacity to adapt to the needs of the human services. It is unlikely to seek genuine client involvement in planning service delivery, or to value the practice wisdom of those at the front line; it is unlikely to involve the community in any more than a token way; it is unlikely to pay much attention to factors in service delivery that may be difficult or impossible to measure; and it is unlikely to look to social, political, cultural or structural issues that may impinge on the problem at hand. In defining service delivery in management terms, it is unable to see beyond the management perspective in providing better services or solving problems. That management itself may indeed be part of the problem rather than part of the solution is not acknowledged.

This limited perspective of the managerial paradigm has significant limitations and problems for social work, and for the effective delivery of social services. It imposes a top-down rationality allowing little room for worker discretion. The idea of a profession is that workers need to be able to exercise professional judgement, but this is heavily circumscribed in a system that devalues professional judgement in favour of managerial expertise. Social work not only requires dis-cretionary judgements to be made by social workers, but more importantly insists on them also being made by clients. Ideas of client self-determination do not sit comfortably with a managerial mode that contains an implicit assumption of wisdom residing with managers. By contrast, social work's commitment to self-determination requires an assumption that wisdom lies with the client, who is in the best position to determine her/his own future and has a fundamental right to be empowered to do so. The language of the managerial discourse labels clients as 'consumers', which implies a relatively passive 'service recipient' role, incompatible with empowerment-based practice (Beresford and Harding 1993).

The managerial approach also offends social workers' traditional understandings of accountability, by replacing accountability 'downward' to the client, or 'outward' to the

63

community, with accountability 'upward' to management. Social workers tend to define their primary accountability as to their clients, or, if working from a community development perspective, to a community. In the managerial discourse, however, accountability is defined in terms of reporting to management, with appropriate statistics about service delivery representing the positivist obsession with measuring and counting everything, even processes that do not lend themselves to being readily measured or counted. This has the effect of marginalising much of what social workers regard as being of greatest importance (Wilkes 1981), as well as disempowering the client and the community by allowing them no active role in the process.

The managerial discourse is therefore fundamentally at odds with social work values as they have been traditionally understood (see Chapter 1). While some social workers have taken a position of uncompromising opposition to what they see as the inadequacies and injustices of managerialism (Rees and Rodley 1995), others have sought an accommodation with the current orthodoxies, in order to retain their jobs and their influence, and in an attempt to maintain some level of service to the disadvantaged. In order to operate within a public sector so heavily influenced by managerialism, social workers have had to compromise their values, and undertake work that is not consistent with principles such as self-determination, empowerment and community accountability. In adapting to the requirements of the managerial paradigm, some social workers have engaged in a process of redefinition of their roles and of social work principles, which to many represents a betrayal of the essence of social work.

One trend has been for social workers to seek to join the management elite. This has been achieved by undertaking MBA degrees, by seeking to prove managerial competence within the terms of the new managerialism, and in many cases by renouncing any identity as a social worker in order to redefine oneself as a manager. Many such workers, while not denying their social work origins, prefer not to mention them where possible, and do not define themselves as social workers. While this frequently provokes criticism from their social work colleagues, there is at least a degree of honesty about such a position, as it recognises the fundamental conflict between social work and the new managerialism, and accepts that to operate effectively as a manager within the current public sector environment it is necessary to deny one's social work values. It is a more consistent position than that of other social work managers who persevere with the notion that it is possible to be both a manager and a social worker, and that management is a legitimate social work method (Skidmore 1983). While this may well have been the case in the public sector of an earlier era, when the 'public sector' was called the 'public service' because service to the public was its primary goal (Pusey 1991), it is a much harder position to hold in the 1990s. Many social workers who attempt such a reconciliation of social work and management find their jobs increasingly contradictory, and become prime candidates for burnout as they seek to reconcile two essentially irreconcilable sets of values.

A more subtle way in which social workers may adapt to the managerial discourse is through an increasing acceptance of authoritarian roles. Work in statutory settings, such as child protection and corrections, has always caused considerable difficulty for social workers, with the role of social police officer sitting uncomfortably with social work values of empowerment and self-determination. Social workers in these fields have been acutely aware of the moral and ethical dilemmas, and have been sensitive to criticisms from their colleagues about their role in social control. In the managerial context, however, there is the danger that social workers may become more comfortable in these roles of overt control, see their work in authoritarian settings as rather less problematic, and be more readily able to justify such 'intervention' as part of a mechanism of state control (e.g., Palmer 1983; Dworkin 1990). Social workers who have successfully defined themselves as 'the experts' in areas such as child protection can readily assume roles that may be seen as more authoritarian as well as more authoritative. The 'appropriate use of authority', 'representing the best interests of society' and 'acting in the best interests of the child' are phrases with which social workers seem to be becoming increasingly comfortable, yet they beg some serious questions. Who defines the 'interests' of the child or of society? What is our justification for 'using authority'? How much 'authority' should we use, and how? And how can 'authority' be reconciled with empowerment? There is an increasing danger, within the managerial paradigm, of these questions being treated as non-problematic and answered without a great deal of moral anguish, or with little participatory decision-making by those most affected.

With increased emphasis on competency, intervention and professional authority, it appears that empowerment as a basis for social work practice is becoming devalued. It is significant to note that in Australia social workers were among the first to use the term 'empowerment' and to specify what it means in terms of social work practice (Liffman 1978; Benn 1981), but now that this very powerful word has entered the general vocabulary many social workers seem less concerned with it, and can readily dismiss the notion of empowerment as meaningless in the contemporary context. The ready acceptance of authoritarian roles, and the corresponding marginalisation of empowerment, is fully consistent with the dominance of the managerial paradigm, incorporating its top-down assumptions of power, and its positivist assumptions of knowledge.

Another way in which contemporary social work has sought to incorporate itself within the managerial paradigm is through its acceptance of the idea of 'case management' (Rose 1992; Moxley 1989; Raif and Shore 1993). This represents the essence of the managerial paradigm, translated into the casework setting, though it has also figured in the more market-based approach of 'purchase of service' brokerage models. No longer are clients people to receive a service, or even people to be 'helped'. Rather they are 'cases' to be 'managed', and the consequence is that the casework role is seen as one of management, requiring management skill, management jargon, and management notions of results, outcomes, efficiency, productivity and accountability. By giving tacit approval to case management (e.g., by applying for case manager positions, by acceding to being called case managers, or through running case manager training programs) social workers in many instances have lent their support to the managerial discourse, and have sought to redefine social work within these terms. It should be noted, however, that some social workers have seen case management as an opportunity to practise from a specific empowerment position, and have sought to align themselves closely with clients in an attempt to 'manage' together the fragmented and contradictory human service system, thereby seeking to ameliorate the worst effects of managerialism.

The above comments, of course, do not apply to all social workers, as many have been vocal and assertive in opposing the managerial discourse of service delivery. Nor should the social workers who have accepted managerialism necessarily be criticised for their actions; in many cases social workers have apparently been presented with little or no choice, especially if they want to remain in employment. The managerial discourse is powerful and seductive; its apparent rationality has strong appeal in an era that seems devoid of certainty, and social workers are as prone as other professionals to a model which potentially gives them authority and status if they are able to play the management game. Social workers, in addition, have not been well equipped to mount an effective opposition to managerialism, and many social workers have accepted the current managerial orthodoxies because they feel powerless to articulate or effect a viable alternative. The way in which social work has been conceptualised and taught has left many social workers ill-equipped to deal with the crisis in which they find themselves, and simplistically to blame social workers is nothing short of 'blaming the victim'.

Just as it is too simplistic to blame all social workers for the incorporation of social work into managerialism, or for that matter for the incorporation of managerialism into social work, it is also too simplistic to blame the field of management for the current inadequacies of managerialism. Some writers within management are also questioning many of these orthodoxies (Reisman 1986), and the long history of the human relations approach to management (Jones and May 1992) has much in common with social work values. The problem is that this perspective is under-represented in contemporary public sector management, for reasons outlined by Pusey (1991) in his analysis of the senior bureaucrats in the Australian Public Service.

Market-based social work

The other dominant discourse of service delivery for contemporary Australian social workers is the market. One of the primary tenets of economic rationalism, or neo-conservative economics, is the priority of the market as the preferred mechanism for allocating goods, resources and services. This is based on an assumption that the consumer knows best, and that consumer choice is maximised through the unrestricted operation of market forces. Thus it is consistent with a 'from below', or anarchist, position on the vertical power dimension of the model, but it also contains a strong positivist element, emphasising the universal laws of supply and demand, and based on the positivism of conventional neo-classical economics. Economic rationalism requires that the market be given priority, and be allowed to operate in an unregulated environment. It also requires that government activity be reduced to a minimum, and private sector (or quasi-private sector) activity be maximised, in order to increase efficiency and productivity. To achieve these goals, as discussed in Chapter 1, government policy has had five major thrusts: *privatisation*, which seeks to sell government activity to the private sector; *encouraging competition* by allowing alternatives to government services to be established; *contracting out* as much government activity as possible; requiring non-profit and profit sector agencies to tender for specific services; *marketisation*, which involves the setting up of internal markets or quasi markets, for example, in the brokerage model of services used in Home and Community Care; and *corporatisation*, which involves making public sector agencies as like their private sector counterparts as possible (it should be noted, however, that there is some inconsistency in the usage of these terms in the literature).

This approach to social policy and human services causes significant problems for social workers. The welfare state, and in large measure the profession of social work, came into being precisely because of the inability of the free market to meet human need in an equitable way. The history of capitalism suggests that while it is an excellent economic system for stimulating growth and technological development, it does not distribute the resulting benefits fairly. Reliance on the market exacerbates the gap between the advantaged and the disadvantaged (Stilwell 1993; Titmuss 1976). As pointed out in Chapter 1, social work has its foundations in the Fabian welfare state ideal, and has defined itself within this context. For social work to operate in a market context is to deny what for many social workers is a significant part of their heritage and justification.

The inadequacies of the market are not simply confined to its historical failure to meet human need (Martin 1993; Rees, Rodley and Stilwell 1993). The ideal of the market contains its own fundamental contradictions, which render it an unstable mechanism on which to base social policy, social work, or indeed any human activity. Even a cursory examination of the operation of the ideal free market shows that the market constantly erodes its own context. In order to operate effectively, the market requires an absence of regulation, the discipline of competition, and opportunities for customers to make free and fully informed choices. However, success in the market can often best be achieved by eliminating the competition through buy-outs or takeovers, or by co-operating with potential competitors through cartels. Market success can also be achieved by ensuring that consumers are not fully informed, but rather are given a distorted picture of the choices available through one-sided advertising and marketing. Thus success in the market is achieved by eliminating the very conditions that make an ideal market possible, and the only way in which effective market mechanisms can be maintained is through regulation, which itself is antithetical to the idea of the market. To put it simply, the market cannot operate properly *without* regulation, but it cannot by definition operate properly *with* regulation.

Another problem with the market is that it rewards those who exploit individuals and the environment, who can externalise their costs (especially environmental and social costs) and who can operate only just within the letter (rather than the spirit) of the law. The employer who wishes to give additional pay or benefits to workers, to minimise environmental damage, or to 'be a good corporate citizen' is likely to return a lower profit than competitors who do not care about such matters, and so will be at a disadvantage. The Marxist assertion of the essentially exploitative relationship between owners of capital and sellers of labour is as true of modern capitalism as it was in Marx's day, and an inevitable consequence of reliance on the market is the entrenchment of the exploitation both of people and of the earth.

Further problems with the market are evident in the global operation of capital. Globalisation of the economy has resulted in what Brecher and Costello characterise as 'the race to the bottom' in which nations compete with each other to provide favourable environments for international investment, by lowering wages and living conditions, reducing public services such as health and education, and repressing the dissent which inevitably follows such policies (Brecher and Costello 1994).

As the principles of the market are applied to the social services, it is interesting to note that the effect is frequently the opposite of the rhetoric. Part of the appeal of markets is their 'from below' perspective, arguing for greater power to the grassroots in the form of consumer choice. The process of contracting out social services, however, has frequently been to increase the power and control of central government. Non-government agencies that were previously supported with an operating grant are now required to tender for specific services that the government purchases. No longer is the agency free to develop its services in the way it thinks best, to establish innovative programs, or to provide an alternative to government; these used to be the chief justification for non-government welfare. Under the current system of contracting, the control of central government is much stronger; the agency must meet the government's agenda or it will not receive funding. Thus the rhetoric of the market mode belies the reality. In this case, it is actually the managerial discourse of centralised, top-down control that is operating, using the rhetoric of the market to achieve very different ends.

As with the managerial paradigm, social workers have reacted to the increasing popularity of the market discourse partly by seeking to oppose it, and partly by trying to accommodate it and to survive within the new environment. Again, this has meant that social workers have had to compromise on some of their long-held principles in order to keep their jobs, and to seek to influence the system from within. Some social workers have enthusiastically embraced the market mode, especially those in private practice. The gradual acceptance over the last fifteen years of the legitimacy of social workers operating in private practice has been accompanied by very little debate within the profession, despite the reservations of some social workers who believe that private practice is simply reinforcing the structures of oppression social work seeks to oppose, and that it can be of little benefit to the most disadvantaged who remain the major concern of social workers. This is an example of the way social work has accommodated itself to the market discourse, and other examples can be seen in the way social workers have accepted, and indeed advocated, brokerage models, and have been prepared to tender for services that used to be provided by government.

As with the above discussion of managerialism, it would be simplistic just to blame social workers for this acceptance of a discourse that is so at odds with their professional heritage and values. In many cases it has simply been a necessity in order to retain a job, and it is often motivated by the intention of providing as good a service as possible; 'If we don't tender for this, then who will?' is a common, and in many cases appropriate, sentiment. And again, it can be suggested that social workers have not been provided with an adequate base from which to form a critique of the market discourse and to develop viable alternatives.

The market and the managerial discourses are the dominant contexts of service delivery, and represent economic rationalist and managerial orthodoxy. Neither of them represents a comfortable environment for social workers, as they both contradict the values and the heritage of social work. Social workers have been used to social policy debate cast as 'the market versus the state', but by 'the state' they have understood the welfare state based on a commitment to some form of equity and social justice, and hence social workers have enthusiastically supported the 'state' side of the debate. In the current context, however, the 'market versus the state' debate is carried out largely on the left hand side of the diagram in Figure 2.2. It is a debate between the market and managerial discourses. The 'state' is no longer the generally benevolent welfare state, but the managerial state dedicated to economic rationalist ends and with little emphasis on social justice. The values of social work have been left out of this debate, and in order to reinstate them it is necessary to recast the debate more towards the right hand (humanist) side of Figure 2.2.

Profession-based social work

The third quadrant of Figure 2.2 is the professional discourse, combining an essentially hierarchical or top-down approach with a commitment to the values of humanity rather than a blind faith in the empiricism and the universal laws of positivism. This has historically been the discourse within which social work has felt most comfortable, and has represented the context for social work education, accreditation and organisation. It most closely fits the assumptions of conventional social work as described in Chapter 1. There are, however, three major problems about the professional discourse as a location for present and future social work practice committed to the promotion of social justice.

The first is simply that the professional discourse is becoming increasingly out of step with current orthodoxies in social policy and administrative practice. The dominance of the managerial and market discourse has left the professional discourse seeming somewhat out of date. Other professions such as nursing and occupational therapy have moved to redefine themselves more aggressively within the managerial and/or market discourses, and represent a threat to social workers through the provision of services that social workers have regarded as their own responsibility. Maintaining a strong professional (in the traditional sense) definition of social work is unlikely to find favour with managers, politicians or funders, and can represent a fast road to oblivion. The ideas of professional discretion, accountability to a code of ethics, independence and professional authority may be still applicable to medicine and law, but are becoming harder to legitimise for social workers and others who do not have the same power and status, and who are forced to operate within the current 'wisdoms' of managerialism and the market.

The second problem with the professional discourse relates to issues of power (Wilding 1982). The very nature of the professional relationship assumes an inequality of power, because of a claim to special knowledge and skills on the part of the professional that are denied to the client. Indeed, professions characteristically exclude others from access to this knowledge and skill, by the use of mystifying jargon and by seeking to place restrictions on those who are 'licensed' to practice. This is inherently disempowering and is contradictory to models of practice that seek to empower people to have control over their own lives and destinies (Liffman 1978; Rees 1991). Illich has argued that professionals assume the power to define people's needs for them, and hence are by their very nature 'disabling' (Illich et al. 1977). The twentieth century, in Western societies, can be regarded as the era of the professional, with professionals of various kinds assuming the right to define people's needs and prescribe how people should live. There are professional experts in everything from cradle to grave: how to have a baby, how to raise children, how to eat, how to drink, how to work, how to play, how to exercise, how to relax, how to make love, how to retire, and how to die. There seems to be no aspect of human activity in which there are not professionals trying to tell people the right way and the wrong way of doing things, and as a result one can argue that people have been effectively disempowered, and spontaneity and freedom of choice have been circumscribed.

Social workers, by adopting a professional model, lay themselves open to such criticism. The particular problem for social workers is that they espouse a commitment to self-determination and empowerment, which is evidently at odds with the reality of 'professional practice'. This dilemma is not new for social workers, and fuelled much of the debate about deprofessionalisation in the 1970s (Wilding 1982). Although that debate does not currently have the same intensity within social work, the argument remains strong, and the contradiction of trying to be an 'empowerment-based profession' remains unresolved.

A related argument sees the main beneficiaries of profess-ional social work as social workers themselves. Given the relatively flimsy evidence for the effectiveness of much social work intervention, and the way in which social workers often do not seem to have the impact that they seek, it is tempting to conclude that the whole enterprise has existed largely for the benefit of social workers themselves, who have benefited from established career paths, professional power and prestige, and structures that enable the 'myth' to be perpetuated (see particularly Polsky 1991; also Illich et al. 1977 and Jamrozik 1991). While this argument may well be considered an over-statement, it raises the important question of who benefits most from professionalised social work, and it questions the cost-effectiveness of professional services in terms of client benefit.

The third problem associated with the professional discourse relates to resources. An approach to meeting human need that relies primarily on individualised professionalised services is very expensive. It could be questioned whether a society could ever afford to have all human services delivered in such a way, but certainly in the current political and economic climate it is quite impossible for sufficient resources to be made available to support such an approach. It is simply impractical to consider the professional model as the way in which all people can have their needs adequately met, and hence a professionalised ap-proach will inevitably lead to some form of rationing, as supply will be inadequate to meet demand. In the current context of economic rationalism, this will almost certainly be rationing through the market, which favours the more advantaged members of the community, and does not provide adequate service to the disadvantaged. Other forms of rationing—for example through waiting lists, by age, or by defined level of need—all have their particular problems, both technical and ideological. It is necessary to develop an alternative to the professional model for many human services, though there will no doubt always be a place for some services to be delivered in this way, particularly services to specific disadvantaged groups, or services that require highly specialised skills.

If social work is to have a significant future, and if it is to be relevant to the changing patterns of service delivery in a changing world, it will need to establish its identity beyond the professional discourse, and to define itself in such a way that it is not limited by the ideological contradictions and resource limitations of professionalism.

Community-based social work

Of the three discourses of service delivery so far discussed, the managerial discourse and the market discourse were seen to be fundamentally in contradiction to social work values and principles, and the market and professional discourses were both seen to contain inherent contradictions. The fourth quadrant of Figure 2.2, the community discourse, represents an approach that is at least consistent with social work values, and that does not contain the internal contradictions of either the market or the professional discourses. It therefore, at least in theory, represents a more viable basis for the development of social work.

Community-based social work has a long tradition. It has found its expression in various models of community organisation or community development (Ife 1995), in 'community social work', in empowerment based models (Rees 1991) and in much of the literature on 'radical social work' and social action (Mullaly 1993). It seeks to combine the bottom-up or anarchist approach with a commitment to human values and a rejection of the certainties of positivism.

It could be suggested that one of the reasons for social work's apparent inability to cope effectively with the challenges of the managerial and market discourses is that social work has in the past been preoccupied with a debate between the professional and community discourses. The community discourse has been the location for much of the oppositional element within the social work profession (Tomlinson 1977), and many social workers have defined their practice from within this quadrant, rather than from within the professional model.

Elements of the community-based model will be discussed in later chapters, as it is the contention of this book that this represents the most fruitful position from which to develop significant alternatives to the managerial and economic rationalist orthodoxies. Seeking to oppose them from within the professional paradigm is effectively operating from a position of weakness, given the contradictions and difficulties mentioned above. By contrast, the promise of a significant alternative from within a community-based discourse represents a source of potential hope and future direction.

It is important to emphasise, however, that the community-based quadrant is not without its problems, and does not represent a magic answer to the dilemmas of the other three discourses. Community structures and processes can be oppressive, and can operate to exclude, marginalise and oppress. Human rights, a critical component of the Western individualist world view, can be too easily devalued in the interests of community solidarity. Because the community-based approach requires a significant shift away from the extreme individualism that characterises much of the political, social and economic orthodoxy of modern society, it is difficult to generate much support within the wider community if the community-based approach is couched in the familiar language of socialism. The analysis and ideals of socialism may be as valid as ever, but with the decline of European communism, and the betrayal of their socialist origins by most of the social democratic parties of the West (including the Australian Labor Party), socialism is an ideology that is hardly in good currency. It is therefore necessary to use other terminology to define and articulate a future direction for social work, and consequently the discourses of postmodernism, feminism, humanism and critical theory will be explored in the following chapters.

3

Formulating an alternative

Reworking the model

The model proposed in Chapter 2, and summarised in Figure 2.2, has been presented with two axes perpendicular, implying (at least for the mathematically inclined) that the knowledge and power dimensions are independent. This, however, is an obvious over-simplification, and it is now time to re-examine the model from a different analytical position.

Power and knowledge are not separate, but are closely related, and to treat them as distinct and independent 'dimensions', as was done in Chapter 2, is both artificial and contradictory. The popular phrase 'knowledge is power' clearly identifies their close relationship at the level of 'common knowledge', and indeed seeks to equate them by implying that acquiring knowledge enables people to exercise greater power. At a more sophisticated level, Foucault maintains that it is in the construction of knowledge that discourses of power are defined and redefined, and that knowledge and power are not unitary 'objects', but are legitimated through social and institutional relations. Power is a consequence of struggles to legitimate and be legitimised by 'knowledge'. Individuals may embody power/knowledge through 'expert status' associated with institutional membership and personal identity, and because social institutions are populated by individuals it is necessary to examine the individual embodiment of power/ knowledge. Foucault thus locates power not in formal organis- ational structures but in the constantly changing redefinition and control of discourse, and in 'sites of power' occupied by individuals (Foucault 1972, 1975; Rabinow 1984; Rouse 1994; Simons 1995). This also bears some relation to Marxist notions of hegemony (Gramsci 1973), where control of the production and communication of knowledge is one of the ways by which relationships of power and oppression are maintained and reinforced. Foucault's conception of power as an entity that is manifest in social relations, rather than as something some people 'have' (in differing quantities) and others do not, has significant implications for notions of 'empowerment', and this will be taken up in the discussion in Chapter 5. In the meantime, it is sufficient to note that power and knowledge cannot be regarded as separate and independent, and this calls into question the assumptions behind the representation of Figure 2.2.

Positivism and hierarchical practice

There is a significant relationship between the positivist paradigm and the hierarchic or top-down approach, implying a link between the top and the left hand side of Figure 2.2. By examining the practice implications of positivist knowledge, Brian Fay (1975) has shown that this relationship is logically necessary. In summary, positivist social science seeks to discover universal laws, of a causative nature, which govern social and political life. The goal of positivism is thus to be able to predict the consequence of certain social events, and to understand what conditions will lead to particular results. The ability to predict in this way leads to the ability to control; for example, a powerful nation that understands the factors that will cause or prevent political revolutions will be able to use this knowledge to ferment revolutions in countries of opposing ideologies, and prevent revolutions in countries considered 'friendly'. At a more individual level, positivist knowledge can lead to the control of the behaviour of another person, through, for example, behaviour modification, therapy, or other forms of direct intervention. Positivist knowledge is therefore inherently linked to the capacity to control society and individuals, through an understanding of causal laws and the manipulation of circumstances to bring about desired ends. The capacity to manipulate and control within the positivist paradigm will inevitably be greater for those who have access to resources, that is, those who are already powerful. Positivist knowledge, therefore, is most likely to be used to entrench the legitimated power and resources of the powerful, rather than to support the disadvantaged or marginalised. This is often denied by arguing that the universalism of positivist knowledge means that all people have access to it, and that it can be used by the disadvantaged as much as by the powerful. This argument, however, ignores the structural causes of power and access to information in modern society—the capacity of the powerful to utilise positivist knowledge will always be greater. Far from being value-neutral and ideology-neutral, positivist social science is by its very nature strongly conservative and will primarily serve the interests of any dominant group that controls access to information and to resources.

This is all totally consistent with the top-down approach, emphasising control from above, the importance of elites, and 'rational' planning and management. Fay argues that a necessary outcome of positivism is the establishment and enhancement of the 'policy science' approach to social change and control, employing policy experts who are in possession of specialised knowledge, and who are able to plan ways for society to meet its desired ends. This leads to the disenfranchisement of ordinary people, as increasing areas of social and political life are defined as the domain of the expert, and as problems (such as unemployment, the economy, crime, poverty or ill health) are seen as far too complicated for ordinary people to understand. Thus these problems are increasingly left to technocrats to solve, rather than being subject to genuine informed public debate.

It can be argued that social workers have played a part in this process of mystification and disenfranchisement, by establishing themselves as the 'experts' in certain social problems and by seeking to become policy technocrats. For present purposes, however, the important point is that positivism implies a form of top-down practice.

Similarly, top-down practice lends itself naturally to positivist forms of knowledge. If one assumes that wisdom and knowledge lie at the top of the organisation, that top-down rational planning is the most appropriate form of change, and that qualified experts are in the best position to plan and deliver services, then the rationality and certainty of positivist social science is very appealing. It simply provides managers with the tools they need in order to manage and control more effectively. In Foucault's terms, top-down practice enables managers to be legitimated as knowledge-experts, and to operate in a hierarchical way, in the process of which positivist constructions of reality are reinforced.

This clear link between positivism and top-down practice can be seen in their common origins in modernist Enlightenment thinking. They both derive from the rational, logical and scientific world view of modernism, and are part of the process of defining the world in a rational way. Indeed, as one looks more closely at positivism and top-down practice they become more like two different aspects of the same phenomenon, rather than the extremes of two independent dimensions as is implied by the diagrammatic representation of Figure 2.2.

Humanism and anarchism

Just as there is a relationship between positivism and hierarchy, so it can be argued that there is a relationship between the other two ends of the dimensions of Figure 2.2, namely humanism and anarchism. The anarchist position (Marshall 1992a; Ward 1988) derives from a value which insists that people are more important than structures, and that structures oppress rather than liberate. It thus has at its core a commitment to humanism, and, to use common social work terminology, to the inherent worth of the individual (see Ragg 1977). In opposing structures of domination, anarchism also opposes the knowledge base on which those structures are built, which is the positivist paradigm.

Just as anarchism can be seen to imply a humanist position, similarly a case can be made that a primary commitment to humanity leads naturally to a bottom-up perspective. A humanist commitment requires that people should be able to articulate their needs and aspirations and should be empowered to act in order to have them met. It is hardly surprising that some of the world's greatest exponents of the human ideal, such as Gandhi, Martin Luther King, Nelson Mandela and Vaclav Havel, had so little time for established structures of authority and accountability in their efforts to make the world a better place (see Chapter 4). Even though Mandela and Havel subsequently themselves became politicians within the system they had helped to transform, both have remained special among politicians in that their motivation is primarily to humanity rather than to their own advancement (Havel 1992; Mandela 1994), and they have become the outstanding exceptions to the otherwise depressing conclusion that political power corrupts, at least in the moral sense if not the material.

While some would suggest that the ideal of people being able to articulate their needs and aspirations, and act to have them met, can best be achieved through a strong socialist state, the experience of socialist states and of large welfare state bureaucracies suggests that they tend to be disempowering rather than empowering. The alternative view can be expressed simply as the belief that, as long as they have access to adequate resources, people and communities will be able to do a better job of meeting their needs and organising their lives if left to themselves than they will by having solutions and structures imposed on them from above, however well-intentioned the managers, technocrats and social workers may be. From this perspective, the values of humanism and of bottom-up, or anarchist, social work practice are clearly closely related, and are no more independent of each other than are positivism and hierarchy.

Combining the dimensions and crystallising the contradictions

As a consequence, the diagram in Figure 2.2 must now be reconceptualised to show the close links between positivism and hierarchy, and between humanism and anarchism. This suggests a single 'dimension' as the basis of analysis, which might for the moment be described as hierarchic/positivist–humanist/anarchist. This, however, raises the danger of reducing the discussion to a simplistic binary opposition, with all the implications and inadequacies of dualistic analysis (Plumwood 1993). It is in fact much more complex than this, as will be shown in the remainder of this chapter and in Chapters 4 and 5.

Recognising the compatibility of hierarchy with positivism, and of anarchism with humanism, is important for the four discourses of human service delivery, and social work, as described in Chapter 2. It suggests that the market and professional discourses are internally contradictory, in that they are attempting to reconcile two opposing paradigms (positivism and anarchism, hierarchy and humanism). In Chapter 2 such contradictions were indeed identified, and seen as the causes of significant problems both for the market and for notions of professionalism. Both market and professional modes of service delivery are essentially unstable, and there are constant pressures to draw them into either the managerial or the community discourse, each of which has the advantage of internal consistency in its approach. The market approach is always subject to incorporation into managerialism; small enterprises tend to grow into larger bodies, competition is limited, and a few big players tend eventually to dominate the market as monopolies or cartels, unless specifically prevented by regulation. Such regulation is essentially managerial rather than market-based; in order for the market to work properly it needs to be 'managed'. As managers of large organisations, the managers of the 'big players' in the private sector will tend to operate in managerial mode, and indeed it is from the experience of the large private corporation that much management 'wisdom' is derived. Eventually, privatisation only achieves the substitution of large private sector bureaucracies for large public sector bureaucracies, each seeking to operate essentially within the same managerial paradigm, and the idea of free market competition becomes largely a myth.

This inevitable trend can clearly be seen in the way the free-market rhetoric of tendering and contracting out has resulted in the strengthening of the larger more bureaucratic non-government welfare agencies at the expense of the smaller community-based organisations, and in tighter bureaucratic control over non-government agency operations. A policy of apparent decentralisation of power has in fact had the opposite outcome, and an approach apparently based on the primacy of the market is in reality serving to entrench a managerial approach to the delivery of human services

For the 'ideal' market to survive, with effective and genuine consumer choice, and with market decisions taken by small competing players responsible to consumer demand, it may indeed be necessary to move to the community discourse, and advocates of LETS systems (systems where a local community currency is used to facilitate the local exchange of goods and services) will maintain that it is only within such localised exchange systems that the ideal of the market can be realised in such a way that it genuinely advantages the consumer (Dobson 1993; Dauncey 1988). This moves the market into the domain of community-based practice models, as LETS schemes require a genuine community base, and have been used and advocated by social workers and others working within a community development model (Dobson 1993).

Similarly, there are significant pressures on practitioners in the professional discourse to realign their practice either with the managerial or the community-based approach. As was discussed in Chapter 2, many social workers have found it necessary to adapt their practice to the managerial model, and the top-down assumptions of professional practice make this an easy transition as long as one is able to resolve the consequent value conflicts. On the other hand, a number of social workers, challenged by the essentially disempowering nature of conventional professional practice, have sought to develop more bottom-up approaches to their work, thus moving to the community-based quadrant of Figure 2.2.

Both market and professional discourses, therefore, face significant pressures to incorporate them into one of the other two discourses. From this perspective, the major rationalist threat to social work values comes not from the market discourse (which is as tenuous as the professional), but from the managerial discourse. Managerialism can only become stronger as the contradictions of the market require changes in policy and administration, and as the ideals of the 'free market' are incorporated into top-down managerialism and control, surviving only in the form of legitimising rhetoric. Such an analysis also suggests, however, that for social work to base its opposition to managerialism and economic rationalism from within its traditional discourse of professional models of practice is unlikely to be successful. Like the market discourse, the professional discourse is both contradictory and vulnerable. Hence, the only likely base for a robust alternative to the inequitable orthodoxies of economic rationalism and managerialism is the community-based discourse, despite its current unfashionable image.

It appears, then, that the collapsing of the two dimensions of Figure 2.2 into one may serve as a basis for conceptualising the problematic context of contemporary practice, and the articulation of an alternative. But before doing so, it is important to look at the resultant single 'dimension' more closely. In particular, what is involved in the humanist/anarchist position, which has emerged from the previous discussion as a likely location for alternative practice? The dominance of positivist and hierarchical discourses has meant that such an alternative has not been well conceptualised, and in itself it is potentially contradictory. For example, the use of the term 'humanism' is problematic, given the dominance of an idea of humanism at the centre of the same Western world view that has spawned positivism and rationality. This issue will be discussed in Chapter 4, where an attempt will be made to articulate a humanism that is liberated from such constraints.

The idea of a single dimension, or dualism, juxtaposing positivist/hierarchic practice on the one hand with humanist/ anarchist practice on the other, relates closely to two other important dualisms that have been significant in the social sciences. These are modernism/postmodernism, and patriarchy/feminism. Each has been widely discussed within the social sciences, and it might be suggested that the humanist/ anarchist approach at which our journey has now arrived is simply postmodernism or feminism (depending on one's theoretical orientation) by another name. It is important, then, to examine postmodernist and feminist arguments, and to ask two questions of both the postmodernist and feminist critiques. The first: *how can postmodernism and feminism help to articulate an alternative approach to social work practice?* The second: *is either of them adequate and sufficient by itself as a conceptual base for social work?* In the following sections it will be argued that each is extremely important, indeed *necessary*, in informing the critique and establishing the alternative, but it will also be suggested that neither is *sufficient* as a conceptual base, and that something more is needed.

Modernism and postmodernism

The positivist/hierarchic discourse can be readily equated with modernism, which is the subject of the postmodernist critique.

Postmodernist thought emerged from the humanities rather than the social sciences, and in some ways its critique (or more accurately, its critiques) of modernism can be seen as parallel to the social science critique of positivism. Its origins in the humanities mean its language is the language of the humanities, using terms such as 'discourse', 'text', 'narrative' and 'author'. It now permeates much social science writing, even in unacknowledged forms; as an example, the frequent use of the idea of 'discourse' in the previous chapter signifies a reliance on postmodernist understandings.

A brief summary cannot hope to do justice to the substantial and varied body of theorising that can be described as 'post-modernist', and that incorporates the work of such differing and complex theorists as Derrida, Lyotard, Lacan, Baudrillard and Kristeva (Harvey 1989; Kumar 1995; Seidman 1994; Rose 1991; Lechte 1994). It is closely related to the poststructuralism of Foucault, which adds a further dimension to an already complex picture. With that acknowledgement, for our present purposes it is still necessary to attempt such a summary, if only because of the inaccessibility of many of the original works of postmodernist and poststructural writers caused by the density of their arguments and the obscurity of their language, and also because of the relative absence of such a perspective in social work literature prior to the 1990s (Hartman 1991; Howe 1994; Solas 1994; Camilleri 1995; Pardeck et al. 1994; Latting 1995; Leonard 1995).

One of the central themes of postmodernism is the denial of a single rationality, discourse or narrative within which to understand the world and interpret 'reality'. The 'death of the meta-narrative' (Lyotard 1984) has significant implications for social science, and indeed for all human understanding. There is no single reality, but rather different realities are constantly being defined and redefined by different actors in different contexts. Thus any attempt to develop a universalist under-standing of history, politics or society, based on universally applicable generalisations, is simply an attempt to impose one particular definition of reality on others, and has no intrinsic validity. This is the perspective that leads Foucault to discuss power in terms of discourse rather than in terms of structure; it is through discourse that power is both defined and exercised, and relationships of power are constantly being reshaped through the development of different discourses.

Modernism is regarded as being based on the idea of unifying discourses, contained in ideas of history, progress, and rationality. Postmodernists reject the modernist notion that there is one 'right answer', or one 'best' way to do something, or even to understand something. Instead they posit a world of relativism, where 'reality' is always contextualised, and where there are no universals.

Postmodernists reached this position through an understanding of the relationship between 'author', 'text' and 'reader'. Modernism has been seen as giving priority to the author, who is regarded as the source of the text, with the reader passively consuming the author's product. From this perspective, the text has a timeless and objective reality, and is the creation of the author. By contrast, postmodernists emphasise the role of the reader in interpreting the text, and, in doing so, also constructing the author. Each reading of a text is different, and in the process of interpretation the constructions of both text and author change. The text, and even the author, are thus the creation of the reader. This process applies not just to the writing and reading of a book, but in other acts of interpretation and definition. A building, for example, can be seen as a 'text', in the way its form is defined and given meaning by the people who look at it, live or work in it, and use it. They are much more important in the 'construction' of the building than the architect or the builder. The building is given significance by the meanings people attach to it; these change with different people, and at different times. Similarly, the human body can be seen as a text, and is read by others in different ways depending on the social and cultural context. In that way the physical person is constructed within a context of, for example, racism and sexism, and the 'identity' of a person is determined by the constructions of those who 'observe' her/him rather than by that person's essential being. The person will thus be constructed differently at different times and in different contexts. As further examples, social phenomena such as a family, a community, a welfare agency, supervision, an interview or the social work profession are all read as texts by those who observe or participate in them. Rather than regarding them as having some form of independent objective existence, postmodernists would concentrate on the ways they are constructed and reconstructed by those who read the texts, and would seek to deconstruct these social phenomena in order to understand the way they are defined and interpreted within dominant or competing discourses.

Postmodernism also does not accept ideas of historical progress, as the very idea of progress implies the acceptance of a meta-narrative. It does not accept notions of objectivity, or of 'reality' existing in any sense other than in the constructions and reconstructions of different readers, and in constantly changing discourses. Reality is fragmented, disjointed, and cannot be understood within a single system or framework. Postmodernism also does not accept traditional disciplinary boundaries, as these are particular attempts to define reality and to impose a modernist perspective on knowledge.

A postmodernist position suggests that the age of modernity is coming to an end. This was an age in which a modernist paradigm was an adequate representation of a reality that was dominated by modernist art, music, literature, philosophy, history and science. The era of postmodernity, on the other hand, is one in which the meta-narratives of modernism are called into question, and which will be better understood through the fragmented and relativist realities of postmodernism. This view does not articulate an objective or a single vision for the new order (this would, of course, be thoroughly modernist), but instead sees a world that becomes fragmented and disjointed by relativism. Simply put, it is a philosophy of 'anything goes', and can be seen as opening up possibilities for new forms of expression, where things do not necessarily have to 'make sense' in a way that will also make sense to others (i.e., fit neatly into a single modernist framework). Postmodern art, music, literature, philosophy, history and science are contradictory, non-linear, fragmented, different, and are not required to be consistent or to 'make sense' in modernist terms.

The methodologies of postmodernist inquiry are character-ised by the interpretive methodologies of the humanities. Typically they involve the analysis of discourses and narratives, in order to understand the realities within which they are defined. Because the idea of construction is important for postmodernists (it is in the process of construction that we make sense of things), *deconstruction* is of major importance as a postmodernist form of inquiry. This requires the pulling apart of the construction of a phenomenon (e.g., 'social work', 'interview', 'client') in an attempt to understand its meaning within a particular context or discourse, for a particular person or group, at a particular time.

For social workers, one of the most important aspects of postmodernism is its allowance, and indeed advocacy, of difference. Acceptance of the idea that there is no universal reality, or meta-narrative, allows for alternatives to develop, and values activity that may be otherwise seen as on the margins of mainstream society. Postmodernists have advocated a politics of difference, suggesting that it is through the constant redefinition of different realities that change can occur, and this gives hope to people seeking to articulate a view that is outside 'mainstream' discourse. Hence a number of post-modernists (referred to by Rosenau (1992) as *affirmative* postmodernists) see postmodernism as having liberatory or emancipatory potential, as legitimising difference, as valuing diversity and as freeing people from the bonds of an oppressive universal discourse that demands conformity and inhibits freedom.

This brief summary of postmodernism has not done justice to a very rich and diverse literature. However it does provide a basis for answering the two questions posed at the end of the previous section, namely what has postmodernism to offer an alternative social work, and is it in itself sufficient as a basis from which to formulate such a practice?

The postmodernist critique is undoubtedly of considerable importance in developing an alternative social work. Specifi-cally, it both allows for and advocates the establishment of alternative discourses and realities. The current context of social work practice is overwhelmingly dominated by a single discourse, namely economic rationalism, and postmodernism allows for the possibility of establishing alternative discourses. The process of deconstruction allows one to seek to understand economic rationalism not as a disempowering system of control to which there is no alternative, but rather as a discourse of power that is constantly being redefined, and that is open to critique. Further, it suggests that an effective counter to economic rationalism may be the development of alternative discourses at the margins of 'mainstream' society, with the aim of invading and fracturing the dominant discourse. This serves to recognise, legitimise and value social workers who are working with disadvantaged groups and communities. From this perspective postmodernism can empower social workers to seek many and varied solutions, and has the capacity to demonstrate that their oppositional efforts are worthwhile. There is another way in which postmodernism can be seen to be potentially empowering. In reading the text, the emphasis on the reader and her/his capacity to construct reality leads to a reformulation of the role of expertise, which is no longer seen as being handed down by experts and simply absorbed by others (the passive reader). The reader, whether a student 'reading' a social work 'text' (understood in its broad sense), or a client, 'reading' a social work intervention or an agency decision, has an active role in defining and in constructing 'reality'. There is thus a capacity for students or clients themselves to be seen as agents of change, rather than as passive recipients of 'intervention' or education. Such an approach emphasises dialogue and shared realities, rather than a necessary power relationship of active worker/teacher and passive client/student. It therefore completely reframes the understanding of 'client' or 'student', and implies considerable potential for empowerment.

Postmodernism has been a powerful discourse from which to attack the positivism at the core of the managerial and economic rationalist approach. Indeed in many ways it parallels the other critiques of positivism in the social sciences, for example, that of Brian Fay (1975), which were articulated before postmodernism became a dominant social science discourse. Such critiques attacked positivism's claims to value neutrality, identified its internal contradictions, criticised its dependence on rationality and universalism, emphasised the inadequacy of a positivist world view in taking account of the full range of human and societal experiences, noted the tendency of positivism to lead to a politics of technical and managerial control, and advocated instead a social science based at least in part on interpretive understandings of human actions. This mirrors much of the postmodernist critique of modernism; the language is different, but the substance of the argument is remarkably similar, though postmodernism has a more ambitious and far-reaching agenda than did the social science critique of positivism.

Postmodernism also requires a greater acceptance of uncertainty, ambiguity, paradox and contradictions. The modernist, or positivist, position is characterised by a search for certainty and for definite answers. It assumes there is one right way to understand the world, and one best way of doing things (e.g., social work), so it is the task of the social scientist to discover them. In a world characterised by uncertainty and contradiction, the modernist approach seeks to impose rationality, order, clarity and uniformity as the answer. Postmodernism, however, accepts uncertainty and ambiguity as natural and indeed inevitable. It allows people to live with the tensions of the current practice environment, and to identify those tensions and paradoxes as likely points for the development of an alternative discourse. The perplexing and uncertain environment of contemporary social work, therefore, represents opportunities for creative practice rather than cause for despair.

Postmodernism also helps to legitimise forms of knowledge other than those that can be empirically verified. The modernist world view, because of its reliance on objectivity and rationality, tends to discount feelings, emotion, intuition, religion, magic and spirituality as valid sources of knowledge or forms of experience. It is essentially a white, male, heterosexual, adult, able-bodied world view, which marginalises other voices and the knowledge they represent. Just as positivism refuses to acknowledge the existence of anything that cannot be measured, modernism is similarly dismissive of non-objective forms of knowledge. Such a restrictive understanding of the human condition is at odds with the experience both of social workers and of their clients, and so an alternative view such as postmodernism, which readily acknowledges and validates different forms of experience, is of considerable value.

It is clear that postmodernism has a good deal to offer the formulation of an alternative social work based on the anarchist/humanist perspective. The question to be asked, then, is whether this perspective is sufficient to develop such an approach. Is the anarchist/humanist position simply postmodernism by another name, or does it incorporate something else? The next stage of our exploration will suggest that although postmodernism has a lot to offer, and can make a very important contribution, there are significant areas in which it is inadequate as a basis for an alternative social work, and that a further perspective is required.

Although postmodernism allows for the development of alternative realities, narratives or discourses, it does nothing to indicate what these might be, and there is no normative element suggesting what may be a 'good' or 'better' direction. Indeed, postmodernism's relativism, its rejection of historical progress, and its rejection of meta-narratives and hence of any notion of universal morality, make such normative prescriptions incompatible with postmodernism. This is a major contradiction of the postmodernist position. If one accepts, with the anti-positivists, that value-free knowledge is impossible and that values and knowledge are inextricably entwined, if not the same thing, then any argument that does not take values into account and that pretends to be value-free must be suspect. Postmodernism, while not necessarily making a claim of value-freedom, does not acknowledge any particular value or ideological position as inherent in its approach, and this must raise serious questions if one accepts that there is no such thing as ideology-free analysis or practice. The ideology of postmodernism, in effect, is pluralism. Postmodernism has been used to justify and legitimise a pluralist approach to politics, where power is seen as dispersed and as located within different interest groups, and where this is regarded as a better way to organise society than any form that concentrates power in the hands of a few. Pluralist politics, however, has its own ideological bias, as it does not take account of structural oppression such as class, race and gender. For this reason, critics such as Taylor-Gooby (1993) have identified an essential conservatism in postmodernism, and have suggested that it draws attention away from structural issues and from universal notions of social justice. By emphasising difference, postmodernism can detract from the importance of solidarity around common experiences of oppression (Bauman 1991). Postmodernism, indeed, can be a convenient world view for the political right, as it legitimises ideas of the market operating in a deregulated environment, where individuals and groups are free to define things in their own way, and where, as Margaret Thatcher maintained, there is no such thing as society but simply individuals interacting in the market (Rees 1995 p. 289).

A related criticism is that by its rejection of meta-narratives, postmodernism thereby rejects the importance of universal discourses of human rights and social justice. Such universalist arguments have been very important for those involved in seeking progressive change through social movements, including the peace movement, the women's movement and the green movement. Postmodernism therefore has the potential to erode the philosophical bases of some of the most progressive movements for change in contemporary society.

Postmodernism, in other words, does not incorporate a vision of a better future society, though it does allow for a multiplicity of such visions to be defined. It rejects universal understandings of principles such as human rights, and validates the culturally relativist definitions of human rights which accept, for example, 'Asian' interpretations of human rights as being somehow different; an argument which has been used to justify gross human right violations in some countries. Many people would argue that the politics of difference must be circumscribed by some universal principles grounded in universal understandings of what it means to be human, and a universal construction of humanity which unites rather than divides the human race (see Chapter 4). Postmodernism rejects such circumscription, and its opponents might claim that the ultimate consequence of postmodernist politics is Bosnia and Rwanda (though there are alternative readings of such tragedies from a postmodernist perspective, which see them as the construction of abnormal identities within discourses of normality, and related to constructions of citizenship and the nation state (Dillon 1995)).

The above criticisms have not been lost on postmodernist writers. There have been attempts to incorporate humanist or libertarian values in postmodernism, and many advocates of postmodernism would see it as containing within it a politics of liberation. This is a major area of contention within postmodernist debate, but nevertheless the basic criticism remains valid, as by its very nature postmodernism must exclude universal narratives, even those of social justice and liberation.

Further theoretical criticisms can be made of postmodernism but need not be explored here. For example, it can be claimed that postmodernism itself seeks to be a meta-narrative; Haber (1994) suggests that it develops a universal discourse of difference, and is hence contradictory. For our present purposes it is sufficient to note that postmodernism fails to incorporate a vision of a better society, or a universal understanding of social justice and human rights. As such an understanding is fundamental to social work, it is clear that postmodernism, while it has important contributions to make to an alternative social work, is not sufficient to form the basis of such a practice.

Feminism

There are, of course, many varieties of feminism, not all of which relate to the positivist/hierarchic–humanist/anarchist distinction identified earlier in the chapter. As was the case with postmodernism, it is impossible within a brief space to do justice to the full range of feminist thought and scholarship, and to reflect the many different ways in which feminist arguments have been advanced. Although there are different classificatory taxonomies that can be used for the different articulations of feminism, for present purposes a basic distinction can be made between *liberal, structural* and *poststructural* forms of feminism.

Liberal feminism basically accepts the existing social, economic and political order and identifies the oppression of women as able to be addressed within these parameters. It therefore seeks to overcome discrimination against women through anti-discrimination programs and legislation, through education, through affirmative action programs, and through empowering women to compete more effectively for jobs, status, recognition and monetary rewards. It is essentially conservative, in that it does not seek fundamental change, but it rather affirms the legitimacy of the existing system and simply seeks a better deal for women, as a recognised disadvantaged group, within that system.

Structural forms of feminism, on the other hand, see the problem of women's oppression as lying within the basic structures of society, which are characterised as patriarchal. Hence if the oppression of women is to be challenged, those patriarchal structures have to be changed. Patriarchy needs to be dismantled, and alternative forms of economic, social and political organisation developed. It is thus a more radical approach to change. It sees the oppression of women as being embedded in basic structures; change to such structures, a more ambitious project than liberal feminism, requires radical transformation.

Within the structural approach to feminism there are a number of different streams. Socialist or Marxist feminism locates patriarchy in the structures of capitalism, and seeks liberation through the dismantling of capitalism and its replacement with a feminist socialism. Ecofeminism (Mellor

1992) links patriarchy to the exploitation of the environment, and draws a clear link between feminism and the green movement in seeking an alternative society that is ecologically sustainable and that validates alternative feminist values within it. Similarly some feminists are closely aligned with anarchism, seeing the dismantling of patriarchy as part of the dismantling of all hierarchical structures of domination. Such feminists regard patriarchy as predating capitalism or environmental exploitation, and therefore suggest that it is inadequate to combine (or worse, subordinate) feminism with either the green or socialist movements. Radical feminism, separatist feminism, and others differ on appropriate strategies as well as on appropriate outcomes. Nevertheless, the various streams of structural feminism have in common the need to address basic structural issues in some way, even though they may differ on the nature of those structures or on how they should be addressed.

Post-structural feminism is feminism that incorporates the perspectives of postmodernism and poststructuralism outlined in the previous section, and hence equates patriarchy with modernism. The modernist view is seen as being based on patriarchal assumptions, and as having incorporated the oppression and subordination of women in its world view. For such feminists, postmodernism and poststructuralism suggest that patriarchy is maintained through discourses of power and domination, and allow the possibility for the establishment of non-patriarchal, or specifically anti-patriarchal, discourses, and the legitimation of feminist narratives. The emphasis is therefore on the deconstruction of the idea of 'woman', the deconstruction of the discourse of patriarchy, and reconstructing discourses that are more inclusive and allow for women's voices to be heard (Brah 1991; Hooks 1981; Davies 1991).

For the purposes of this discussion, the emphasis will be on structural and post-structural forms of feminism as a basis for an alternative social work. Liberal feminism is clearly inadequate for the formulation of the anti-positivist, anti-hierarchical position outlined earlier in this chapter, as it accepts the basic structures of existing society, and is clearly grounded in positivist and hierarchical understandings. Structural and post-structural versions of feminism, however, seem to have the potential to reflect the humanist and anarchist ideals on which an alternative social work might be based.

The value of structural feminism for social work is more than simply its emphasis on gender and the oppression of women. There are other groups who are the victims of structural oppression, such as the poor, the unemployed, people with disabilities, gays and lesbians, the aged, children, and various race and ethnic minorities. Feminism not only identifies the importance of gender as a form of structural oppression, but it has made a number of contributions to the understanding of structural oppression in general, and to ways in which it might be overcome. As a potential basis for an alternative social work, therefore, feminism can make a contribution that goes well beyond the gender dimension of social work and social problems, and the specific oppression of women.

One of the most important contributions of feminism has been its insistence that 'the personal is political'. The personal suffering of women in the domestic sphere as well as the public sphere has been specifically related in feminist writing to political issues of patriarchal structures and oppression. Hence there is a deliberate link between the individual and the structural, requiring that individual suffering be understood in its political context, and the corollary that political structural issues must be understood in terms of their impact on people's lives, and must not be seen in purely abstract or macro-political terms. The personal and the political are seen as two manifestations of the same thing, and the separation of the personal and the political is seen as one of the consequences of patriarchy, which has drawn a sharp division between the public (traditionally male) arena and the domestic (typically female); this separation of the public and the domestic has served the interests largely of men, has enabled the interests of men to be defined and contextualised differently from those of women, and has been a key feature of women's oppression (Pascall 1986).

For social work, the linking of the personal and the political is of critical importance. Social work deals with both the personal and the political, and is probably the only profession that can claim at least a partial mandate to work with both and to relate each to the other. This is similar to C. Wright Mills' famous distinction between private troubles and public issues (Mills 1970); it is Mills' claim that sociology must concern itself with both in its inquiry. Social work has the added responsibility of actually developing a form of practice

95

that spans the personal/political divide and seeks to bring them together. For this reason, it is clear that social work has potentially much to gain from feminist understandings of the personal and the political, and of what it means to take action within a paradigm that insists that they belong together.

Feminism's attempts to dismantle patriarchal structures are also of relevance to social work, given social work's aim to bring about social justice that, from the perspective of structural social work, requires structural change and the dismantling of structures of oppression. Earlier models of radical social work were largely based on Marxism (e.g., Corrigan and Leonard 1978), and sought to oppose class oppression through attempting to challenge the hegemony that maintains the existing order, and to establish some kind of socialist alternative. It can be suggested that in more recent decades feminism has been more successful than Marxism in developing a theoretical understanding of oppression and in developing forms of practice that will specifically challenge oppressive structures, though in this case it is the structures of patriarchy rather than the structures of capitalism. This is obviously of particular importance for the development of an alternative social work.

A further area in which structural feminism is of particular interest to social work is in its attempts to develop alternatives to the competitive and exploitative structures of patriarchy. Instead of accepting existing structures, as liberal feminism does, structural feminism has sought to use the women's movement to revalue the achievements of women in terms of collective or consensus decision-making, co-operative structures, more egalitarian forms of organisation, and so on. Thus the feminist movement has not been content to criticise structures of patriarchy, but has tried to establish counter-structures to replace them. Such structures have their place not only in women's struggle against oppression, but in the struggles of other structurally disadvantaged groups, and have been the concern of other social movements such as the peace and environment movements (Coover et al. 1995; Shields 1991). Feminism has thus influenced social justice agendas broader than simply those related to gender, and has become a framework for the establishment of oppositional practice and alternative structures. For this reason, its applicability to alternative social work is clear, and social workers have been able to draw on feminist writing and experience in their attempts to establish social alternatives.

Poststructural forms of feminism also clearly have a good deal to offer social work. In the previous section it was shown that postmodernism and poststructuralism are important components of an alternative social work, and attempts to link such views with a feminist analysis are important, as they combine the strengths of both positions. Poststructural feminism requires that a gender perspective informs both the deconstruction of patriarchal discourses of power, and the reconstruction of alternatives. Similarly it requires feminism to allow for and indeed encourage the celebration of difference and the legitimation of different voices or constructions of a counter-patriarchal position, rather than seeking the one 'right' answer to the oppression of women. It locates women's struggle for liberation firmly in the arena of discourses of power, and emphasises the need for women to be able to engage in the process of influencing such discourses and developing alternatives. Such considerations are essential if social workers are to locate their practice in what has been characterised in this chapter as the humanist/anarchist position.

Like postmodernism, then, it is clear that feminism has much to offer a social work that seeks to base itself on the humanist/anarchist perspective. Again, however, it can be suggested that while such an approach must be informed by feminism, an exclusively feminist position is inadequate as a conceptual basis for social work. The criticism of feminism in this regard, however, is weaker than that of postmodernism. While postmodernism was seen to have inherent weaknesses and contradictions, this is not necessarily the case with feminism, though it does depend on which variety of feminism one is considering; many people, for example, would find it hard to reconcile separatist feminism with the broad humanist position incorporated in the anarchist/humanist approach—the subject of the next chapter. Similarly, a purely postmodernist feminism is subject to the criticisms of postmodernism noted earlier. Such exceptions apart, the criticism of feminism does not focus on content, but rather suggests that it does not provide a complete picture on which to base an alternative practice.

Despite its applicability to other forms of oppression, feminism remains firmly grounded in the experience of the oppression of women. While the significance of this form of oppression must not in any sense be undervalued, it remains only one of several significant dimensions of oppression in contemporary society, along with class, race, ethnicity, age, disability, sexuality, and possibly others. While some feminists claim that gender oppression is more fundamental than the others, this is contested ground, and would not be accepted by many social workers, including radical social workers operating from, for example, a Marxist perspective. The debate about which form of oppression is the most 'fundamental', though frequently heated, is seldom very productive, and it is not necessary for our present exploration to engage further in it. What is important to note, however, is that the critical humanist vision of social work, which will be developed in the following chapters, requires a perspective that unites and transcends the differences of race, gender, class, age or whatever, in a common vision of humanity. Feminism can, and indeed must, inform such a vision, but it would be inappropriate to take as the *foundation* of that vision a philosophy primarily grounded in only one dimension of human oppression. Oppression extends beyond the oppression of gender, and must be understood from within such a context if one is to develop a truly appropriate social work for the changing context of contemporary society.

While feminism may come close to providing such an overview (or meta-narrative) of oppression in general, its grounding in the experience of gender-based oppression will mean inevitably that this form of oppression will be represented as paramount, with the corresponding risk that those with other emancipatory agendas may be marginalised. For this reason, more than a feminist analysis is needed as a basis for alternative social work, although it is clear that feminism must play a very influential role in such a development. For the purposes of this book, the feminist critique of patriarchy somewhat resembles the postmodernist critique of modernity. Both are important, and while each represents a significant aspect of the critique of the dominant paradigm and can inform the 'dimension' of analysis proposed at the beginning of the chapter, neither is sufficient as a conceptual base within which alternative social work can be located.

A humanist vision

At the core of social work is a vision of humanity. This is expressed in various ways: the social work commitment to 'the worth of the individual'; the continual reference to some idea of 'social justice'; the code of ethics that enshrines the values of humanism; and so on. The common motivation for students to enter a social work course is often characterised as 'I want to help people'. Although this may often be expressed in more sophisticated and academically acceptable language, this basic human motivation is something to which all social workers can relate. It was out of a desire to help, a wish to make the world a better place, and a commitment to assisting people in their struggle to lead better, more fulfilling and rewarding lives, that social work originally developed. The same motivation continues to draw people into social work in spite of the negative publicity, the poor work conditions, and the repeated assaults on this humanist value coming from the dominant ideology of economic rationalism and individualism.

In the current economic, social and political climate, to assert humanist ideals is to make a radical statement. It is contradictory to the dominant ideology, which values individual achievement, selfishness, a lack of concern for others, and the dominance of economic goals over social and humanitarian goals. We live in a society where 'do-gooder' is a term of abuse; every time the term is used, it serves to marginalise and trivialise the act of helping, doing good, or seeking to implement human values—especially if the recipient of the help can be characterised in some way as 'undeserving'. Doing good is seen as misguided, as having little to do with 'real life', and as distracting people from what is really important. Social workers, the professional do-gooders, are the most visible representation of this unpopular philosophy of altruism, and so are often labelled as irrelevant, misguided or dangerous. The marginalisation of social work, and of do-gooders in general, says much about the values of society, and emphasises the hostile environment within which social workers attempt to articulate the values of humanity. It suggests that humanism is more than simply making worthy statements in codes of ethics, but rather that it is a major challenge for social workers in the contemporary setting. It also suggests that a common societal commitment to humanitarian values can no longer be assumed, yet this is an assumption that social workers have tended to make. Rather, this commitment must be assertively and publicly articulated, and social workers need to be looking for ways in which a discourse of humanity can re-enter the public domain. This has been strongly advocated by, among others, Stuart Rees (1994, 1995), as providing a basis for progressive social work in an age of economic rationalism.

In its period of flirtation with positivism, social work was in danger of losing its humanist commitment. By its very nature, positivism separates fact and value, and emphasises empirical facts while marginalising value, ethical and moral considerations. During the 1970s and early 1980s social work's basic commitment to humanity was in danger of being swamped by its obsession (at least in universities) with positivist theory, scientific models, measurement and empirical research. It took writers such as Ruth Wilkes (1981) and Nicholas Ragg (1977) to argue the necessary centrality for social work of a concern for the person, and to help to turn social work concerns back towards those of its founders. This took place in academic social work, but at the present time the hostile organisational and political context of practice suggests that the same argument needs to be made in the wider arena; this is a critical task for contemporary social workers.

It is important, therefore, to look at what is involved in a commitment to, and advocacy of, humanist values. There are varieties of humanist positions, as is exemplified by the two social work writers mentioned in the previous paragraph, Ruth Wilkes and Nicholas Ragg. Writing in the heyday of positivism in university social work departments, both argue eloquently and powerfully for a rejection of positivism and a re-emphasis on the centrality of the person, and human values, in social work. Their conclusions, however, are very different. For Wilkes (1981), the answer is a very existential and individualist social work, while Ragg (1977) uses his critique of positivism to develop a social work based on 'critical humanism' with a clear commitment to social change at a more macro level. Ragg is thus able to link the personal and the political, and to see his humanism as providing a justification for change at the political level, whereas Wilkes is not.

The aim of this chapter is to examine what is involved in articulating a humanist vision, and to seek to develop one that specifically links the personal and the political, and hence it is more in keeping with the humanism of Ragg than that of Wilkes. This will be done initially by examining several of the tensions inherent in a discourse of humanism. Significant criticisms have been made of the humanist position, and these need to be acknowledged if humanism is to be adopted as a basis for critical social work. In discussing the tensions inherent in a humanist position, the problems of relying *exclusively* on a humanist discourse for the foundation of a critical social work will become apparent.

Tensions in humanist discourse

Humanism as a Western tradition

Humanism has been so tied to the Western world view, that it could be questioned whether it can ever transcend its Western origins. The origins of contemporary humanism can be seen in the Renaissance, where 'man' was given a new priority at the centre of existence, and where human achievement and human values were celebrated in a way unknown in medieval times. Humanism thus had its origins at the same time as the Western intellectual, artistic and scientific tradition began to be established in its modern form. As the Western world view developed further, humanism was always very much at its centre, and a driving force in its achievements. The notion of progress became established as part of the Western consciousness, and the goal of progress was essentially a humanist one—working for the betterment of humanity. The period of the Enlightenment, in the late 18th century, further cemented the place of humanism at the centre of the Western tradition. The philosophy of Locke was particularly important in this regard. Locke sought to free 'man' from the constraints of religion, superstition and ignorance, and his philosophy of secular individualism represents a final break with medieval constructions of 'man' as simply a part of God's world, designed to play a passive role as part of some divine purpose. From Locke's philosophy, 'man' emerged as the dominant species, destined to control the world, and to subjugate the forces and resources of nature for 'his' own benefit (and hence unleashing the greatest ever human assault on the global ecosystem, which continues today). The centrality of 'man' was further reinforced by the central figure of the Enlightenment, Voltaire, with his world view characterised by reason, tolerance, and respect for humanity (note that the term 'man' has been deliberately used to emphasise the patriarchal assumptions of the Western world view—this will be discussed later in the chapter).

The Western world view, now also characterised as 'modernity', is facing increasing criticism. While it has undoubtedly resulted in many great achievements, it is also criticised as patriarchal, colonialist, racist, and as providing the context for capitalist and colonialist exploitation and the environmental devastation of the last 200 years. This criticism has led to the advocacy of alternative world views such as postmodernism, which specifically rejects and criticises the human-centred notion of humanism, and to the re-valuation of other cultural traditions that were devalued and marginalised in the colonialist enthusiasm of the West. Different views of history, art and literature, placing less value on the works of 'dead white males' and validating the experience and cultural achievements of other groups, have more recently been given increased prominence as a result of this criticism.

The question, then, is whether humanism can survive the attack (and presumed demise) of the Western world view, of which it is so much a part. Some writers (e.g., Carroll 1993) equate humanism with the Western world view, and celebrate its demise. Foucault sees humanism as essentially modernist, and regards humanist notions of emancipation as a myth that disguises the changing discourses of power (Simons 1995). Another view, however, maintains that a vision of humanity and the human spirit transcends cultural boundaries, and can (indeed must) be part of whatever new paradigm will in time replace the Western modernist tradition. From this perspective it is wrong to assume that the West, or modernism, has a monopoly on humanist values. This tension is reflected in the debate about the universality of human rights, which will be discussed later in this chapter.

It is also inappropriate to condemn the entire Western intellectual tradition as having no value, and nothing to offer an alternative social work. While there is much to criticise in Western society and culture, there is also much to admire, in terms of artistic, scientific, cultural, social and material achievements. Perhaps the most important contribution of the Western tradition is indeed its humanism, and rather than simply condemning it as a product of a paradigm whose end is near, it is more appropriate to see how the values of humanism, and a vision for humanity, can be articulated in such a way as to open up possibilities for future action.

Indeed, if one is to abandon humanism as a result of a criticism of the Western tradition, one may as well also abandon social work itself. Social work, after all, is a product of the Western world view as well, and is in effect one of the ways in which the humanism of that view is given expression at a societal level. If social work is to survive in a changing world, and to have something important to contribute in terms of social justice, then it is necessary for both social work and humanist values to be redefined in such a way that they can thrive in a more varied cultural and social context.

Individual and collectivist notions of humanism

One of the characteristics of humanism as it has been constructed within the Western tradition has been its individualism. It is 'man' rather than 'men' (let alone 'men and women'), which has been the central focus of the humanist vision. Human achievement, human potential and human rights have all been described from within a largely individualist perspective. Individuals are given credit, even when it is the efforts of groups that have been important. For example, it was Captain Cook who is credited with the great voyages of discovery, not those who sailed with him and actually did the work. Similarly, 'Montgomery defeated Rommel' in North Africa, as if they were two individuals locked in a heroic personal combat like Hector and Achilles, rather than generals commanding large armies of men who actually did the fighting and the dying. Lenin is almost single-handedly given credit for the Russian Revolution. Herbert von Karajan is the one who gets the credit for the sound of the Berlin Philharmonic. Sir Edmund Hillary climbed Mt Everest, Gough Whitlam was responsible for the Labor Government's triumphs and disasters in the 1970s, and so on. The achievements of individuals take pride of place in the Western history of human accomplishment, and the achievements of groups, or of the loyal supporters of the great leaders, are scarcely acknowledged. That the great leaders mentioned above are all white males suggests further problems for traditional humanism, which will be discussed below; for the moment it is the individualism that is at issue.

The individual understanding of humanism can also be seen in the discourse on such matters as human rights, social justice and equality before the law—all central to the humanist vision. These are articulated almost exclusively in individualist terms; rights, justice and equality for groups or collectives are seldom recognised. In the human rights area, for example, this is particularly clear. The so-called first generation of human rights were civil and political rights, such as freedom of speech, the right to a fair trial, freedom of religion, and so on, all highly individual in their definition. The second generation, namely economic, social and cultural rights, can be understood collectively, but their common conceptualisation remains primarily individual. These include the right to education, to adequate health services, to housing, to social security, and to employment. It is only with the recent emergence of the so-called third generation of rights that collective rights have begun to be identified. These include the right to development, the right to a clean environment, and so on.

Collective understandings of the humanist ideal have the potential to move humanism beyond the confines of the indivi-dualised world of the current social, economic and political order. They are necessary in order to provide a rationale for opposition to the individualism of economic rationalism, and to promote the rights of oppressed groups. However they also hold certain dangers if individual discourses are abandoned. Specifically, there is the danger of the individual being swamped by the collective, and suffering in the interests of the larger group. The way in which some governments have sought to define human rights collectively rather than individually, thereby justifying the brutal repression of dissent, is an example of the need to balance individual and collective notions of human values.

It is necessary to maintain some degree of balance between individualist and collectivist notions of humanism, and both should form part of the discourse of an alternative social work. There is an inevitable tension between individualist humanism and collective humanism, and both need to be taken into account. In cultures dominated by economic considerations, individualist notions of humanism predominate, and it is therefore important that alternative collectivist forms of humanism also be recognised.

Unitary discourse

The essence of a humanist account is the idea of a universal discourse of humanity, which transcends differences, and which seeks in the common humanity of all people something that can, in the words of *The International*, 'unite the human race' (Benn 1984 pp. 299–300).

This unitary approach contradicts the discourse of difference, which is of such importance in social work and the social sciences, and which has been significantly reinforced by postmodernism and its 'celebration of difference'. The discourse of difference has emphasised the things that divide humanity and fragment the human experience: race, gender, class, culture, ethnicity, language, age, wealth, and so on. While these are clearly important, an exclusive concentration on difference can blind one to the things that unite all people. These are the things that are seen by humanists as in some way inherent in the human spirit, and that are experienced by all as part of their common humanity. Two people, who may differ from each other in terms of gender, race, class and culture, will still have many things in common. They will both feel anger, pain, joy, suffering and the full range of human emotions. What they share, to the humanist, is more important than the things that divide them, and this leads to a powerful case for social justice based on the universal bonds of a common humanity, regardless of gender, race, culture or class. Such a vision has inspired many of the great social movements of the last century, and has led to many of the greatest achievements of the international community, including the Universal Declaration of Human Rights, which, with its associated Protocols and Conventions, perhaps represents the finest achievement of the United Nations.

The universalist structural position, so popular in radical social work writing, has by contrast had the effect of creating dichotomies and emphasising dualisms; it belongs to the discourse of difference. Thus a gender analysis will tend to reinforce the two categories of 'man' and 'woman', and to set them in opposition to each other. Similarly a class analysis pits 'ruling class' against 'working class', and a race analysis emphasises differences between people of different racial and cultural backgrounds. If one takes a structural perspective, this is of course essential. Structural issues such as class, race and gender have resulted in particular groups being disadvantaged, and hence structural issues must be addressed in order to overcome oppression. The problem, however, is that by creating such dualisms, the tendency is to divide rather than to unite. And in terms of power the division is normally into two (or more) unequal groups, creating or reinforcing a society of winners and losers: men and women, ruling class and working class, Anglo-Celtic Australians and Aboriginal people, and so on. In such circumstances, one is setting up a conflict in which the loser will most often be the disadvantaged, and the dominant or oppressing group, simply because it has more power, will usually 'win'. By conceptualising in terms of division, one is therefore simply reinforcing the socialisation of people into roles of 'winners' and 'losers', or 'oppressors' and 'oppressed', thereby entrenching the exploitative power inequalities of the existing order. This also results in a linear analysis, where everything is seen in terms of gender, class or race. While these three forms of structural disadvantage are undoubtedly of critical importance, any analysis that only takes one—or even all three—factors into account will ignore much of the complexity of the human experience. A good deal of the popular opposition to both feminism and Marxism, as portrayed in the popular media, is because their perceived attempts to reduce everything to an issue of gender or class simply do not ring true to the lived experiences of ordinary people, who tend to think that life is rather more complex. If one takes a position that values grounded theory, and that seeks to start with the people's real-life experiences and their attempts to construct their world accordingly, the 'meta-narrative' of a structural analysis is not always a very useful analytical framework.

The difference between the discourse of unity and the discourse of difference can be seen in the construction of race issues. The discourse of unity belongs to Martin Luther King (despite his use of the gendered language of the Declaration of Independence):

> The marvellous new militancy which has engulfed the Negro community must not lead us to distrust of all white people, for many of our white brothers, as evidenced by their presence here today, have come to realise that their destiny is tied up with our destiny and their freedom is inextricably bound to our freedom. We cannot walk alone ...
>
> I say to you today, my friends, that in spite of the difficulties and frustrations of the moment, I still have a dream. It is a dream deeply rooted in the American dream. I have a dream that one day this nation will rise up and live out the true meaning of its creed: 'We hold these truths to be self-evident: that all men (sic) are created equal' ('I have a Dream', speech, Lincoln Memorial, Washington DC, 28 August 1963).

The discourse of unity also belongs to Nelson Mandela, whose extraordinary achievements in refusing to succumb to the politics of hate, despite his experience of brutal repression, now give South Africa a real chance to move beyond a culture of racial mistrust and hatred, towards a culture based on common human destinies. By contrast, the discourse of difference belongs to Louis Farrakhan, with his advocacy of separatism and a different destiny for people of colour in the USA.

It is worth noting that one thing King, Mandela and Farrakhan share, in their different ways, is the marginalisation of women. One can hardly blame Martin Luther King for his use of 'all men' and similar phrases elsewhere is his 1963 speech, as he was simply using the language of the time, well before inclusive language became an issue. None the less, it represents the gendered nature of the civil rights struggle of the time, gives offence to many today, and reduces the impact of his otherwise powerful speech for the contemporary reader. In Nelson Mandela's autobiography (1994) there are several incidents showing that he viewed the role of women as somewhat marginal in the struggle for liberation, and saw them as supporting the men rather than having a major role in their own right. Both of these, however, pale into insignificance compared with the exclusion of women from Farrakhan's 'million men's march' on Washington in October 1995 in support of his black separatist campaign.

This suggests that a humanist discourse of apparent unity can also serve to reinforce a politics of difference, unless a view of humanism is taken that includes *all* people, and that takes account of *all* forms of oppression. The danger of basing a humanist discourse on one form of oppression alone is that it will, by omission, unintentionally entrench other forms of dehumanising oppression. In Chapter 3, this was raised as an issue in relation to an over-reliance on feminist discourse. The vision of humanity must rise above the uni-dimensional discourses of class, race or gender oppression (though clearly drawing on their wisdom and experience), and seek to incorporate all of them in a broader, greater vision. It thus provides an antidote to some of the dangers of an extreme postmodernist position and its amoral celebration of difference, which can encourage the politics of hate and lead to the tragedies of Bosnia, Rwanda and Northern Ireland.

This is not to say, however, that there is no place for a discourse of difference, or that we must abandon a structural analysis that seeks to understand the cause of difference and to seek ways of redressing structural disadvantage. Indeed, a unifying discourse that ignores such structural disadvantage may simply become an affirmation of the dominant discourse of the powerful, and enshrine positions of colonialism, sexism, racism and so on. How to incorporate such an analysis without reducing the power of an over-riding unitary vision of humanity is another of the tensions inherent in the adoption of humanism as a basis for an alternative social work.

Internationalism

A humanism that seeks to incorporate a discourse of unity, rather than simply a discourse of difference, must have an internationalist dimension. Nationality can readily divide people, and nationalism has been one of the causes of much war and human conflict. Any approach seeking to develop a vision of a common humanity must do so in a way that transcends national boundaries, and hence internationalism is an important part of the humanist vision. In this regard it is not surprising that many of the most powerful expressions of a common humanity have been seen in international organis-ations—not only in the United Nations, but also in internat-ional NGOs (non-government organisations) such as the Red Cross, Amnesty International, Oxfam (Community Aid Abroad), the Women's International League for Peace and Freedom, and several others. All these groups are based on an international humanist vision affirming that humans have fundamental rights to basic freedoms and a decent standard of living wherever they were born. It insists that oppression, war, starvation, poverty, disease and pollution cannot be tolerated wherever they occur. It also insists that any preventable death is one too many, and is cause for equal outrage whether it be a death from malnutrition in the Sudan, from death squads in Brazil, from a chemical explosion in India, from fallout in Chernobyl, from war in Bosnia, from the death penalty in the USA, from diseased meat in the UK, or from domestic violence in Australia.

An international humanist perspective requires social workers to be concerned about human suffering wherever it occurs, but it also allows them to be inspired by the example of those who have struggled for social justice, human rights and a fair society, wherever that struggle has taken place. It allows social workers in Australia to understand that they are part of the same struggle as their colleagues in the Philippines who worked to overthrow the Marcos regime, their colleagues in India who are working to reform the bonded labour system, and other social work colleagues around the world. It allows all to draw strength from the extraordinary efforts of people such as Gandhi, Nelson Mandela, Aung San Suu Kyi, the Dalai Lama, Vaclav Havel, Martin Luther King, Chico Mendez, and many others less well-known, whose actions have inspired thousands and led to social change. Although each acted in a particular national and cultural context, such people are the heroes of humanity, and their achievements transcend the artificialities of national and cultural boundaries. Such people embody the humanist ideal, which insists that the human spirit cannot be broken, but rather that the struggle for a better world remains the central concern of those who define themselves in terms of a common humanity.

An internationalist perspective is particularly important at the present time, when internationalism is being defined increasingly in economic rationalist terms. The deregulation of national economies, and the almost universal acceptance of the value of free trade, has led to a global economy over which few if any national governments can exercise control. Economic wisdom dictates that we are encouraged to interfere in the economies of other nations, and to allow others to interfere in our own economy, and any attempt to restrict such interference is seen as a barrier to free trade, and therefore to be condemned. It is ironic that this is happening at a time when many nations are becoming resistant to the idea that we can intervene across national boundaries over matters to do with the environment or human rights. Economic rationalism, at a global level, has largely succeeded in appropriating the internationalist agenda for its own justification, and the older forms of internationalism, which were actually to do with the humanist ideal of the well-being of people, seem to be in retreat. As national boundaries are opened up to economic activity, they are closed on matters that are to do with human rights and social justice, and the humanist ideal of internationalism has been replaced by the economic ideal of globalisation.

The international arena is likely to be an increasingly important one for social workers, if indeed they are to seek to counter oppression which has increasingly international origins, and this will be taken up again in Chapter 7. But it is also important to sound a note of caution about internationalism. It can readily lead to a decontextualising of the human experience, and in an attempt to develop a universalist human discourse the importance of cultural difference can be undervalued. This in turn can lead to colonialist attitudes, which attempt to impose the world view of the West onto other nations and cultures. This has prompted the criticism from other cultures of ideas such as human rights being simply a Western construct, and part of a continuing agenda of colonialism. This is not to say that one should abandon the internationalist dream, but rather that one must be aware of this tension between the universal and the local context, and that any attempt to develop a universal humanist discourse must be tempered with an understanding of and sensitivity to the significance of context. Later in this chapter an attempt will be made to do this, within the context of a discussion of rights and needs. For the moment, it is sufficient to identify the tension, and note that it is potentially problematic.

Gender

A significant problem with the vision of humanity as understood within the Western tradition is that it has been largely a male construction. The centrality of 'man' in the humanist discourse has only recently been challenged, and it can be suggested that the humanist vision is still largely masculine. Of the people cited in the previous section as providing inspiration in the struggle for the human spirit (Gandhi, Nelson Mandela, Aung San Suu Kyi, the Dalai Lama, Vaclav Havel, Martin Luther King, Chico Mendez), all but one are/were men. While they were representative of varying cultural and racial groups, indeed most were from non-Western traditions, there is still a clear gender bias in this list of humanist heroes. It would certainly have been possible to add some women, such as Mother Teresa and Mary McKillop, to the list, but this would have been to alter the list of my own selection of the most significant recent public humanist leaders in the interests of maintaining an appearance of gender balance (or 'political correctness' as some conservative commentators would suggest). Leaving the list as it is serves to emphasise the gender bias in the construction of humanism, and the need to do something about it.

The reason such a list of humanist heroes is almost exclusively male lies in the way the ideal of a humanist hero has been constructed, and relates to the distinction between the public and the domestic spheres. Like many other phenomena, humanism has been constructed primarily within the public (largely male) domain, rather than in the domestic (largely female) domain. The visible heroes of humanism are those who have made an impact in public, changed governments, achieved a significant public following, been granted plenty of media coverage and played the role of public hero or public martyr. We have not as readily defined as humanist heroes those who have patiently worked in voluntary service, put time and effort into making the local school a more liberating and humane environment, campaigned at a local level for more public open space,

111

struggled to establish adequate child care facilities, written letters for Amnesty International for twenty years, worked to set up a refuge for the victims of domestic violence, looked after their elderly relatives for years because of genuine feelings of love and concern, and sought to bring up their children as caring, non-violent people aware of their citizenship responsibilities. These, the majority of them women, also need to be recognised as the heroes of the humanist vision, and although they are not acknowledged in the same way as the high-profile men in the public domain, they give substance to the humanist ideal, and the world is an incomparably better place as a result.

A vision of humanism, therefore, must not rely simply on the stories of the (largely male) public heroes, important as these stories can be as a source of hope and inspiration. Alongside them must also be the stories of the humanist ideal worked out in the local or domestic spheres. This is in no way to diminish the status or the achievements of Gandhi, Mandela, King and the rest; they are some of the great human beings of the age. Rather we must set their well-publicised achievements alongside those of others whose names are not household words and who persevere in the struggle for humanity in a more modest, but equally significant, way, without seeking public recognition, but simply because of a profound belief that this is the right thing to do. In doing so, such 'street-level humanists' also change the world. Among their number are many social workers, who, both in the workplace and in their private capacities, have been part of the struggle to achieve a more human and tolerant society.

One of the goals of the humanist movement should be to balance the legitimation and recognition of both public and domestic versions of the humanist hero, and also to seek ways in which a gender balance can be achieved among the humanist heroes of both the public and private spheres. However for present purposes it is sufficient to note that gender represents another significant tension in the discourse of humanism that needs to be taken into account in formulating a humanist vision on which to base an alternative social work.

Ecology

Another criticism which can be made of humanism is that its human-centredness denies and diminishes the importance of other living, and indeed non-living, beings in the global eco-system. The more that 'man' (or even 'men and women') is seen as the central concern, the more justification there is for the exploitation of animals and of natural resources, all in the interests of humanity. Writers such as Eckersley (1992), Fox (1990) and Marshall (1992b) have pointed out that the human exploitation of nature increased significantly from the time of the industrial revolution, and the Enlightenment world view of Locke gave this environmental exploitation a philosophical justification. A medieval world view saw 'man' as merely a part of God's creation, and as being interconnected with the rest of the natural and supernatural world. The Enlightenment, however, set 'man' apart, and gave 'him' mastery of the world, and the right to exploit it for 'his' own ends. Since then, the exploitation of the natural world, and the extinction of many species, has continued unabated until the recent dawning of a Western environmental consciousness.

Humanism, grounded in Enlightenment thinking, has encouraged this anthropocentric world view, and hence the humanist perspective is challenged by a number of writers from the green perspective. Eckersley (1992) has advocated the replacement of the anthropocentric world view with an eco-centric perspective, which values not just humans but all living things, and which therefore seeks to act in the interests of the eco-system as a whole rather than seeing human beings as being in a particular privileged position. The same thinking is, of course, an important justification for animal liberation groups, who argue that animal rights demand recognition. Indeed, from a truly eco-centric perspective, animal rights should not be subordinated to human rights, and the humanist insistence on the primacy of a discourse of human rights is seen as simply reinforcing the exploitation of non-human species.

The ecological crises currently facing the world, and indeed threatening the long-term existence of human civilisation (let alone the survival of many non-human species) have emphas-ised the importance of a holistic perspective, and of seeing humans as part of a larger ecological system rather than separate from it. This requires humanity to re-establish its contact with the earth, as well as its interconnectedness with other living beings (Ife 1995). A humanism that sets 'man' aside from the rest of nature, and allows 'him' to dominate it for 'his' own interests, is no longer acceptable in a world threatened with ecological disaster (note again that the male pronoun has been deliberately used to emphasise that there is also a patriarchal element to the human domination of nature; see Mellor 1992).

This criticism, however, need not invalidate a humanist position. The interconnectedness of all living things means that a contemporary humanism must take account of the wider ecological context of humanity, and indeed it can be argued that human beings will not reach their full potential, and realise their true humanity, unless they do so consciously as part of the eco-system. Many of the most profound experiences of humanity are grounded in the natural world: looking at the ocean, climbing a mountain, experiencing wilderness, interacting with animals, gardening, sailing, swimming, bushwalking, and so on. It is often in such experiences that people feel more keenly what it is to be human, and it is only a small step from such experiences to an eco-centric position that defines humanity in relation to the eco-system, and that therefore intrinsically values other living and non-living entities. By enriching the natural world, the human experience is also enriched, and far from humanism implying the exploitation of the natural world, it can be argued that a humanist position requires respect for, acceptance of, and identification with the world in which humanity is located, and of which it is a part.

The anthropocentric world view can be regarded as part of the Western Enlightenment paradigm, and it was argued above that it is necessary for a humanist vision to break out of this paradigm and to redefine itself in the different context of the 'postmodern' world. This would include a rethinking of the anthropocentric implications of the Western world view. Indeed, the imperative of the ecological crisis requires that ecological sustainability be seen to be just as significant as social justice as a goal for humanity, and it is out of a synthesis of both a social justice and an ecological perspective that future policy and practice must be developed (for further elaboration of this argument, see Ife 1995).

Sources of a humanist vision

Despite the difficulties noted above in a discussion of the various tensions inherent in any definition of humanism, such a vision remains a critically important part of an alternative social work. This is partly because social work, whether one likes it or not, is inevitably bound to a humanist vision, given its value base, historical origins, and political location. Indeed one of social work's strongest claims to legitimacy is precisely that it does represent an expression of humanist values in a society that increasingly marginalises them; within that society there are still many people who believe such values to be fundamentally important, and who will support social workers in their attempts to realise their social justice aims. Another reason for the importance of the humanist vision is its power to motivate and mobilise. Reading, for example, Nelson Mandela's *Long Walk to Freedom* (1994), Vaclav Havel's *Open Letters* (1991), Aung San Suu Kyi's *Freedom from Fear* (1995) or Martin Luther King's *I Have a Dream* speech not only restores one's faith in the human spirit, but can inspire one to a new commitment to activism and to doing one's bit to follow their example.

The humanist vision can be found in other sources as well. As suggested above, the lives of 'ordinary people' who have lived out a commitment to humanist values are also a powerful source of inspiration. Such people are to be found everywhere, and their influence pervades those with whom they come into contact. One does not have to look very far in one's own personal experience to find the unsung heroes of the humanist ideal, and their lives and achievements fly in the face of the those writers who triumphantly celebrate the 'death of humanism' (Carroll 1993), or the economic rationalists who assume that individual self-interest is the principal motivator of human behaviour.

A further source of inspiration lies in the rich cultural heritage of literature, poetry, art, music and drama. The creative arts have been the source of some of the most insightful and inspiring interpretations of humanism, whether in the romanticism of Beethoven, Keats, Tennyson, Dickens and Tolstoy, the more distant Shakespeare, Milton and Michelangelo, the more recent Picasso, Henry Lawson, Bob Dylan, Arthur Miller and Shostakovich, or contemporary voices from David Williamson to Michael Leunig. This list, it should be noted, is exclusively male, again emphasising the need to make women's representations of the humanist vision heard and seen. It is also characteristically white and Western, representing the cultural tradition in which this particular author, like the majority of

Australian social workers, was raised. The list thus serves to highlight the very limited vision of humanity that is part of mainstream Australian culture, and the need to hear and validate other voices. Limited though the list is, it nevertheless contains many powerful and inspirational renditions of the human spirit.

The sources mentioned in this section—merely examples, representing only the tip of the iceberg of the great humanist tradition—are seldom integrated in models and visions of social work. They do not normally belong on the reading lists of introductory or even advanced social work units, are not the subject of continuing professional education seminars, and are not incorporated in practice models. Their absence, in a profession committed to humanist values, is significant and says a good deal about the way social work and 'legitimate' social work knowledge have been constructed. The legacy of positivism is still strong, as are the demands of the managerial discourse, and it is not easy to specify the inspiration gained from a Mahler symphony or a Shakespeare play in terms of specified behavioural outcomes, competencies, or evaluated intervention skills. This simply emphasises the need for a strong alternative discourse of social work education and practice, and the need to move away from the constraints of positivism and managerialism.

Is humanism sufficient?

Before proceeding to develop an approach to social work based on the alternative discourse discussed in the previous two chapters, it is necessary to ask the same question of humanism as was asked of postmodernism and feminism in Chapter 3. It is clear that humanism has a lot to offer an alternative social work, but is it in itself sufficient to act as a basis for social work theory and practice? Again, as with postmodernism and feminism, the answer must be 'no'. Humanism is able to provide the over-arching discourse missing from postmodernist accounts, and in doing so ties social work closely to a view of social justice. It also provides a broader and more inclusive discourse than feminism, despite the limitations and tensions identified earlier in this chapter. However it is missing another important element, namely a structural analysis of oppression and disadvantage. There are difficulties in incorporating the discourse of conflict inherent in a structural analysis with the discourse of unity inherent in humanism, but it can also be argued that a humanist position need not be incompatible with a structural analysis, and that such an analysis can readily be incorporated in a vision of humanity. Indeed, from a social work point of view a commitment to humanity makes no sense unless it contains, at its core, a structural analysis of oppression and disadvantage. Hence there is a need to balance the tension between the competing narratives of unity and difference.

As mentioned at the beginning of the chapter, Nicholas Ragg's critique of positivism ended with the advocacy of what he called 'critical humanism'. So far we have simply explored humanism, and have not looked at the 'critical' component of such a perspective. At various stages in the preceding sections it was noted that humanism does not always account for issues such as gender and race, and one could readily add class to this criticism. Without a structural analysis, humanism can readily become a conservative position supporting the status quo and entrenching existing relationships of power and oppression, reframed in a positive and progressive rhetoric. It should also be noted that the single 'dimension' developed at the beginning of Chapter 3 advocated a position that was not just humanist, but also incorporated the anarchist perspective represented by the vertical dimension in Figure 2.2. A commitment to an anarchist, or bottom-up, approach, opposed to hierarchical structures of domination, requires by definition an analysis of those structures, and for this reason too, the structure-free humanism outlined earlier in this chapter, while important, is not sufficient.

Universal rights and relativist needs

Underlying much of the discussion in both this and the previous chapter is the tension between universalism and relativism. Universalist accounts, such as humanism, allow a focus and purpose for social work, and enable social work to be linked to a vision of social justice. On the other hand, universalism can reinforce marginalisation, and it has been shown above that the humanist discourse does not necessarily allow adequately for the separate voices of women, racial and ethnic minorities, and other oppressed groups to be heard. Relativist discourses, such as postmodernism and poststructuralism, get over this problem by allowing for the establishment of creative alternatives and for the legitimation of the voices of those at the margins, in their rejection of the dominance of a single explanation or meta-narrative. In doing so relativism frees social work from the shackles of positivism, but it may also remove it from the humanist agenda, and from a universal commitment to social justice, which is at the core of social work.

This tension between universalism and relativism can be seen in the use of the term *humanist/anarchist*, which has been used to characterise the vision of social work this book seeks to articulate. The *humanist* element, by its very nature, seeks some form of universal discourse based on the idea of a common humanity. By contrast the *anarchist* component suggests the need for a relativist understanding, allowing for diverse voices and constructions to emerge 'from below'. The two thus do not seem to be as compatible as they appeared in the discussion at the beginning of Chapter 3.

As a way of resolving this tension, the remainder of this chapter is devoted to developing a vision for social work practice that incorporates both a universalist view of social justice and, at least in part, the relativism of grounded theory and poststructuralism. This will be done in terms of a *universalist* discourse of *human rights*, grounded in a vision of humanity, balanced with a *relativist* discourse of *human needs*. The discourses both of human needs and human rights have been locations for a contest between universal and relativist understandings. In order to develop a framework incorporating both needs and rights, the relationship between the two must be further explored.

The idea of need implies some form of desired end. One does not need something as an end in itself, because the very idea of need incorporates necessity; one needs something *in order to do, have or be something else*. Thus we need food in order to stay alive, a patient needs medicine in order to relieve symptoms of illness, an abused child needs out-of-home care in order to be protected from abuse, a person needs counselling in order to cope with post-traumatic stress, a community needs a child care centre so that parents can work or be otherwise occupied, and so on. In each case, the 'need' is not an end, but is something that enables a desired end to be reached; it is a statement of necessary conditions for the achievement of something else. If it can be shown that the desired end can be met in another way, the need might cease to 'exist' (for example, a patient's symptoms may be removed by a change of diet, removing the 'need' for medicine, and extra supports for the family may also prevent child abuse, thereby removing the 'need' to take the child into care). It is actually the desired end that is important, rather then the 'need' *per se*.

This may seem to be an obvious point, but its implications are profound. Often the language of social work and social policy does not take account of the desired goal, and speaks of needs as if they are ends in themselves, for example: to measure the needs of a community; to assess the level of need for particular services; to assess the needs of a family; and so on. This has two consequences: it ignores the value and ideology questions associated with the desired end (e.g., should parents really have the right to be able to place their children in child care?), and it makes 'needs' sound as if they are objective, value free entities, instead of them being seen as value laden.

When the desired end is considered, it is very easy to see the relationship between needs and rights. Whether a need can be justified depends very much on how one views the right implied in the desired end. Thus in the examples cited above, the need for food implies a right to remain alive, the need for medicine implies a right to be free from pain and suffering, the need for out-of-home care implies a child's right to be free from abuse, and so on. These are fundamental issues of human rights, and such claims of need can be seen to be resting on claims of rights; the language of needs and the language of rights are thus clearly linked.

There has been a good deal of philosophical debate about whether 'needs' imply 'oughts', for example, whether a statement that a community needs a child care centre implies that one ought to be supplied. In a strict philosophical sense it can be argued that there is no such implication, as a 'need' should only be met if a moral case can be made on the basis of rights. If I tell my supervisor that I need a new office chair, my supervisor is likely to want to know why; in other words, what is the right implied in my claim of need. If it is because I have been experiencing back pain and a doctor or physiotherapist has said that a different chair is required, this relates to a right to a safe workplace as guaranteed by Occupational Health and Safety legislation. On the other hand, I may simply be offended that my chair does not match the colour of the carpet; here my need is based on a 'right' to aesthetically pleasing surroundings, presumably a weaker case than the right to a safe workplace. In each case, the 'need' is the same, and is undeniable; a new chair is necessary to achieve the desired end. But *on the basis of right* the strength of each claim is very different, and it is the right, not the need, that my supervisor will in effect be evaluating in making the decision as to whether I should be provided with a new chair. To take an example more closely related to social work, the statement that a community 'needs' a community centre may be made simply because a neighbouring community has one, and this community wants to be seen to be as well served. Alternatively it may be 'needed' as a memorial to a prominent local councillor, or it may be needed as a location for a variety of youth and family programs that help to foster social cohesion and development. Although the need for the centre is the same, there are three different associated rights (the right of a community to 'look good', the right of a prominent former councillor to be memorialised in bricks and mortar, and the right to a genuine experience of human community), and these will obviously be differentially evaluated by any potential funding body.

A discourse of competing rights is therefore behind claims or assessments of need. In social work this discussion is usually omitted, as 'needs' are treated as existing on their own, and this tends to mask the important rights issues behind the assessment and determination of need. Because of this, it is also true that in the context of social work and social policy, a statement of need does imply a claim that the need ought to be met, even though in the strict philosophical sense this is not a necessary implication. However to evaluate the strength of that claim, in the light of other competing claims, it is necessary to explore the rights that are implied in the need statement.

In an attempt to counter the potentially conservatising implications of relativism, which have been mentioned above, some writers, most notably Doyal and Gough (1991), have sought to develop a theory of universal human needs, a project with a long history in social work (Towle 1965). This has been seen as important because of the perceived need for a universal discourse based on principles of common humanity and social justice, to override the injustices and continuing inequalities caused by relativism. For the purposes of this book, it is clear that such a universal discourse of humanity is critically important, if the task for social work is to move public debate and social work practice back towards the humanist/anarchist paradigm. However, because of the nature of the relationship of needs and rights, the starting point will be a universalist discourse of human rights, rather than a universal approach to needs as advocated by Doyal and Gough.

Because of the pseudo-scientific nature of 'needs', which in many cases are treated as objectively existing and measurable, a theory of universal human needs is likely to have aspirations to a scientific base. It thus lends itself to a process of rationalisation, objectification and operationalisation, and in doing so it not only falls into the positivist trap, but it can easily be diverted from the most important aspect of a universal claim to social justice, namely a vision of what it means to be fully human. A universal approach to human rights, however, makes no claim to scientific justification, but seeks its foundation in a consensus of values. Inspired by a common vision of humanity, a universal approach to human rights seeks to delineate those rights which can be claimed by all people, on the basis of their humanity, and which can form a basis for a struggle for justice. In that sense, it represents the search for a common definition of humanity and its aspirations. Indeed, there has been considerably more progress down the road towards establishing universal rights than is the case with universal needs. Universal needs have been understood in the rather limited sense developed by Doyal and Gough (1991), or by writers such as Maslow (1970), but a universal and comprehensive definition of human rights, which has received at least token acceptance from the vast majority of governments, is found in considerable detail in the Universal Declaration of Human Rights and other associated United Nations covenants and protocols. Despite the limitations that might be associated with these UN statements, they nevertheless represent a remarkable achievement of international consensus about what it means to be truly human, and the rights we should all expect as members of the human race.

Another reason why *rights* represent a more fertile ground than *needs* as a focus for a universalist discourse is the link of rights with the law. Human rights can be legislated for, and indeed such legislation is a feature of international law, bills of rights, constitutional guarantees and the statute books of many states. Human needs, on the other hand, have not been enshrined in legislation, and claims of need cannot generally be supported with laws. A discourse of human rights is therefore more likely to be supported by politicians and law-makers in terms of legislative action, while a discourse of human needs is more likely to remain at the level of rhetoric or of pious statements in social work texts. If a person feels their rights have been violated they have recourse in law to have the situation reversed, whereas if a person feels their needs have not been met, they can only resort to making a moral case. One reason for the stronger legislative backing for human rights is that rights have a much stronger claim for being met—a right, by its very nature, implies an imperative for the state to ensure that the right is recognised and met, whereas a claim of need carries a much weaker imperative. There is, however, a negative side to the legal nature of human rights. The legal framework allows rights to be legally challenged and debated, and requires legal action if one feels one's rights have been violated. In a system where access to the processes of law is not equal, and where the law and the legal system operate in favour of the rich and powerful and against the interests of the disadvantaged and marginalised, a discourse of human rights can become another mechanism simply for reinforcing the dominance of the powerful. Despite this difficulty, however, the legal aspect of a human rights perspective does represent, at least potentially, significant advantages for those concerned with achieving social justice.

A universal discourse of human rights, therefore, represents a more promising direction as a foundation for social work practice than does a universal framework of needs. This then allows for a relativist understanding of human needs to complement a universal understanding of rights. Needs are the way that rights are translated into the local context, and they become the contextualised statement of rights for particular people in particular circumstances. For example, the right to education may be universal, but it will be translated into very different need statements in different social, cultural and economic contexts: the need for school buildings, the need for textbooks, the need for computers, the need for qualified teachers, the need for children to have a place to study at home, the need for audiovisual equipment, the need for school buses, and so on. In some settings, some of these needs will be much more important than others, and will be expressed in different ways (e.g., the type of school building 'needed', or even whether a building is needed at all, will vary with climatic conditions). The claims of educational need will therefore vary considerably depending on the context, and it would be foolish to attempt to universalise what is 'needed' for an adequate education. But they will all be based on the universal right to an education, which is claimed for all people regardless of who they are or where they live.

Developing a common vision of humanity as the core of social work practice therefore requires a vision of universal human rights. Until recently, there was widespread acceptance of a universal human rights framework, usually stated in the words of the Universal Declaration of Human Rights, and it has formed the basis of much social justice and development work in both government and non-government organisations. In recent years, however, this universality has been challenged, from four different perspectives.

The first challenge comes from the categorisation of human rights. Commonly human rights are thought of in three categories: civil and political rights; economic, social and cultural rights; and the so-called 'third generation' of human rights. *Civil and political rights* include rights such as the right to vote, freedom of speech, freedom of assembly, fair trial, etc.; the preconditions for full participation in civil society and political life. *Economic, social and cultural rights* include the right to work, the right to education, the right to social security, and so on; the things necessary for full participation in, and benefit from, the economic activity of the nation and the institutions of society. The *third generation* of rights incorporates collective rather than individual rights, such as the right to development, environmental rights, and the right to community. This categorisation has led to claims that some rights are more important than others. Conservative politicians, for example, while happy to uphold the importance of civil and political rights, are often rather less keen about economic and social rights, as these can be seen as intruding on market forces. The leaders of some Asian nations have argued that for a developing country the right to development (a third generation right) must take precedence over civil and political rights. Thus the categorisation of human rights can easily lead to a form of relativism, and a trade-off of one set of rights for another.

The second challenge to a universal human rights discourse comes from arguments about cultural specificity. This view argues that the definition of rights is itself culturally determined, and hence that universal definitions of human rights represent a form of cultural imperialism, or the imposition of Western understandings of rights on other cultural traditions. This view has also been strongly expressed by leaders of some Asian countries, who have argued that an Asian understanding of human rights is necessarily different from a Western position. One needs to question the validity of such arguments, as they have become a justification for the continuation of repressive measures and have been used in an attempt to stifle international criticism of human rights abuses. It is certainly a view of human rights that has been defined by—and is in the interests of—some very repressive regimes, and it is a perspective that is undoubtedly not shared by the many victims of human rights abuses in those countries. Opposition leaders such as Aung San Suu Kyi (1995) and the Dalai Lama do not share such a view of 'Asian' human rights being somehow different. There are, however, arguments advocating cultural specificity in human rights that need to be taken more seriously than the politically convenient posturing of the leaders of repressive regimes. One such argument is that of Galtung (1994), a noted peace researcher and activist, and a long-standing advocate of universal human rights, who is now suggesting the importance of allowing human rights to be defined in different cultural contexts as a form of liberation rather than of repression. His argument supports a view of human rights that is closer to the position on human needs advocated below.

The third challenge to universalism in human rights comes from postmodernism, which sees such universalism as a metanarrative and a leftover from modernism, with no place in a postmodernist world. The dangers of such a perspective have been discussed in Chapter 3, and need not be reiterated here, but postmodernism, and its influence on contemporary Western thinking, remains a powerful critique. The challenge is to adopt some of the important insights of postmodernism, without allowing universal notions of social justice and a vision of humanity to be undermined as a result.

The final challenge to universal understandings of human rights comes from feminism. Many definitions of human rights, and attempts to articulate human rights and to oppose abuses, have been located in the public sphere, and human rights have been conceptualised in terms of the relationship between the individual and the state. This has largely been a male domain, and the understanding of 'citizen' incorporated in human rights is that of the active participant in civil society, still a predominantly male activity. By contrast, the human rights issues that most affect women tend to be located in the domestic sphere, such as domestic violence, rape, genital mutilation, and the denial of freedoms in domestic life rather than in civil life. The conventional human rights discourse, characterised by the Universal Declaration, does not adequately deal with such issues, and hence is biased against the protection and promotion of the human rights of women. It should be emphasised that this is not a criticism of a universal human rights discourse *per se*, but rather of the way in which it has been defined on the basis of certain patriarchal assumptions. The task is therefore not to dismantle the idea of universal human rights, but rather to redefine them so that the domestic arena is adequately included.

Thus the idea of universal human rights is not without its critics. Much of the criticism, however, comes from positions that themselves pose significant threats for the hope of a vision of humanity. It is precisely these arguments that have made human rights somewhat unfashionable, but also make them all the more important in the current social, political and economic context. For the moment, however, more has to be said about a relativist discourse of needs, and its importance for social work.

Social work as a profession is very much in the business of defining needs, and having them met. The word 'need' is one of the most widely used by social workers, who seek to assess the needs of clients, families, children, communities and institutions. As Illich (Illich et al. 1977) maintains, social workers have become professional need-definers, but often this is achieved without acknowledging Illich's criticism of how this disempowers, and in the absence of any sense of puzzlement about the nature of 'needs'. 'Need' is a concept philosophers have argued about for centuries, but this has not stopped social workers from using it as if it is non-problematic (Ife 1980).

If needs are derived from a universalist approach to human rights, the definition of need can become the way in which rights are contextualised. The definition of need, however, must also be looked at in terms of the power dimension of the model in Figure 2.2, i.e., in terms of 'top-down' versus 'bottom-up' approaches. From a top-down perspective, as in the professional or managerial discourses, needs are defined by experts, such as social workers, policy-makers or managers, because need definition is seen as being something that requires expertise. From the bottom-up perspective, on the other hand, need definition is a matter for the people or communities directly involved; expert professional need definition is seen as disempowering and as representing a form of control. For this reason, if the humanist/anarchist approach is to be the basis of social work, need definition must be a democratic, participatory process, and is an essential component of empowerment. This links with the work of writers such as Fay (1975, 1987) and Freire (1972), who each emphasise the importance of not only allowing and encouraging people to define their own needs, but also of providing a context within which this can happen, enabling the personal to be linked to the political, and providing opportunities for action to achieve change. This approach to social work will provide the basis for the next chapter.

A universalist understanding of human rights, linked to a relativist understanding of needs as being the way those rights are defined and contextualised, therefore allows for both the universal vision of humanity and the freedom for alternative voices to be heard, and hence for a plurality of different systems to develop. It allows social workers to engage both with the grand narratives of humanism and also with the varying ways in which individuals and communities define their needs and seek to have them met. It also relates to the two dimensions of Figure 2.2; the universal discourse of human rights is a way of asserting the value of the humanist end of the horizontal dimension, while the relativist discourse of needs legitimises and values the bottom-up approach of the anarchist end of the vertical dimension. In summary, it allows social workers to make confident claims for social justice on the basis of universal understandings of human rights, and to establish a powerful normative argument in support of a better world, while at the same time it fully endorses an empowerment-based model whereby the voices of a variety of people are heard and legitimised, and they are enabled to act to meet their needs and aspirations in culturally appropriate ways. The linking of universal rights and relativist needs requires that the two activities become part of the same practice, rather than being seen as separate and competing discourses.

126

CHAPTER

5

Critical theory and social work practice

The two traditions of radical practice

Attempts to develop a radical, or alternative, social work fall into two categories. The first can be called the *structural* approach, which has sought to base social work analysis and practice around an analysis of structural oppression, specifically in the areas of class, race and gender. Much of the radical social work literature of the 1970s was based on a Marxist or pseudo-Marxist analysis of class (Corrigan and Leonard 1978; Bailey and Brake 1975), and other formulations have used a gender analysis (Marchant and Wearing 1986). More recently, Mulally (1993) has integrated these approaches into a more comprehensive account of 'structural social work'. These structural accounts characteristically depend on a form of universalist discourse, seeing class, race and/or gender oppression as transcending cultural and national boundaries, and as requiring analysis at a more general and abstract level. Thus they rely on a universal discourse about the nature of oppression, though of course they allow for more relativist and culturally specific definitions of appropriate action.

The other tradition of radical social work writing has been the *post-structural* tradition, drawing on the work of writers who have rejected universalist discourse and have advocated relativism, difference, and a world of multiple realities. This includes the post-structuralism of Foucault (1972, 1973, 1975; Gutting 1994; Rabinow 1984), and the various writers within the post-modernist tradition (Harvey 1989; Lechte 1994; Haber 1994). The 'death of the meta-narrative' (Lyotard 1984) implies that universalist accounts, even of oppression along class, race and gender lines, are unacceptable. Alternative forms of analysis and understanding are sought by valuing or celebrating difference, and by understanding the way in which power relationships are constantly defined and redefined as part of a fluid and changing discourse (or a number of changing discourses). Although social work writers have not been as prolific in this tradition as they have in the structural tradition, there are some interesting explorations of how social work might thus be conceptualised (Rojek et al. 1988; Solas 1994; Howe 1994; Hartman 1991; Latting 1995; Leonard 1995; Camilleri 1995).

The contribution of feminist writers has spanned both traditions. Some have written within the structural perspective, using an essentially universalist understanding of women's oppression to seek paths to liberation, in much the same way as Marxist writers in relation to social class. Other feminist writers, however, have used feminism to develop a politics of difference, and as a way of challenging universalism, equating universalism with patriarchy as a system of domination (Rothfield 1991; Brah 1991). This demonstrates how feminism has been able to draw on both traditions, and has been informed by both a structural and a post-structural perspective. In being able to bridge this dualism and other dualisms (Plumwood 1993), feminism has demonstrated that discrete dichotomies, even between structural and post-structural accounts, need not be regarded as universally valid, and this opens the way for an analysis that seeks to benefit from the insights of both the structural and post-structural approaches. This will be the position taken in this chapter.

In attempting to develop a perspective that draws from both traditions, one is essentially abandoning an extreme post-modernist position, as postmodernism does not allow for meta-narratives about such issues as social justice and human rights (Rothfield 1991; Davies 1991). Although the discussion below,

128

and indeed much of the discussion in previous chapters, has drawn on postmodernist understandings and interpretations, it is not a postmodernist social work that is advocated in this chapter. Rather it is a position which reasserts the importance of principles of humanity and social justice, as specified in the discussion on universal rights in the previous chapter, but which also seeks to contextualise them through an empowerment-based approach to practice. The theoretical paradigm within which this can best be developed is critical theory, and the discussion below uses a critical theory perspective to define an approach to social work that is consistent with the humanist/anarchist perspective discussed in previous chapters.

Critical theory

The field of critical theory contains some of the most inaccessible literature in the social sciences. It is a complex area, with many differing viewpoints and theoretical formulations, and is characterised by writers who frighten off even the bravest readers with their dense argument and obscure vocabulary. This is ironic given that one of the central aims of critical theory is to enable people to be empowered through equipping them with the tools to analyse their own experiences by relating them to social and political structures (the personal is political) and thus to take action. How they are supposed to do this, when the texts are so inaccessible, remains a mystery. This issue of accessibility is important, and will be taken up again in the next chapter, as it directly relates to a potential role for social workers.

It would be impossible in the following pages to convey a complete summary of the field of critical theory, with all its subtle nuances, layers of argument and points of contention; this would be a task quite beyond the scope of this book. There are various formulations of critical theory (Morrow and Brown 1994; Calhoun 1995; Ray 1993; Geuss 1981; Dryzek 1995) differing in many important aspects, and to summarise them into a single entity would be inappropriate. Rather, what is presented is a particular version of critical theory which draws on some of the previous discussion, and directly relates to the articulation of an alternative social work. It is only one version of critical theory among many, and draws specifically on educative forms of critical theory (Ray 1993, p. 22) as discussed by Leonard (1990), Fay (1987), and others, with particular reference to the work of Freire (1972, see also McLaren and Leonard 1993; McLaren and Lankshear 1994). This version of critical theory is significant because it has sought to relate critical analysis to ideas of political practice, and hence it is relevant to developing a form of social work that can address both the practice and policy dilemmas posed by the context of economic rationalism.

This approach to critical theory also incorporates the humanist vision discussed in Chapter 4. A number of writers have sought to use a critical theory approach to overcome the shortcomings of humanism, and to develop a 'critical humanism' that incorporates a power analysis alongside the humanist vision. In the Australian context, Janet McIntyre (1995) has developed such a perspective in her model of community development, which in some ways parallels the discussion of social work outlined in this chapter.

Critical theory specifically rejects the positivist paradigm of objectivity, empirical measurement and the quest for universal laws. The critique of positivism has been discussed in earlier chapters, and need not be reiterated here. Instead, critical theory can be seen as starting with a position that values an interpretive understanding of reality. Interpretive social science is concerned to uncover the meanings people attach to actions, and the social rules that guide people's behaviour and interaction (Fay 1975). These are not the universal abstracted rules of positivism, but rather are contextual rules grounded in particular cultural experiences. In its attempt to uncover these rules and make them explicit, interpretive social science seeks to improve communication and understanding between people, both within a particular cultural context, and also across cultural boundaries. It also is concerned with understanding how communication breaks down, and explains this through inadequate sharing of symbolic meanings, different cultural definitions and expectations, and inadequate communication. Interpretive social science aims to promote interaction and understanding, and so inter-personal communication is regarded by Fay (1975) as the form of political practice that is necessarily connected to interpretive social science, in the same way that technocratic managerialism and social engineering are the forms of practice associated with positivism (see Chapter 3).

Interpretive social science is a paradigm with which many social workers are familiar. It reflects the reality of a good deal of social work practice, which is about understanding and interpreting the reality of a client, family or group, and which seeks to understand the patterns of communication that may result in misunderstanding or 'pathological' behaviour. Family therapy, for example, is largely built on a tradition of interpretive social science, as are other accepted forms of social work, especially in casework and work with families. The techniques of interviewing and of establishing empathy are characteristically interpretive, and the interpretive paradigm represents a way of working with people in which social workers have been prominent, and where social workers have made significant contributions to the literature (family therapy being an outstanding example). It is, however, a form of practice that is out of step with the positivism and empiricism of the managerial discourse, and hence has not reacted well to the demands to measure, to specify outcomes and to adopt a form of scientific rationality.

This leads inevitably to a concern with language, as it is through language that symbolic meanings are shared and defined, and it is primarily through language that communication is established and maintained. The skill of a social worker in family therapy or counselling is primarily in her/his use of language, and it is through the interpretation of meaning implicit in the language of others that the social worker attempts to understand the reality of a client. Interpretive social science would stop at this point, but critical social science seeks a more powerful role for language, not only in terms of understanding and interpretation, but also in terms of articulating change and opening up possibilities for liberation, or 'emancipation' to use a favourite term of critical theorists. We shall return to the issue of language a little later.

Interpretive social science, in isolation from a broader contextual analysis, tends toward conservatism. Fay (1975) argues that this is an inevitable consequence of the interpretive paradigm. Interpretive social science, by seeking to enhance communication and understanding, and by resolving tensions and misunderstandings at an individual level, leads to a form of practice that simply reconciles people to their position in society rather than working towards change. Interpretive social science does not contain within it a view of a direction for

131

change (whether towards liberation or control), but simply works to enable people to live more happily within the existing order. Such practice is, by its very nature, conservative. The criticism of casework as conservative echoes this point within social work, and was behind much of the radical critique of the 1970s, which saw social work as primarily social control, helping to reconcile people to their lot in an unjust society, rather than seeking to change it. This critique is important, and applies just as readily to a good deal of social work in the 1990s. What is needed, however, is a more sophisticated response than that of the radicals of the 1970s, when a number of babies were thrown out with the bathwater, and much of the practice wisdom and the value of the interpretive tradition within social work was devalued. This in turn opened the way for the domination of positivism within social work discourse, in the mistaken belief that the answer lay in being 'more scientific'. A more sophisticated approach, however, is offered by critical theory, which does not reject an interpretive understanding on account of its conservatism. Rather it accepts the need for an interpretive understanding but seeks to add to it a politics of liberation.

Interpretive social science is also compatible with the relativism of postmodernism. It allows for the establishment of multiple realities, for the death of the meta-narrative, and for the valuing of diversity at the expense of a universal discourse. In some ways interpretive social science can be seen as a forerunner of postmodernism and is subject to many of the same criticisms. In seeking an alternative, critical theory thus takes on board a dismissal of totally postmodernist accounts. Again, this is done not in the spirit of complete rejection; it accepts the validity and the importance of much of the postmodern critique, but in the recognition that something more needs to be added if one is to develop an approach to both theory and practice that is able to achieve change towards a more just society.

Critical social science therefore seeks to add a structural perspective to the understandings of interpretive social science. It insists that to interpret, to understand and to communicate are not enough, and that one also needs to incorporate a perspective that can lead to action and change, and can point to the direction in which that change ought to occur (e.g., towards liberation rather than towards further oppression). This requires some form of structural analysis, which identifies the causes of people's oppression or structural disadvantage within a wider context. The felt needs and sufferings of people may be the consequences of forces of which they have little or no knowledge and understanding, given the global and often hidden nature of the forces of capitalism, patriarchy etc., and the limited analysis presented by the mainstream media, and hence an interpretive approach alone is insufficient to enable them to take effective action. However if one adds a structural analysis, there is the potential for a powerful force for change. This enables people to relate their own experience of oppression at the level of social practice to a broader political understanding. It is, effectively, the linking of the personal and the political in a paradigm which says that each by itself is insufficient, and that our understanding of the human condition, and of the events impacting on ourselves and on others, must incorporate both. The structural analysis provides the overall perspective within which individual constructions of meaning, and individual actions, occur.

Critical social science, then, is normative. It is not simply content to describe the world of society and human relations, but is also concerned to change it. The critical approach incorporates a view of the direction of desired change, based on an articulation of social justice, human liberation, or some other high-level account. The structural analysis involved in a critical approach will typically involve the components of structural oppression, such as class, race, gender, ethnicity, age, disability, sexuality, and so on. It makes no pretence to value freedom, but rather will inevitably be based on value premises about what would make a better, fairer, more just or more liberated society. Many critical theorists use the term 'emancipatory' thereby underlining the importance of notions of freedom and liberation, whether from the structures of patriarchy, the oppression of class, the denial of human rights, the cultural invasions of colonialism, or from some more complex interaction of these oppressive forces. It is therefore necessary for one's theory and practice to be acknowledged as normative, and any notion of practice as essentially technical and value-free is specifically rejected. All practice, by its very nature, is political.

The important thing for critical social science is that both the interpretive and the structural accounts are not only important, and indeed necessary, but they must be somehow integrated into a single understanding, rather than separated. It is not simply concerned with the personal *and* the political, but requires an incorporation of the idea that the personal *is* political and *vice versa*. This is one example (several more will be discussed below) of the essentially integrative nature of critical theory, which seeks to break down many of the dualisms inherent in traditional Western thought. As such, it represents a challenge to the conventional paradigm, and draws heavily on feminist thought, which has been significant in breaking down dualisms, and which was the origin of the phrase 'the personal is political'. Critical theory therefore is readily compatible with feminism, and this underlines the importance of feminist analysis as a way of informing both theory and practice.

Integrating an interpretive approach with a structural analysis, however, is easier to say than to do. They are characteristically defined from very different standpoints, and their compatibility is not helped by the positivist elements of some structural accounts (Marxism, or at least some forms of it, being a particular example). Habermas, one of the most influential writers on critical theory, has attempted to bridge this gap through his analysis of language (Habermas 1987; White 1995; Pusey 1987). He has sought to demonstrate how language is not used simply to define local realities and specific discourses, but also that by its very existence it represents some form of universal rationality, which thus provides a framework for a higher order discourse. His theory of 'communicative action' attempts to extend this to an analysis that sees language and action as inextricably linked, and sees the potential in the universal rationality of language for the establishment of dialogue that can be free of domination and therefore has the potential for liberation. While Habermas is more pessimistic about the potential for achieving such liberation than writers such as Fay (1987), his work is important in establishing the significance of the link between the personal and the political within the way language is used.

The integration of interpretive and structural under-standings, therefore, can be identified as being located in the field of language, and this is an area where critical theory can draw heavily on the work of poststructuralists such as Foucault (1972, 1975), who describes the way power is defined and redefined in relation to discourse. The discourse then can provide the means for the definition of alternative views of power, and hence can be related to a specific agenda of empowerment. Because people are always part of discursive structures and networks, which have power relations implicated in them (Davies 1991), they are in fact always part of the discourse of power. Foucault describes how different discourses have been used to define, legitimate, entrench and embody relations of power, and the corollary is that working to change the discourse can lead to changes in power relations. This is why the analysis of the current context of social work in Chapter 2 was undertaken in terms of discourse, as it is the orientation of this book that social workers can—and indeed should—work to change the nature of this discourse that defines their work. How this might happen will be the subject of Chapters 6 and 7.

Another important way in which the significance of language affects critical theory is in the notion of practice. Traditionally, use of language has been seen as important for those social workers who are concerned with individual constructions of social problems, such as caseworkers and therapists. Language is, after all, their main tool, and the medium within which they help their 'clients'. On the other hand, action at a more macro level was not seen as relating particularly to language skills. It was more about social action, organising and community development, and while language is a useful (indeed essential) skill for this form of practice, it was typically not seen as the most important skill for such a practitioner. Linking the personal and the political, however, means that language has a greatly increased role in progressive change-oriented social work. Talking to clients becomes not just a matter of the traditional interview, but a dialogical consciousness-raising relationship leading to action, in the kind of practice advocated by Freire (1972), which will be discussed below. This puts a very different focus on the language skills of the practitioner, and on the nature of the communication that takes place between worker and client. In doing so, it removes the 'interview' from the essentially conservative position it has occupied in much traditional social work, and sees the development of inter-personal skills, understood from a specific perspective of empowerment, as vitally important for radical practice.

Critical theory is specifically oriented to a discourse of liberation. It is therefore directly concerned with change and empowerment, and is oriented to the kind of social justice that is such an important part of social work. Because of its link between the personal and the political, it is able to define human liberation and social justice both in individual and structural terms. Thus it is able to acknowledge the legitimacy of both the individual and structural approaches to empowerment, both of which are evident in the social work literature. The tension between these two approaches to empowerment has been an area of difficulty for some social workers. The individual approach requires the worker to seek to empower clients or families to take control of their lives, to have access to resources, to set goals, and to articulate and achieve their ambitions. Structural approaches to empowerment, however, have demanded the empowerment of groups such as women, Aboriginal people, gays and lesbians, people with disabilities, and so on. This requires a structural analysis, and can be achieved only by structural change. The conflict between the two approaches to empowerment has caused tensions, with structural social workers maintaining that individual approaches to empowerment are simply liberal affirmations of the status quo, thereby devaluing the skilled work of many social workers. By contrast, those who work for individual empowerment may feel that the aims of the structural social workers are unattainable, at least in the short term, and that they devalue the importance of change and empowerment at the personal level.

An approach based on critical theory would require the incorporation of both approaches to empowerment, within the social work profession as a whole, and in the work of each social worker. It would assert that individual empowerment is not possible unless links are made to structural empowerment issues, and the client is helped to see the connection between individual powerlessness/oppression and broader political questions, through a reflection on her/his own experience not simply of personal oppression, but as a member of one or more oppressed groups. Similarly, it would maintain that empowerment at the structural level must incorporate the lived experiences of the people concerned, their own stories of oppression and disempowerment, and the impact of structural change on individual lives. Thus the idea of empowerment inherent in a critical paradigm is one that requires it to incorporate the personal and the political in the same process. The link between the personal and the political is made not just at the analytical or theoretical level, but also in practice, and this results in the dialogical consciousness-raising approach to practice spelled out below.

An important aspect of the critical approach of this chapter is that it accepts and validates wisdom and expertise 'from below' as well as 'from above'. In the interaction between worker and client, it is not only the worker's expertise that is brought to bear on the problem at hand. The client also is seen as having wisdom and expertise, as a result of life experience, and from having lived through the experience of oppression in a way the worker probably has not. Similarly, working at a community level, the community is seen as being the location of knowledge, wisdom and understanding. This is not to deny that the worker also has wisdom and expertise. But it is different from the wisdom and expertise of the client/community, and therefore the essence of practice from a critical perspective is that *both sets of wisdom and expertise are valued, and are brought together.* This is essentially a *dialogical* relationship, where each will enter into a dialogue with the other, each will respect and learn from the wisdom of the other, and as a result each will develop and grow. It is an equal relationship in terms of power, in terms of respect, and in terms of the value each places on the other's wisdom. Within this dialogue, the problem or issue is defined, the links can be drawn between the personal and the political, and action can be initiated.

It is important to emphasise that this dialogical relationship includes the posing of the question, problem or issue to be addressed. The worker does not come with an already deter-mined definition of a problem, or a frame of reference within which that problem can be understood. It is up to the worker and the client, together, to formulate the issue and to develop the framework within which it can be addressed. The worker does not impose solutions, but works alongside the client so that together they can ask the questions as well as think about the answers. From the perspective of the worker it is problem-posing rather than problem-solving practice, as the problem-solving takes place through dialogical action. In establishing such a dialogical relationship—whether with a client, a community, a student, a colleague, a supervisor, an employee, a politician, a manager, or whomever—the social worker must be aware of the power implications, and must ensure that it is a relationship in which power is genuinely shared, where each has a sense of ownership of the outcome, and where each sets out to learn from the other so that the result is *mutual* empowerment for both worker and 'other'. As a result, both will better come to understand the issue, both will learn, and both will act.

There is therefore in this approach a particular understanding of the relationship, and of the way it is constructed, which differs from the way in which the social work relationship is often conceptualised. It is seen as a mutually empowering and mutually educative process, and does not have the power imbalance of the traditional 'professional relationship'. There is no room in it for 'the use of authority' in the sense often understood in the social work literature. It incorporates Freire's (1972) critique of a banking concept of education (where knowledge is essentially commodified, and is something that is transmitted from teacher to student), and instead promotes a model of mutual empowerment. This model of education is as applicable to social work as it is to teaching, and indeed is perhaps more so, given Freire's work was developed against a backdrop of oppression and structural disadvantage that is also the arena in which most, if not all, social work is practised.

An essential component of the critical approach is that it should lead to action. It is not enough to understand and interpret, as is the case in the interpretive paradigm, but this understanding and interpretation must result in the people concerned being able to take action in order to have their articulated needs met. This, according to Fay (1975), is a key criterion for the success of a theory developed from the critical perspective. Within positivism, a theory is successful if it helps to predict and hence to control; within the interpretive paradigm, a theory is successful if it helps understanding, and hence communication. Within a critical paradigm, on the other hand, a theory is successful if it enables people to articulate their needs and to act in order to have them met. Hence social action becomes not something that is somehow separated from other aspects of social work, but a necessary component of all practice.

Another important link made within the critical paradigm is the link between fact (or knowledge) and value. The positivist world view sees them as distinct, and necessarily so. Indeed social work texts from the positivist perspective, such as Compton's and Galaway's *Social Work Processes* (1994) insist that it is essential for workers to make a clear separation between knowledge and value statements, and to think about knowledge and values in different ways. From a critical theory perspective such a separation is quite untenable, and in this regard critical theory again draws on postmodernism and poststructuralism in understanding how 'knowledge' is socially and linguistically constructed in such a way that it is by its very nature value-laden. To attempt to separate knowledge and values is to deny the value basis of all knowledge, and to reduce social work to a potentially value-free technical activity. Such a separation is a requirement of economic rationalism, where the market is seen as operating in a value-free way, and where the constructed knowledge of economics is at least implicitly understood as value-free or value-neutral. Ideology is an inevitable part of any discourse of power and any construction of knowledge, and critical theory's insistence on the link between knowledge and values (i.e., that they are really the same thing) represents an important leverage point for the critique of economic rationalism, and of the managerialist and market discourses of human services.

A further important link in critical social science is between theory and practice. Instead of understanding each as separate, and then agonising about how they can be related (as social workers are apt to do) the critical paradigm insists that they are part of the same thing. It is only by changing the world, according to Marx, that we can understand it, and to assume that we can learn without doing (i.e., develop the theory separate from the practice) is to adopt a very precious and ultimately useless understanding of 'theory' or 'knowledge'. The integrated approach of critical theory maintains that it is by practising that we will develop our theory, just as it is by developing theory that we practise. This is related to the notion of reflexive practice as developed by Jan Fook (1993, 1996) and in the earlier work of Donald Schon (1987), and also relates to the Marxist notion of *praxis*, where learning and doing, or developing theory and practice, are the same process. From this perspective, any attempt to develop theory in a practice-free context is nonsense. Theory for social work emerges from practice; the 'client' has as much of a role in formulating that

139

theory as the social worker, and any idea of 'theory' being accessible to the social worker but inaccessible to the client is unacceptable. This in turn leads to the notion of 'grounded theory', which emerges from the specific social and cultural context, and represents the constructions of the people who live in that context rather than the abstractions of a social worker, sociologist or psychologist. Social work practice, from the point of view of the critical perspective, must emerge from and be part of grounded theory, namely theory that the 'clients' or 'community' have actually formulated and own. This is a very different understanding of theory, and indeed of knowledge from the traditional social work perspective, and it requires a very different relationship between worker and client.

This approach to theory would not be accepted by all critical theorists, and indeed it represents a direct challenge to those critical theorists who have undertaken their work purely in the cloistered halls of academia and who have produced works that are quite inaccessible to the vast majority; such writing is contradictory to the approach to critical theory/practice discussed here. It must be emphasised that the critical theory described in this section is only one construction of critical theory, and not an attempt to encompass the entire field with its various strands of analysis. However the incapacity of critical theorists to put forward their case in clear and accessible language points to an important role for social workers who have much greater skills of reframing and of grounding their work in the lived experiences of their 'clients'. In some ways, the development and progression of critical theory is a task that social workers are perhaps uniquely equipped to accomplish.

As has already been mentioned, one of the most important writers for this particular version of critical theory is Paulo Freire (1972, see also McLaren and Leonard 1993; McLaren and Lankshear 1994). In his literacy programs, Freire sought to help people define their immediate experiences and articulate their needs, and to relate this to a political analysis of oppressive structures that affected their lives and defined their life chances. This led to programs of action, arising out of the shared analysis of oppression. Thus his education programs were specifically both liberating and empowering. Freire's work has been particularly important for social workers, and has been used by many in the radical social work tradition and in community development. One of the reasons for its importance is that, in the tradition of critical theory, it provides a framework for analysis linked to practice (or praxis) that requires the personal to be linked to the political, and the political to the personal, so that action to achieve liberation is seen as taking place in both arenas. This, it can be argued, is fundamental to social work because of social work's location on the boundary of the personal and the political; it suggests that non-political social work is an impossibility.

It is also important to note that Freire incorporates both a universalist discourse of structural oppression and a relativist, grounded analysis of specific personal, social and cultural contexts. Indeed, he maintains that such an incorporation of both the universal and the relativist is a requirement for effective action to achieve change, which is aimed towards countering oppression and achieving liberation. This suggests that for social workers the structuralist/post-structuralist issue need not be seen as a simple dichotomy, and that genuine radical practice can, and indeed must, incorporate both. As suggested in Chapter 1, social work has always had to struggle with reconciling apparent dualisms (theory/practice, knowledge/skills, etc.), and so such a synthesis should be more comfortable for social workers than for others who are more completely socialised into dualistic thinking.

Social work and critical theory

It has been suggested throughout the above paragraphs that there are ready parallels to be drawn between critical theory and social work, and that critical theory presents a possible model for the establishment of an alternative social work to address the issues and dilemmas outlined in earlier chapters. Critical theory, at least in the form outlined above, is clearly located in the lower right quadrant of Figure 2.2, in the community-based or humanist/anarchist discourse of human services. It incorporates the humanist position, in that it values the expression of the human ideal and allows for the kind of universal humanist position articulated in Chapter 4, while it also emphasises the 'from below' approach, acknowledging the importance of reality as defined by the people rather than by experts, and encouraging this reality to be the location for both theory and practice. It therefore represents a good basis for a discussion of social work theory and practice, and for creative practice opportunities in opposition to the dominant managerial and market discourses of economic rationalism.

There is much in traditional social work that is fully consistent with a critical theory perspective, and many social workers, perhaps a majority, would find little with which to disagree in the approach taken so far in this chapter. That in itself is significant, as it suggests that a critical alternative can be developed from within a construction of social work which is understood and supported by many social workers. It is not a case of establishing a social work that comes from right outside the mainstream, thereby potentially alienating many practitioners, but rather of drawing on traditions that are already present in social work, bringing them to the fore, and seeking ways to articulate their vision in more substantive and influential ways (see Chapter 7). There are, however, some aspects of the conventional construction of social work, as described in Chapter 1, which are not easily reconcilable with the critical theory approach. It is appropriate at this point to identify these tensions, and the issues that each of them raises for any attempt to develop a social work based on the critical paradigm.

Professionalism

One of the most important areas of contention is that of professionalism, as critical theory requires either an abandoning of a professional mode of practice, or a considerable redefinition of what is involved in practising as a 'professional'. The inequality of power implicit in a traditional professional relationship is not acceptable within the critical theory approach outlined above. The relationship between 'worker' and 'client' becomes one where power is shared, and where each is seen as bringing specific wisdom and expertise, with neither being given the superior status implied by the term 'professional'. The reification of professional knowledge and expertise, and its being rendered inaccessible by the use of jargon, is similarly unacceptable.

There are, of course, obvious advantages to a professional approach to practice. If being professional involves a commitment to the highest practice standards, and a commitment to ethical practice, then few could argue with it. And the additional credibility social workers can claim, as a result of their professional status, enables them to take some actions and to have a degree of influence that would not be possible if they renounced their professional identity. These potential advantages, however, may not be as positive as they seem, and a critical theory approach leads one to question even these claims for a professional model.

The commitment to the highest standards of practice begs the question of who defines those standards, and how they are operationalised. Traditionally, this is done by senior members of the 'profession', by the professional association, or, in the current context, by managers. In each case, the definition of what counts as high standards can be a limitation on creative practice, and can become a way of seeking to ensure that social workers conform to the dominant definition of what counts as 'good' service. As this is increasingly being defined by managers, working within an economic rationalist paradigm, the danger of using 'high standards' as a form of control are even greater. A critical theory approach would question this construction of 'high standards', and instead would seek a definition derived from the perspective of the 'client' her/himself. While many social workers will support the idea of some form of client feedback as part of evaluation, to expect clients to be the ones who define what is meant by 'high standards' of practice is a rather more radical notion.

This relates also to the question of competencies, which has become an increasingly important part of the context of social work. The competencies required of social workers now have to be specifically defined for employment and accreditation purposes, and indeed the AASW has produced a significant document that attempts to achieve this. But the role of clients, consumers, customers or citizens (depending on which of the discourses of Chapter 2 one is using) in this definition has been minimal. In any case, even if clients had been actively involved in preparation of this document, it would still not meet the requirements of critical theory, which would expect that the idea of competencies be contextualised, or grounded, in particular practice experiences. Simply defining social work competencies in the abstract, and applying them to all possible locations for social work practice, is removing the idea of competency from its practice context, where critical theory would require it to be located. The notion of competency is surely relative to many differing conditions, and defining competencies in a generalised way is simply to accept the positivist paradigm of universal generalisations and context-free evaluation, and to impose a definition of social work from above, with the consequent potential problems of control.

A similar argument applies to ethics, and the professional ideal of high ethical standards, adherence to a code of ethics, and so on. While ethical behaviour should of course be encouraged, who defines ethical behaviour, and on what basis? A code of ethics, however carefully formulated, will, like a set of competency standards, be divorced from the reality of the practice context. It leaves little or no room for an alternative approach based on situational ethics, where ethical issues are seen as not being able to be resolved by reference to an abstracted code, but rather have to be understood within the specific context in which they are located. This of course may be done by reference to values such as equity and social justice, or affirmations of human rights, but the expectation that a code of ethics can be readily applicable, and that it will result in genuinely ethical behaviour, is problematic. Further, it again represents an attempt by a particular group of people, however well-intentioned, to define what is and what is not acceptable behaviour for a social worker, without reference to the views of those with whom that social worker has to work. Like a statement of competencies, it has the potential to be used as a mechanism of control, to ensure that social workers accept the discipline of an 'official' professional view of how they should behave. However, like competency standards, a code of ethics is not entirely negative, and can also be a powerful political document that can be used by social workers as a justification for making a stand on a particular issue of social justice, especially where this involves a conflict with an employer. Just as it represents a discourse of power that can be used to control, it can also be harnessed in order to legitimise a stand taken for liberation and empowerment. Whether critical social work is better off with or without a code of ethics is therefore a debatable question, which exemplifies the contradictions of professionalism and the complexity of the professionalism debate.

The other apparent advantage of professionalism is the extra status and legitimacy it gives social workers to operate in the public arena. This was one of the primary motivations for social workers seeking professional status, as it was felt that this would empower social workers in their attempts to achieve change. Such power is indeed important, and will be a focus of discussion in the following chapters. However, this argument too is problematic from the point of view of critical theory. It locates the significant area of analysis and change away from the interaction between social worker and client, and defines a significant area for social work 'professional' action as in the rarefied 'policy' arena, away from 'practice'. This raises the whole issue of policy and practice, which will be discussed in more detail in the next chapter. For the present, it is sufficient to say that critical theory requires social work to redefine its concern with 'policy' in such a way as it includes the kind of dialogical relationships discussed above. Hence policy must become part of practice, and 'clients' must be incorporated in policy intervention, so that it is a genuine result of the dialogical action inherent in critical theory. If this is the case, and the cause can be advanced by the status of 'professionalism' claimed by social workers, then it may well be that a professional label is a useful one for social workers to wear.

Professionalism, then, cannot be understood or evaluated in a context-free way, but must rather be contextualised and evaluated in terms of power and the particular social, economic, political and organisational location. Whatever one's position on professionalism, the structural analysis of power inherent in critical theory requires that social workers take seriously the power aspects of practising as a professional, and if they choose to use that power, that they do so in ways that are consistent with the emancipatory aims of critical theory, and not in such a way as to entrench and reinforce inequalities and structures of oppression. If professionalism is unable to be constructed except in disempowering terms, then it has no place in a social work based on critical theory. If, on the other hand, a form of professionalism is constructed that is genuinely compatible with empowerment-based practice, then incorporating professionalism into social work becomes quite appropriate.

It is likely that professionalism will remain an unresolved dilemma for social workers for some time to come. From a critical social work perspective, however, it is important not to accept uncritically either professionalism or anti-professionalism. Rather, it is necessary to engage in the task of deconstructing professionalism, and of helping social workers to reconstruct a form of professionalism more consistent with critical practice that allows them to use their professionalism in a positive, creative and liberating way.

Authority and control

Another area where there is a tension between mainstream social work and the critical theory approach is in the area of authority and control. Many social work positions require the social worker to take an authority role, especially in the areas of corrections and child protection, where there is a statutory function to perform. This is at odds with the idea of practice under a critical theory model, as the power relationship effectively prevents the establishment of the mutually respecting dialogical relationship described earlier.

The question, then, is whether social workers should continue to define such roles as legitimately within the arena of social work. On the one hand, authority roles seem to be totally opposed to the social work approach developed above, and a critical social worker would surely seek to avoid such positions. On the other hand, they are locations for social work practice, where many social workers are employed, and they perhaps represent the most likely areas for continued employment of social work graduates, given the social control agendas of conservative governments. To deny social workers the opportunity to apply for such positions could be to deny a future for social work and for social work education. It can also be argued, and it is a strong argument, that if social workers were not to fill these positions they would simply be filled by others, and that it is better to have social workers doing such jobs, as at least they can be expected to act with humanity and a concern for equity and social justice. The challenge for social workers is whether it is possible, even in such an authoritarian setting, to introduce at least some of the elements of a critical practice, and to retain social work's integrity from a critical theory perspective. Child protection, public welfare and corrections are, after all, at the critical edge of social control, and as such they can perhaps provide an opportunity for creative practice. It is easy to talk about an alternative social work paradigm when working in, for example, a community centre or a welfare rights and advocacy service, but the real test of progressive social work is whether it can be located in the more hostile and authoritarian environments within which social workers are currently required to work. There is no easy answer to this question, and it will be resolved differently by different social workers, but it represents a continuing source of tension for workers seeking to operate within the critical paradigm.

Supervision and accountability

The social work understandings of supervision and accountability have been very much affected by the economic rationalist context. Supervision has often been defined in largely top-down terms, where a social worker, or student, is 'supervised' by a more experienced and more senior worker. The very understandings of 'experienced' and 'seniority', however, imply a particular construction of social work and what makes a good social worker. This does not value the experience the social worker may have achieved outside 'the profession', and in terms of life experience, wisdom and the first-hand experience of oppression, it may well be that the supervisee is far more experienced than the supervisor. In the conventional supervisory relationship, however, qualifications, formal position in a hierarchy, and length of time in the profession are defined as more important. Moreover, the relationship, like the traditional casework relationship, is characteristically one-sided. It does not (at least formally) allow for the possibility that the supervisor may learn from the supervisee, or that both may develop a dialogical relationship from which each may grow, with the potential to lead to action for change. In this way, the supervision relationship is defined as parallel to the conventional casework relationship, with its built-in disempowerment and its reinforcement of relationships of power and control; hardly an appropriate environment in which to develop a critical form of practice.

Fortunately, many supervisory relationships do not work out that way in practice. There are many social workers who realise that the relationship can be redefined as one of mutual empowerment; these tend to be reported by both supervisor and supervisee as good supervisory experiences, but they do not always fit the supposedly ideal model. There remains, however, the potential (and in many instances it is more than potential) for supervision to become simply another form of control of a social worker, and a way of reinforcing the power of orthodox professionalism. The unequal supervisory relationship is also reflected in the apparently increasing practice of a social worker paying for private supervision from a more experienced colleague, because 'good supervision' is not available in the agency. The very idea of the supervisee paying, and the supervisor accepting payment, suggests that the whole experience is something of a burden for the supervisor, for which she/he needs to be compensated, and that all the benefit flows to the supervisee; hardly the mutual empowerment of the critical perspective.

All this is not to say that social workers cannot benefit from the wisdom and experience of their colleagues. Any responsible social worker, however experienced, will seek opportunities to benefit from such wisdom. It is rather that 'supervision' has been defined in a way that reflects a top-down approach of managerial or professional control, which is incompatible with the critical paradigm. Supervision should in this regard mirror practice, and the same principles of empowerment, dialogue and mutual learning should apply. This could be achieved by other forms of 'supervision' (preferably not even using the word, with its strong connotations of hierarchy and control), where workers meet on a more equal footing, where 'peer support' rather than the more controlling 'peer review' is the norm, and where all workers, however experienced, are seen as having valuable wisdom and expertise to contribute.

Like supervision, accountability has also been defined primarily in top-down, or managerial, terms. The critical paradigm emphasises a form of accountability that is either 'downward' to the client, or 'outward' to the community, rather than 'upward' to management. Social workers have, understandably, been very willing to accept obligations of accountability, but these have been incorporated into a top-down managerial approach that assumes it is the managers who know best, and that social workers owe their primary public accountability to management. This is the discourse of the managerial strand of economic rationalism, and again contributes to structures of control within which very conservative practice models can be reinforced, and which make the development of creative alternatives extremely difficult.

It is important for social workers to be exploring other mechanisms of 'accountability', by involving consumers and the community as those to whom social workers are accountable.

This in turn leads to the idea of agencies or programs that are run or 'managed' by the community, or by the 'clients' themselves, as in the empowerment model of the Brotherhood of St Laurence (Liffman 1978; Benn 1981). For this reason, an understanding of community work principles of participation and community-based decision-making are vital for social workers who are seeking to practise within the critical paradigm.

Services

It was noted in Chapter 1 that social work has largely been conceptualised in terms of the delivery of social *services*, and that social workers are regarded as social *service* workers. It was also pointed out that the idea of a 'service' has changed significantly from its original meaning, and has become a commodity that is delivered to a consumer or client, or is purchased in the market (depending on whether the managerial, professional or market discourse is used). In any event, the recipient of the 'service' plays essentially a passive role, and has little part in defining the nature of the 'service' or in 'delivering' it. This is hardly consistent with the active, dialogical, partnership role required in the critical paradigm. The empowerment of the recipient requires that the very idea of 'service' be either abandoned or totally redefined.

The language of 'services' is so dominant within social work and social policy that it is very difficult to move away from it, and to think of another way to characterise the work social workers do. This presents a major challenge for the critical paradigm, as the pervasiveness of the idea of social or community 'services' effectively leads to a restrictive social work discourse incorporating the power of the service 'provider' and the relative powerlessness of the passive service 'recipient' (as pointed out in Chapter 1, this is the reverse of the original understanding of the idea of 'service'). The language of 'services' helps to commodify the work of social workers, and is totally consistent with the managerial paradigm and the desire to measure social work competencies.

Reconstructing social work outside the language of 'services' is a major task for social workers. Critical theory provides a paradigm within which this can be done, and has the potential to help recast social work in more emancipatory terms, but this is a challenge social workers have not yet adequately faced.

Skills

The idea of skills within the critical paradigm is very different from the understanding of skills in conventional social work discourse. Critical practice requires that skills not be seen as the sole prerogative of the social worker, to be carefully applied, and to be kept out of the reach of those who are not professionally accredited. The critical paradigm requires that skills be shared between worker and 'client', that the 'client' be seen as possessing skills that are just as valid and important as those of the worker, and that each should share their skills with the other in a process of mutual empowerment and mutual education.

Social work skills, therefore, are not to be confined to social workers, nor are they only able to be used after lengthy training and accreditation. Social workers do have skills, certainly, but critical social work requires that these be shared with others, and the challenge for the critical practitioner is how to communicate and teach these skills, while at the same time being open to valuing and learning the many skills (though not formalised and accredited) that the 'client' will also possess.

The critical paradigm, as noted above, does not separate knowledge and skills, but sees them as two aspects of the same thing. Hence the sharing of knowledge and understanding, implied in the dialogical relationship, extends to the sharing of skills between the social worker and those people or communities with which she/he is working.

Developing a critical approach to social work

Because of the above difficulties, it must be emphasised that many social workers will not be able to work entirely, or even occasionally, from within a critical theory perspective in their work within the contemporary managerial welfare state, or in private agencies that are forced to operate in the market arena. The approach to social work inherent in a critical perspective must rather be seen as an *ideal paradigm*, a goal to be aimed for, rather than a form of practice that must be instituted in all agencies tomorrow, and about which social workers should feel characteristic guilt if they are unable to live up to the ideal. It represents a goal to work towards, and a vision of what social work could be, in terms of its potential to contribute to a better world.

On a more positive side, however, it should be noted that much of the critical perspective is entirely consistent with social work, its history, tradition, values and practices. Social workers are probably on the whole better than most other professionals at linking the personal and the political, and at taking a holistic perspective that incorporates a structural as well as an interpretive account of human behaviour and social issues. There has long been a tradition of linking practice with the ideals of social justice and human rights. Before 'empowerment' became a word used even by conservative politicians, social workers (most notably at the Brotherhood of St Laurence) had undertaken significant work in defining empowerment and in trying to put it into practice in working with the disadvantaged. Much about social work is consistent with critical theory, and in many ways what has been presented as the critical theory approach to social work is familiar to many social workers, and is what they have been trying to implement in their practice, often against significant opposition.

The assertion of a critical theory base for social work therefore serves more as an affirmation of the critical and alternative spirit in social work, which can be traced back to Jane Addams (Woodroofe 1962) and to many who came after her, who saw social work as an essentially critical practice to bring about a better, fairer and more just society, rather than merely providing professional interventions to individuals and families.

Critical social work, as it has been described, clearly falls within the humanist/anarchist discourse, which was identified earlier as the necessary location for an alternative formulation of social work. In Chapter 7 this will be further explored, in terms of what such an approach means for practice, theory and education, and directions for the development of such an alternative will be identified. Before doing so, however, it is necessary to consider the relationship between social work and social policy, and to look at the interaction of policy and practice. This will be the task of the next chapter.

CHAPTER

6

Policy, practice and change

Much of the powerlessness experienced by social workers in the current political and economic climate is a result of the problematic relationship between practice and policy. This has long been an area of difficulty for social work, both at the conceptual level, and also in the reality of the work place.

One of the motivations for the professionalisation of social work was to enable social workers to be taken seriously in policy debates and in policy-making. The respectability and authority of a profession was seen as enabling social workers to be more influential, and more able to pursue a social justice agenda for the disadvantaged. During the period of social work's professionalisation, this was the way in which social workers saw the solution to the dilemma of policy and practice; if social work became a recognised profession, it could influence policy more effectively, and could have a greater say in the development of more just, fair and progressive social policies. This dream, unfortunately, did not become a reality. Once professional status was achieved, it was discovered that influencing policy was rather more problematic than had been earlier assumed. In Australia this was particularly clear at two critical stages: the period of

153

the Whitlam government in the 1970s, and the move to managerialism in the late 1980s and early 1990s.

The Whitlam government (1972–75) seemed like the realisation of social workers' dreams. Suddenly there was a government in Canberra that appeared to be committed to the same social justice values, and was sympathetic to social workers. The Prime Minister's wife was a social worker, and was herself an important part of the new vision. The government was committed to a more institutional view of welfare, and clearly valued social work and social workers. Specific funding was made available to expand significantly the number and size of social work education programs. From having been politely ignored, social workers were suddenly at centre stage; they were appointed to senior positions in the public welfare sector, and there were meteoric rises through the hierarchy, with recent graduates finding themselves responsible for the initiation and operation of national programs. In those heady days, it soon became clear that social workers were not always able to deliver the goods. From a position of complaining about being on the margins of policy, social workers who were suddenly thrust to positions of prominence found that it was a good deal harder to put their ideas into practice, or even to crystallise their ideas in such a way that they could be implemented as viable programs. Much of the Whitlam period was characterised by well-intentioned chaos rather than well thought-through policies and programs. By the time social workers became used to this new responsibility, and began to develop expertise in program development and management, the window of opportunity had already closed. Even before the momentous political events of November and December 1975, by the August 1975 budget economic constraints had begun to curtail the capacity for initiatives and new programs, and many of the opportunities of the previous two years had not been fully realised. Social workers, in retrospect, were not well prepared for the opportunities provided by the Whitlam government, and by the time they began to take advantage of these opportunities it was already too late. As a result, social workers surrendered much of the social policy initiative, in an area that might have been thought to be their own field of expertise, to other groups such as political scientists, economists, public policy specialists, and to professions such as medicine, psychology and education. That lost ground has yet to be made up, and this is one of the reasons for the relative (though far from complete) absence of social workers from contemporary Australian social policy debate.

The other significant policy failing of social workers was their incapacity to respond appropriately to the new managerialism of the late 1980s and early 1990s. While complaining about the assumptions of the new managerialism, and about its impact on services to the disadvantaged, social workers were in general unable to articulate a coherent critique, or to establish a viable alternative. There are, of course, exceptions, for example in the work of Stuart Rees (Rees, Rodley and Stilwell 1993; Rees and Rodley 1995), but by and large social workers reacted to the new managerialism either by seeking to join it, or by keeping their heads down and pretending it would go away. With few exceptions, social workers have been largely absent from the public opposition to managerialism, and while in private conversations they are only too aware of the contradictions and inadequacies of the managerial paradigm, this has not been translated into public action.

This is in spite of the fact that social workers have given a good deal of attention to 'social policy' as an important part of social work discourse. Social work courses, in order to be accredited, are required to include a substantial component of social policy, though it is significant that in a number of social work schools this material is not taught by staff with a social work qualification. Social policy is studied at much greater depth by social work students than health policy is by medical students, legal policy by law students, planning policy by architecture students, arts policy by art or music students, and so on. A number of social work texts have identified social policy not merely as an area of foundation knowledge for social workers, but as a method area of social work practice. In this too, social work is perhaps unique among professions. The medical profession, for example, does not see doctors involved in health policy as actually *practising* medicine, nor does the legal profession define lawyers in policy positions as *practising* law, though in each case presumably their professional background will inform their decisions. Social workers, however, have unashamedly defined policy as part of social work practice; social workers employed in policy positions are not simply informed by their social work values and knowledge—they are seen as actually practising social work. Given

155

this concern with policy, social workers' relative lack of input into major policy debate is remarkable.

A more modest view of social work and social policy sees policy not as a method of social work, but as the context within which social work is practised, and as setting the parameters for social work practice at any given time. In this view, social workers will still wish to have an impact on policy development and change, as they seek to change the boundaries of their practice, but policy itself is not seen as a form of practice. Social work thus has the same relationship to social policy as medicine does to health policy—it is clearly related, and social workers make a special contribution because of their expertise, but this is not part of social work practice. Such a view, however, does not imply any lesser role for social workers in social policy debate. There is still an important contribution social workers can make, and indeed it could be argued that social workers, if they are to be true to their values, their code of ethics, and their commitment to the link between the personal and the political, have an obligation to engage actively in social policy development and change.

A contrary view is that of the anti-professional critics, such as Illich (Illich et al. 1977) and Polsky (1991). This view suggests that social workers, because they have a vested interest in social policy outcomes, should not play a dominant role in social policy debate. Professionals, as a consequence of their social-isation and interests, will inevitably see the solution to social problems as the provision of more services, especially services that require professionals to deliver them. Social workers will advocate the employment of more social workers, and their own professional and career interests will become confused with (and will supplant, according to the cynics) the interests of the disadvantaged. If one takes the view that the profes-sionalisation of human services and of caring has done more harm than good, and is largely for the benefit of the professional rather than the consumer, then the lesser role professionals have in policy debate, the better. In popular discourse, this view is encapsulated in the phrases 'health is too important to be left to doctors', 'education is too important to be left to teachers', and so on. The point is that other people (consumers, parents, citizens) have a legitimate and important role to play in policy, and that professionals, who have a particular point of view and set of interests to protect, must not be allowed to dominate on the basis of their apparent expertise, which is often reinforced by their use of professional jargon.

This view argues for less involvement in the policy process by social workers, rather than more, and would regard social workers' relative lack of policy impact as positive. Such a view, however, takes a rather simplistic perspective on social work. Certainly it is a powerful argument if social work is conceptualised from within the professional discourse of the top right quadrant of Figure 2.2. If social work is defined within the critical community discourse of the lower right quadrant, however, the relationship of power, policy and practice is viewed very differently.

For present purposes, it can be suggested that the issue is primarily one of discourse, and that the reason social workers have not been as effective as they would like (or as their rhetoric demands) in relating policy and practice is that they have not located their view of policy within an appropriate discourse. The four discourses identified in Chapter 2, and summarised in Figure 2.2, account for the policy–practice relationship very differently, and it is therefore appropriate to use the framework of Chapter 2 for a consideration of these differences and the development of an alternative approach to policy/practice consistent with a critical humanist approach. An examination of the inadequacies of the managerial, market and professional discourses will be followed by a more detailed examination of the relationship between policy and practice within a critical approach, as outlined in earlier chapters.

The managerial approach to policy/practice

The managerial discourse, from the top left quadrant of Figure 2.2, separates policy and practice. Policy is seen as essentially a top-down exercise, involving technical expertise. The technocratic, policy-science approach to social change, characteristic of both the positivist paradigm and the top-down hierarchic paradigm, incorporates an understanding of policy based on the wisdom of those in authority (whether managers, policy-makers or politicians), informed by technical analysis and advice.

Policy is seen as essentially rational and technical. It is the selection of the most effective means to meet specified ends. The separation of means and ends, an important feature of the positivist paradigm, separates policy analysis from value-laden debate, and does not require policy to be the concern of the wider society. A good example is the current approach to economic policy. There are a few generally accepted policy goals about which there is assumed agreement, for example, full employment, 'sustainable growth' and rising levels of personal income. Beyond this, however, debate on economic policy is couched in language that is inaccessible to the majority of the population, and this is readily justified on the grounds that the policy experts are simply engaged in a technical (and hence value-free) debate about the most effective and efficient means of meeting these desired ends. There is no perceived need for the wider population to be involved, any more than they need to be involved in any other technical exercise, such as designing a motor car or programming a computer. This enables the debate on economic policy, which in reality is far from value-free, to be carried out among an elite group of economists who feel no compelling need to make that debate accessible to the general population or to involve other sections of society (Pusey 1991).

The same processes can be seen to be operating in social policy. The idea of the social policy 'expert' had led to a good deal of social policy debate being cast in language which, while not as intimidating as that of economists, is hardly accessible to the general population. For example, the debate about poverty, especially its measurement and effective alleviation, is carried on in such a way that the poor themselves are unable to participate in it. The debate about equivalence scales, transfer payments, poverty line methodologies, the social wage, and real disposable income is hardly one with which the people actually experiencing poverty are able to engage. Within this perspective, the 'expert' in poverty is not a single parent seeking to raise several children in a public housing estate on Social Security benefits, but is rather a person with a PhD in economic and social policy analysis who has undertaken research on the computer modelling of expenditure patterns, and who may never have experienced poverty or even spoken to a person on a low income.

This construction of 'expertise' in such a way as to exclude the people most directly concerned is characteristic of the managerial discourse. It is replicated throughout the public sector, and in public policy discussion and debate. It rests on the positivist assumption of the split between value-determined ends and value-free means, which is both inconsistent and contradictory (Fay 1975; Ife 1995).

Such a formulation of 'policy' separates it from the world of 'practice'. Practitioners are seen as those who implement the policies determined by the experts. They may seek to have those policies changed, by drawing attention to certain patterns or issues, and they may engage in wider societal debate about desired ends, but their role in the actual determination of policy is strictly limited. Practice expertise does not equate with policy expertise, and practitioners have no role in the rarefied world of the policy scientists. From this perspective, therefore, the social work agenda of 'integrating' or 'reconciling' policy and practice is highly problematic. In order to influence policy, social workers would need to leave the world of practice and join the world of the planners, researchers, analysts and managers, as these are the actors who are seen as being able to influence and direct policy. A number of social workers, indeed, have made this move, and have become policy 'experts'. In doing so, however, they have left the world of practice far behind, and have removed themselves from what is potentially social work's great strength: its ability to ground its understandings and its practice in the reality of the oppressed and the disadvantaged.

Social workers are potentially in a particularly strong position to link the world of the policy-makers and the world of the disadvantaged. Because of their education and their socialisation, they are some of the few people in society who are able to communicate effectively both with the policy 'experts' and with the people who are experiencing social and economic disadvantage; they should be able to talk to and understand both the single parent on Social Security benefits and the Canberra-based policy analyst. They should be able to interpret the wisdom of each to the other, and to bring them together so that each is enriched by the other's expertise. Unfortunately the structures imposed by managerialism do not readily allow this to happen and this potentially fruitful area for social work practice is largely unfulfilled.

The strength of the managerial paradigm is making this creative approach to social work practice particularly difficult, as social workers (at least those who retain a strong practice focus) are finding themselves increasingly removed from the realities of policy-making. It is becoming harder for social workers to move to significant managerial and policy positions without effectively disowning their social work identity and expertise and redefining themselves as managers. The gap between policy and practice, already large, seems to be widening, and it is unlikely that it can be effectively bridged if one remains within the discourse of managerialism.

The market approach to policy/practice

While the managerial discourse incorporates a clear construction of 'policy', this is much less so within the discourse of the market. The bottom-up laissez-faire assumptions of the market are incompatible with the formulation of deliberate policy goals and strategies. The assumption is that the best outcome will be achieved if the market is allowed free reign, and is not distorted through regulation. The setting of goals, and the development of policies to achieve these goals, is incompatible with the theory of the market, and implies regulation and control. From a purist market perspective, the only effective 'policies' are those that ensure an absence of regulation and prohibit or discourage any interference in the market's 'natural' operation.

Of course in practice this is unachievable, as was discussed in Chapter 2. Policies are required in order to keep the market operating effectively, including policies of regulation to ensure that the preconditions for the market are maintained (e.g., to prevent the formation of cartels and monopolies). However, the discourse of the market remains reluctant about the very idea of 'policy', beyond policies to undo what is seen as the evil of previous interventionist governments, for example, through privatisation. The advocates of the market are inevitably devoid of long-term visions and objectives, and this can be seen in the reluctance or inability of the leaders of conservative market-based political parties to articulate a strong sense of direction and of social goals. A belief in the mechanism of the market as the best determinant of economic and social outcomes requires that we allow the market to take us where it chooses, and prevents us from undermining the will of the market with interventions or 'policies'.

The market discourse, therefore, is inadequate in its construction of the policy–practice relationship, because of its inability to incorporate a strong sense of 'policy'. Practitioners thus need not be concerned with matters of policy, as these are in any case best left to the market. Social workers will inevitably feel impotent if they wish to influence policy, or to participate in the policy process from a position that is stronger than their place in the market determines. The only way they can legitimately concern themselves with policy is through their participation in the market, as both purchasers and providers of services.

The inadequacies of the market have already been discussed in Chapter 2, and need not be reiterated here. These inadequacies mean that an approach of resorting to a market strategy is most unlikely to deliver, in terms of social work values such as social justice and human rights. Indeed, such values are likely to be undermined by a reliance on the market. The discourse of the market does not provide social workers with a capacity to link policy and practice effectively, or to have any significant impact on policy direction and development. It is completely contradictory to a view of social work which incorporates both the personal and the political, and which seeks solutions to social problems at both individual and structural levels.

The professional approach to policy/practice

Within the discourse of professionalism, there is a separation of policy and practice that is not dissimilar to that of managerialism. This arises from the top-down perspective shared by both discourses. Such a view inevitably sees practice as something that takes place at a different level from policy, as wisdom is located at 'higher' levels of structures, while practice is something that occurs at the 'lower' levels, or at street-level to use Lipsky's terminology (Lipsky 1980). The integration of policy and practice is therefore problematic, as the two happen at different locations, and are done by different people.

The professional discourse, however, in allowing more room for social work discretion and more autonomy for the human service professional, gives more scope and legitimacy for a professional to be involved in policy development or change in some way. Within managerial discourse, social workers are seen as having little discretion and as following the policies and procedures determined by managers. The professional discourse, by contrast, respects the professional expertise of social workers and gives them more power to make decisions on the basis of that expertise. In doing so, social workers can effectively create a form of policy, as a result of the cumulative effect of their day-to-day case decisions.

Lipsky (1980) pointed out how 'street-level bureaucrats', including social workers, need to make discretionary decisions in order both to make the job possible for themselves and to provide a realistic and appropriate service to the public. This involves decisions about who will and who will not receive service, how extensively to intervene, and 'creative interpretation' or bending of the rules and regulations. While such deviance is not in accord with the top-down approach of the professional model, and may even appear to be in conflict with ethical principles, it nevertheless represents reality for social workers attempting to do their best in a job where the increasing demands both of managers and of clients simply cannot be fully met.

The importance of Lipsky's work for present purposes is that by making such decisions social workers are in effect making policy. They are determining how services will be rationed, in an environment where demand exceeds supply. Whatever may be written in official documents, passed by executive boards, or communicated by official instructions, social workers in their day-to-day practice are effectively making the actual policies by which the agency operates. In this way, social workers can be seen to have a good deal of power to shape and influence policy, and it is perhaps the way in which social workers have been most effectively able to influence the system that has allocated them little formal power.

There are, however, significant problems with this approach to policy and practice. A major one is that of accountability. If social workers are to be held accountable for their actions, within the conventional top-down understanding of 'accountability', the exercise of discretion must necessarily be reduced. The idea of accountability can, in fact, be used to disempower social workers by instituting measures of accountability that are merely control by another name. The establishment of adequate measures of accountability, while at the same time ensuring a degree of discretion and autonomy for social workers, is a difficult challenge. The conventional social work response to this has been to emphasise the importance of professional supervision, which allows a degree of accountability while at the same time being administered by someone who shares a commitment to professional autonomy. The danger, however, is that this will become a 'professional conspiracy', where social workers get together to reinforce and entrench a position of professional power without a broader understanding of accountability, especially accountability 'downward' or 'outward'.

Another problem posed by the discourse of professionalism is that it creates a contradictory position for social workers, and only partially legitimises social workers to exercise their professional discretion in this way. While the professional discourse accepts, and indeed encourages, social workers making professional discretionary decisions *in relation to individual cases*, it does not allow this to extend to the macro level of 'policy', where decisions are made about groups or categories of people, rather than individuals. At the macro level, responsibility for the decision rests elsewhere. Social workers are therefore allowed to exercise discretion and judgement only at the individual case level, and not extend it to the societal level. For social workers who use the fundamental link between the personal and the political as the foundation of their practice or who can see the natural extension of casework into political action (Barber 1991), this is an untenable position. It drives a wedge between individual and structural explanations, and hence denies forms of practice which seek to incorporate the two.

A third problem with the discretionary nature of practice within the professional discourse is that it can place social workers in an industrially and legally vulnerable position. The necessity for discretionary judgements, and for rule-bending, renders practitioners liable to action against them, either by managers or in the courts by aggrieved clients. In a system that relies on uniformity and consistency and places a high value on them, a practice that questions this by discretionary rule-bending, however justifiable morally or by the dictates of necessity, is likely sooner or later to leave the practitioner highly exposed to disciplinary or legal action.

A critical empowerment approach to policy/practice: opportunities for an alternative

If the inability of social work to deal effectively with the issue of policy and practice is a result of the inability of the managerial, market and professional paradigms to link the two effectively, it would appear that the critical theory approach, which is an elaboration of the community discourse as described in Chapter 2, has more potential for an adequate integration of policy and practice. This is because critical theory is a more integrative framework. The problem of policy/practice can be regarded as a specific instance of the relationship between the personal and the political, which critical theory specifically addresses. Policy, after all, is clearly in the political domain, while a good deal of social work practice is concerned with the personal. A discourse linking the personal and the political will therefore also link policy and practice and see them as aspects of the same thing, rather than as separate phenomena.

The policy process is a very complex one in modern Western democracies (Ham and Hill 1984). In a federal system such as Australia's, the complexity is much greater because of the additional levels of government. It is a confusing amalgam of formal and informal political processes, party platforms, election promises, administrative decisions, strategic and operational plans, media pressure, interest groups, community actions, street-level decisions, global forces, personal agendas, industrial pressure, economic imperatives, environmental imperatives, grand visions, pragmatic choices, rational decisions, irrational decisions, and sheer chance. There are many 'players' in the game, including politicians (federal, state and local), bureaucrats, professionals, lobby groups, unions, consumer groups, media owners, journalists, bankers, managers (in both public and private sectors), economists, entrepreneurs, researchers and academics. It is common for people such as social workers, faced with this complex and overwhelming picture, to feel disempowered and to withdraw feeling that it is all too much. From another perspective, however, the complexity provides opportunities. There are many points of entry into the policy process, and many arenas in which social workers are able to make contributions, whether through the workplace, outside the workplace but in a social work capacity, or in the capacity of a private citizen.

An assumption that has often disempowered social workers in the policy arena is the modernist rationalist assumption that somehow there is a single locus of power, and that one is not effective unless one is able to have access to, and influence, 'where the power really lies'. This leads to a monolithic understanding of policy, and hence to a tendency to define oneself as excluded and therefore powerless, unless one happens to have access to the Melbourne Club, the Cabinet Room, the Prime Minister's Office or Rupert Murdoch's Office, wherever one happens to think 'real' power lies. Even a more pluralist account, which may see all these centres of power as important, can disempower because the very hierarchical way in which such a perspective views power and policy leaves little room for the participation of anyone other than the elites. Post-structural notions of power, on the other hand, help to redefine power as located in a multiplicity of changing discourses, which are much more open to social workers and those with whom they work. This is where poststructural accounts have much to offer social workers, and can help to redefine the relationship between policy and practice in a much more empowering way. From this perspective, there are potentially many opportunities for redefining discourses, and the opportunities to have an impact on 'policy' are many, both in and outside the workplace.

The danger of a purely poststructural account, as has been noted before, is its exclusion of some form of structural analysis of oppression. From a critical theory perspective a structural analysis must be taken into account; indeed, a critical approach would seek to incorporate both structures and discourses. Such a view sees power as not only defined within changing discourses, but as also present in structures of domination—most importantly class, race and gender. Policies, and the policy process, will inevitably reinforce oppressive structures unless such structural issues are specifically addressed, and this means that if social workers are to influence the policy process they must be concerned with countering structural disadvantage. This can be achieved through many of the well-known forms of social work, such as consciousness-raising, education and community action, all of which are part of a good deal of social work *practice*. Thus we begin to see a way in which policy and

165

practice become linked; good social work practice, from a critical perspective, is inevitably about policy, and about policy change.

From the critical perspective, policy only makes sense if it is understood from the point of view of practice, and practice only makes sense if it is understood from the point of view of policy. Social work is concerned with both policy and practice, as a way of implementing its central project of linking the personal and the political. Put another way, by integrating the personal and the political, social work integrates policy and practice, and is inevitably concerned with both. This is hardly a novel formulation for social workers. As soon as social work moves beyond purely individual definitions of social problems (and their solution) and incorporates an understanding of broader systemic causes of disadvantage, action at the policy level becomes an imperative for social work practice (Barber 1991). The task for social work has been twofold: how to legitimate its policy focus in a context that defines social work's mandate only in individual terms, and how to put a concern with policy and policy change into practice. The remainder of this chapter will be devoted to the second of these, namely a consideration of how social workers might be able to implement the policy/practice integration in their work.

The important point to be made is that one need not operate only in the rarefied world of traditional 'policy' in order to have an impact on policy, or to incorporate policy with practice. Rather, *policy action emerges from within social work practice*, and is a necessary component of all social work undertaken from the critical perspective. Working with clients, or communities, is always political, and hence has policy implications. In the case of communities, the link is quite easily made, as it is easier to understand community work within a social or political frame of reference. Social workers in community settings are often active at the policy level, whether in partnership with the community with which they are working, or representing the interests of the community in an advocacy role. Community workers have plenty of opportunity to develop skills in the political process, and operating in the policy arena therefore comes easily. Social workers in more individualised 'direct service' agencies, however, often do not have the same opportunities. The organisational context of their work has insulated them from the political process, even though it impinges on their work, and on the circumstances of their clients. In such settings, it is easier for social workers not to become engaged in policy issues, and to define their practice purely in terms of the private concerns of their clients. The critical approach to social work is a direct challenge to such a form of practice, but this alternative is not compatible with the managerial or economic rationalist definition of social work's role.

There are, nevertheless, frequent opportunities for social workers to make a link with policy, either directly or indirectly, in their work. The way in which a problem is discussed with a client, the terms used, and the way in which a solution is sought, provide an opportunity for linking the personal and the political, and for opening up the possibility for policy-related practice. Simply drawing someone's attention to the increasing numbers of people experiencing the same problem is a way of making a potential link with a public issue. Making people aware of self-help groups or action groups of others with the same problems or concerns is another simple way to make that connection; they may or may not seek to follow it up, but the opportunity has been created. Social workers can have an important role in supporting and possibly even facilitating such action or self-help groups, and this is a logical way in which their work can extend from the personal to the political, as advocated by Barber (1991). Once the problem is taken on in this group context, the possibilities for implementing the policy process become significantly greater, as collective action is potentially much more powerful than individual action. Simply encouraging people to think of their problem in collective terms, rather than purely individually, is a radical step, and has significant potential for empowerment.

This, however, is only one dimension of political practice. Social casework has always been much more than simply direct worker–client interaction. In most social work settings caseworkers are able to help their clients far more by their capacity to 'work the system', to intervene organisationally, to advocate, to make representations in meetings, and to understand the workings of the welfare state, than they are through any interpersonal magic that they can perform in an interview. It is thus in their organisational skills that case-workers provide their most important service, and this is, in many ways, the most significant part of their 'practice'. Such a view of the actual practice of casework opens up many other opportunities for critical policy-related social work.

From such a perspective, one can develop an approach to policy/practice that focuses on work with colleagues, supervisors, managers, clerical workers, other professionals, and indeed all the other workers with whom a social worker interacts. It is here, too, that a social worker can engage in consciousness raising, critical practice and dialogical action. It is important to emphasise that such activity is not separate from the task of conventional social work. It is one of the most important parts of social work, and the policy dimension can be naturally incorporated into a worker's practice. Such work might involve, for example, good use of informal discussions over morning coffee in order to build solidarity and a sense of purpose, involvement of colleagues in community-based self-help or action programs, or bringing people together in order to present a petition or submission about a policy issue, or to advocate for change. It could under certain circumstances incorporate industrial action in support either of better conditions or of a specified political objective. It might mean seeking to support a supervisor or manager in advocating for change. Or it may mean making the most of whatever informal contacts a worker might have.

The capacity to operate effectively in an organisational context, whether in a large bureaucracy, a community-based agency or a private profit-making enterprise, is essential both for good social work practice and for making an impact in the policy arena (Jones and May 1992). It involves a definition of social work that is essentially political, and the capacity to understand one's actions within the broader political context. Social work skills such as advocacy, communication, and group process can be used for more obviously political ends, and the boundary between practice and policy thereby becomes blurred.

Social work practice, from the anarchist view discussed in Chapter 2, can be seen to influence policy in another way. Lipsky's analysis (1980) of the work of street-level bureaucrats was discussed earlier in this chapter, and from this perspective it can be seen that the totality of the discretionary (and often deviant) decisions of front-line workers can actually determine the 'policy' of the agency. This notion of worker-created policy suggests that in their day-to-day practice workers are actually making policy, and creating a counter-policy to the formal policy statements of agencies and governments. Creative practice, in other words, becomes an effective counter to official agency policies which may be seen not to be in the interests of social justice or of individual clients. A social worker will typically start with the needs of a particular client or family, and see how 'the system' can be 'worked' in such a way that those needs can be met as effectively as possible. Policies and programs are therefore of secondary importance to the client's needs, and are interpreted so as to benefit the client. In this constant reinterpretation of 'policy', and the creative 'bending' of rules, social workers effectively make and change the actual policy of the agency. If this is done at an individual level, the overall impact will be minimal, but if it is done as part of a collective consciousness, formed through the kind of organisational work discussed above, the potential for significant change can be far-reaching.

Another level at which social workers can be involved in policy is at the level of the profession. Here there are considerable advantages in the professionalisation of social work; it enables social workers to speak with a degree of authority, it gives them legitimacy in a number of quarters, and it enables them to hold action-oriented meetings under the legitimising label of a 'conference' or a 'workshop' (if social work were, for example, a 'trade', such a meeting would have to be a 'stop-work meeting' involving suspension of salary, and without employer-provided funding for attendance). The social work profession, however, has not been particularly significant in the policy arena, as was noted early in the chapter. Reasons for this lack of impact might include: the apolitical way in which much conventional 'social work' has been conceptualised; lack of political sophistication by many social workers; the separation of policy and practice in social work discourse; and the tendency of the more politically committed social workers to seek a location for action outside the formal structures of the profession, partly as a result of the conservative reputation of the professional association. At the professional level, however, there is considerable potential for social workers to make public statements, to engage in effective lobbying, and to give a much higher public profile to the critique of economic rationalism.

The final arena for social work policy action is the public arena. This involves the political process, the media, and other high-profile activities. Some social workers have entered politics, and others have achieved prominence as media commentators, but again it is not an arena where social workers have made the impact that one would expect given their expertise and social commitment. This suggests that social workers are perhaps not as well prepared for participation in the policy arena as they might be, despite the emphasis on social policy units in social work courses. Such a suggestion leads to the final section of this chapter, on how social workers might be better prepared for the policy arena, and the integration of policy and practice.

Awareness, analysis and vocabulary

Social work courses normally contain a substantial element of social policy, and this is, quite properly, a requirement set by the AASW for successful accreditation. As already mentioned, it is surprising that social workers are not as effective in the social policy arena as they might be. While some reasons for this were suggested earlier in this chapter, another reason, perhaps, lies in the way social policy is defined within social work courses, and the way it is taught.

It is common for social policy to be taught separately from social work practice units. The staff tend to be different, and in the eyes both of teachers and students they are essentially unrelated aspects of the course. Indeed, it is common for social policy in social work courses to be taught by people who are not social workers—typically political scientists, sociologists or historians. While such disciplines undoubtedly have many important contributions to make, such lecturers will be unable to integrate policy with social work practice in the way that was discussed above, or to talk about the policy implications of practice or the practice implications of policy. Instead, social policy tends to be taught as a separate field, which is clearly relevant to social work and sets the context for social work, but does not directly relate to social work theory and practice. Social policy is seen as something that some social workers will become involved with, and hence a specialist field of study, rather than something that pervades all social work. Similarly, teachers of social work theory and practice are frequently not concerned with social policy in their teaching, or in the way they construct social work and communicate it to their students. Social work practice is often constructed as independent of (though clearly impinging on) the social policy context. Thus social policy occupies a place in the course similar to units in health and law—important for social workers to know, but not incorporated as an essential component of the actual *practice* of social work. This perspective of separating policy and practice, and of marginalising policy from the 'real' practice of social work, therefore pervades the consciousness of social work graduates, and determines the way social policy is understood within the profession. It is important therefore, if the aim of a critical approach to policy/practice is to be achieved, that the relationship between policy and practice in schools of social work be reconceptualised so that they become part of the same process, and so that the policy perspective is actually incorporated in the teaching of practice. This is only one of the implications of the critical perspective for the reformulation of social work education, which will be further discussed in the next chapter.

In order to equip social workers to practice more effectively from a policy perspective, and to have more impact on the policy arena, there is a need for increased policy *awareness*, a more sophisticated policy *analysis*, and a more appropriate *vocabulary* with which to address policy issues. The first of these, awareness, requires social workers to be politically aware, both in terms of current political discourse and political structures. Although many social workers have such an awareness, it is also true that many others come to social work without a very good grounding in political issues or a working knowledge of political structures. While some attention is given to these matters in a social work course, it is also true that many social workers do not retain that interest after graduation, and hence fail to appreciate the political and ideological context within which they are practising. This not only makes it impossible to practise a social work that genuinely links the personal and the political, but also makes it difficult to develop a policy perspective as part of one's practice. If they are to be effective, social workers have a responsibility to remain politically aware, to keep up-to-date with current policy issues and broader political trends within the society, and to relate their practice to this political context. It is interesting that in the large range of professional development, continuing education and post-qualifying programs available to social workers, relatively few relate to improving and updating one's political awareness, compared with, for example, the extraordinary number devoted to advanced counselling or family therapy skills. This is indicative of a particular construction of what it is necessary to know for contemporary social work practice, and a lack of effective integration between policy and practice, or between the personal and the political.

Social work is, at heart, an ideological activity, and hence it is important that it be undertaken from within the perspective of a strong ideological *analysis*. An awareness of the nature of ideology, the characteristics of different ideological perspectives, and the ideological assumptions behind the practice environment are extremely important if a social worker is to be able to link the personal and the political and address policy issues as part of practice. A further form of analysis that is necessary is an analysis of the policy process and political systems. Commitment and good intentions are important, but they amount to little if not accompanied by a good analysis of the political context and the ways in which policy is formulated, transmitted and implemented. From this perspective, political analysis is as much a central requirement of social work knowledge as is the knowledge of human behaviour and of society, and it should play as central a role in any construction of social work practice either within schools of social work or the professional body. As discussed in Chapter 1, the political context is hostile to many of the values and practices of social work, and if social workers are to present a viable alternative, and to incorporate it as part of their practice, they need a good analytical basis from which to do so. Simple awareness, achievable through following issues in the media, is not sufficient. Analytical frameworks are needed in order to conceptualise the issues at a more far-reaching level, so that appropriate programs of action can be formulated and implemented.

The final attribute mentioned above was *vocabulary*. There is no sense in social workers being politically aware, and having a strong political analysis, if they do not have the vocabulary to articulate their critique and their alternatives in the policy arena. Use of language is very important in policy-related practice, as indeed it is in all practice. But while many social workers have a very good knowledge and understanding of the vocabularies of therapy (both the therapeutic vocabulary to use with clients and the professional vocabulary to use with colleagues) they are generally not as articulate in the policy arena. The language of economics, of management, of business and of government is often mystifying to social workers, and their inability to understand the language is a major impediment to their capacity to make significant inputs into the policy process, and to debate in a relevant way. A good understanding of the vocabulary of these disciplines, and a basic understanding of their content, is often sufficient to be able to demonstrate the contradictions and false assumptions on which they are based, and to point out the absurdities of both economic rationalism and managerialism. Social workers are not well provided with a vocabulary appropriate for public policy debate, and this renders them unable to participate in that debate in the way they would like. Developing basic literacy in disciplines such as economics, politics, management and public administration can be one of the most empowering educational experiences for a social worker. This does not mean that social workers have to accept the content of these disciplines; rather it provides them with the understanding and the language needed to mount a critique, which is the basis for establishing an alternative.

This chapter has discussed the policy/practice issue for social workers, because it is seen as a particularly important part of developing an alternative or critical social work based on the analysis of previous chapters. It is, however, only one aspect of such an approach to social work, and in the remaining chapter other aspects of critical social work will be identified which will help to complete the picture, and to make some specific proposals for the future development of the profession if it is to continue to address the relevant social issues of the day, within a changing social, economic, political and organisational environment.

Towards critical practice

This final chapter identifies some directions for social work that are consistent with the ideas explored in previous chapters. It will not be a simple guide as to 'how to do it', because there are no simple answers in the complex and contradictory activity known as social work, located in the complex and contradictory context of the welfare state. It is possible, however, to identify some potential areas for further work and exploration that are likely to prove fruitful in developing a critical or alternative social work practice.

Bringing radical social work in from the margins

Up to this point, this book has largely avoided the word 'radical', in favour of the terms 'critical' or 'alternative'. This is because of the marginalisation of 'radical' social work within the profession, as a major aim of this book is to avoid such marginalisation of alternative approaches to practice. It is now time, however, to address the radical tradition in social work, and to locate the perspective of this book within this tradition.

The place of radicalism in social work has always been problematic. The origins of social work reflect its dual concerns with social change and social control, and this contradiction has never been resolved in the history of the profession. Radical change is on the one hand seen as central to social work's concerns (though there will always be disagreement as to how that should be achieved), while on the other hand the radical perspective is marginalised by social work's need to operate in structures of authority and control, and to maintain its professional status and respectability in an essentially conservative environment. Certainly in contemporary social work the tension between social control and change-based practice is keenly felt, and has been heightened by the dominance of managerialism, with its strong control agenda, which has asked searching questions of social work and its commitment to social change and social justice.

There has always been a radical tradition in social work, which has identified social work's basic agenda as being to work towards the kind of fundamental social change necessary if society is to be based on principles of social justice. This radical tradition goes back to some of the key founders of the profession such as Jane Addams (Woodroofe 1962), who achieved international recognition as a peace activist. Even in the conservative political climate of the 1940s and 1950s in the USA, a radical perspective was evident in the socialist practice of Bertha Reynolds (1942). Many community workers of the 1960s and 1970s adopted the pseudo-radicalism of Alinsky (1971), whose radicalism was more in his innovative choice of tactics than in his political philosophy, but who seemed to capture the imagination of social workers studying in the time of the great student protests. In the UK, community workers were influenced by the socialist analysis of writers such as Marjaleena Repo and Marjorie Mayo (Repo 1977; Jones and Mayo 1974, 1975; Lees and Mayo 1984). During the 1970s, the radical tradition was re-established in social work as a whole, rather than just in its community work arm, by writers such as Galper (1975), Corrigan and Leonard (1978), and Bailey and Brake (1975), writing from essentially a Marxist perspective. In the 1980s feminism took over from Marxism as the main location for radical social work analysis (Marchant and Wearing 1986), though more recently Mullaly (1993) has restated the case for radical social work based on a broad structural perspective.

176

There have also been some attempts to reformulate social work from a poststructuralist or postmodernist perspective (Hartman 1991; Howe 1994; Solas 1994; Camilleri 1995; Pardeck et al. 1994; Latting 1995; Leonard 1995).

There have been a number of significant Australian contributors to this radical tradition, including, among others, Harold Throssell (1975), Bill de Maria (1993), Connie Benn (1981, 1991), Wendy Weeks (1994), Jan Fook (1993, 1996), Adam Jamrozik (1991), Stuart Rees (1991, 1994, 1995) and Bob Pease (1990). However in Australia, as elsewhere in the Western world, radical social work remains in an essentially marginal position within the social work profession. The many seminars, conferences and workshops within the radical tradition are attended by those who are interested, and largely ignored by the rest of the profession. They involve a good deal of 'preaching to the converted', together with very important mutual support and encouragement among those committed to radical practice. While such work is tolerated (and indeed seen as legitimate and important) by the mainstream of social work, it is by and large not defined as of central concern. This marginalisation of radical social work is seen in the construction of social work curricula, the contents of professional journals and newsletters, accreditation guidelines, the code of ethics, competency definitions, and the other written manifestations of the way in which social workers construct social work theory, practice and education.

In this context, 'radical' implies more than simply opposing the latest round of cuts to public spending and the increasing privatisation of human services. This has become a significant mainstream concern for social workers and can be the starting point for a more radical position. It does not by itself, however, represent the structural analysis and perceived need for fundamental social change implied by the idea of radicalism. Indeed, many social workers, in the tradition of Alinsky (1971), have developed the art of adopting a pseudo-radical stance by using apparently radical rhetoric, when all they are effectively doing is seeking to preserve the liberal welfare state and the comfortable and familiar professionalism represented by the top right quadrant of Figure 2.2. From the analysis of previous chapters, this is clearly insufficient for the establishment of a critical practice that will enable social work to confront the challenge of economic rationalism and develop a viable alternative practice.

177

The critical position adopted in earlier chapters leads to the conclusion that *social work is, by its very nature, radical.* The linking of the personal and the political implies that change is necessary on the political level, and the structural analysis required in the version of critical theory adopted in Chapter 5 further underpins the need for fundamental, or radical, change in the arenas of class, gender, and race/ethnicity. Social workers, by the nature of the task they have taken on, are concerned with seeking to alter relationships of power, domination and oppression in society (however they are defined), and this requires radical practice. It is therefore essential for social work to come to terms with its necessarily radical agenda, and to examine what this means for practice in the current environment.

For this reason, the marginalisation of radical social work within the profession is a cause for concern. It is not sufficient for radical social workers to talk only to each other, and to support and reinforce each other, in forums (formal or informal) that are ignored by other members of the profession. It is also not appropriate to define and articulate radical social work in such a way that it alienates other social workers, or presents radical social work as something that need not be of interest to the majority. Radical social work has been good at defining alternative frameworks for social work theory and (to a lesser extent) practice, but it has not been able to locate itself at the centre of social work. The task, then, is to bring radical social work in from the margins, and to conceptualise social work in such a way that its inherent radicalism is recognised and incorporated into 'mainstream' understandings of social work practice.

A significant criticism which has been made of much of the radical social work literature is that it is stronger on analysis than on practice. While providing a devastating critique of the welfare state and of current practice frameworks, it was often seen as failing to provide a social worker with genuine practice alternatives; indeed many of the practice prescriptions of the radical social work literature would be readily accepted by many social workers who do not identify themselves as radical, and seem to be simply good social work practice under another name. Most of the radical practice prescriptions of Corrigan and Leonard (1978), or more recently Fook (1993), would not be seen as different, problematic or deviant by many mainstream social workers. Certainly a good deal of conventional social work is seen as unacceptable by radical writers (e.g., the way in which 'use of authority' can justify oppressive practice), but it is also true that most of what radical writers advocate as good practice is also very much part of the mainstream. This is clearly evident in Jan Fook's formulation of radical casework, as many social workers who do not see themselves as radicals would find little to argue with in her presentation of 'radical' analysis, goals and strategies. One way of looking at this is to suggest that radical social work has been inadequate in defining radical practice, and to criticise radicals who pretend to be presenting something new but in fact are not. A more interesting perspective, however, is to conclude that there is much that is at least inherently radical in conventional social work practice, and that radical social work need not be something totally different, but rather has its origins in much of the practice wisdom and experience of mainstream social workers. Radical social work writers are simply moving social work from its more conservative vocabulary and theoretical or ideological assumptions, and identifying what social workers do, every day, as at least potentially radical. This is also acknowledged by Fook, who sees 'radical casework practice' as 'derived directly from radical and feminist analysis, *and traditional practice*' (Fook 1993, p. 152, italics added). Indeed Fook implies that it is the analysis, rather than the forms of practice, that is new or different in radical casework. Being radical need not require workers to acquire new skills, but simply that the old skills be applied in perhaps a different way, for a different reason, and in a different context.

As a simple example of this, one can take the problem-solving approach to social work practice, which is very much part of the 'mainstream' and is a form of practice used by many social workers (perhaps even the majority) in their regular work. In this light it is interesting to note that Freire (1972) describes his dialogical approach to education, which is very similar to the critical social work discussed in previous chapters, in terms of problem posing and problem solving. For Freire, joining with another in the process of identifying and then solving a problem can be a very powerful experience of consciousness-raising, and can become the very basis of empowerment. The act of defining and solving the problem is an excellent way to link the personal and the political, and to help people to redefine their personal frustrations and sufferings within a broader political context. Part of problem-solving, then, becomes determining how to develop actions in order to bring about change, at the political as well as the personal level. Casework as 'problem-solving', therefore, has the potential to be some of the most radical practice a worker can undertake, though this requires problem solving to be understood within a political or structural framework that is often absent from conventional casework practice.

Another example is the common social work skill of 'reframing', the capacity to redefine and recontextualise a problem or a statement in order to bring it closer to a person's own experience, and to open up possibilities for creative action, rather than leaving the person immobilised. This too is very much part of radical practice. It is, effectively, a form of deconstruction, and an invitation for the other person to engage in a dialogue around reconstruction. It can be a way of linking the personal to the political, both in terms of understandings and in terms of actions. Its role in consciousness raising is central, and again a Freirian model of practice can be seen as a constant engagement with a 'client' in the constructive reframing of problems and outcomes.

Radical practice, then, involves skills that are central to mainstream social work, and does not require a social worker to learn new skills or necessarily to work in a different way. This perspective is extremely important in bringing radical social work in from the margins and locating it at the centre of social work concerns. It emphasises that the alternative social work perspective of this book, while certainly critical of some aspects of mainstream social work, is grounded in many of social work's traditional understandings and practices, and can draw on the strength of the social work tradition in seeking to develop an alternative form of practice. One does not need to seek a radical practice approach from outside mainstream social work; rather it is clear that social work itself is inherently radical, and has built up a tradition of potentially radical practice, even though it often does not recognise it.

Legitimising the voices of the marginalised

In the current economic and political climate, the marginalised do not have a legitimate voice, and what voice they have is being further devalued. Increasingly, it is the voices only of the powerful, and the economically advantaged, that are heard in what passes for public debate in modern society. This allows economic rationalism and managerialism to continue largely unchallenged, as it is by and large only those who are advantaged by them who are able to have access to the media and who are able to influence policy debates. Critical theory requires that the marginalised not only are enabled to define their needs, but that they should be able to articulate them in such a way that they can be met. The continuing marginalisation of the poor, Aboriginal people, women, people with disabilities, gays and lesbians, people of non-Anglo-Celtic cultural background, children and the aged, has resulted in their effective exclusion from the discourses of power. Attempts to change this, to allow them to express alternative views, and to alter the language of power to become more inclusive, are ridiculed and devalued with the label 'political correctness', which has joined 'academic' and 'do-gooder' as convenient labels with which to marginalise any mildly progressive view.

Social workers, as people who work with, and in the interests of, marginalised people and communities, have therefore a particular responsibility to allow the voices of the marginalised to be heard. This requires a reluctance to move too quickly into an advocacy role, where social workers take it on themselves to speak on behalf of the marginalised, thereby making it social workers' voices that are heard, rather than those of the people they claim to represent. Such advocacy, while well-intentioned, can readily reinforce the powerlessness of the marginalised, and amounts to yet another powerful group, in this case social workers, taking it upon themselves to define the needs of the oppressed. From the critical theory perspective, the authentic voices of the marginalised must be heard, and the role for social workers is to make sure that this becomes possible, by helping the marginalised to gain access to public forums, and by helping marginalised people to develop the skills and vocabulary needed to address the structures of power and domination. This, of course, must be accomplished within a dialogical relationship as discussed in Chapter 5, where social workers are able to work *alongside* marginalised people and communities in an empowerment role.

The legitimising of the voices of the marginalised can occur both at individual and at community level. Many social workers, as part of their day-to-day practice, seek to achieve this for their individual clients, by helping them to articulate their needs and present their cases in a variety of arenas, both within the structures of the welfare system, and in their own social milieu, for example, in a family, a group or a school. Every time a social worker helps a woman to stand up against oppressive or discriminatory behaviour, or helps an Aboriginal person to pursue a claim against discrimination, she/he is a part of this process. The social worker is able to add legitimacy by her/his support of the person or people concerned, making it less likely that they will be ignored or intimidated for their actions, and helping them to make their impact more effectively. However, it remains the marginalised person's struggle, in which the social worker is playing a supporting role. It is not, and must not become, the social worker's struggle in which the marginalised person remains marginalised.

Working on such struggles at a purely individual level, however, is simply reinforcing the dominant individualisation of society and perpetuating the conservatism of the existing system. While such struggles are important, they cannot be the only form of struggle in which social workers are engaged. Legitimising the voices of the marginalised is something that must occur at collective or community level, where the political impact of those voices will be much greater. Again, it is the voices of the marginalised, not of the social workers, that need to be heard. Social workers have a critical role in working with marginalised groups, if they are working on an empowerment model linked to a critical theory approach seeking liberation from oppressive structures. It is worth noting that social workers have played a pioneering role in working on an empowerment basis, and have developed techniques of working at community level as well as in the casework mode (Benn 1981; Liffman 1978; Ife 1995). Legitimising the voices of the marginalised at this level, however, also requires social workers to be well-informed about the political process, and sophisticated in operating within it, so that they can support marginalised groups appropriately. This is an area where many social workers perhaps do not feel as well-equipped, because this has tended not to be a major part of the education and socialisation of most social workers (though many specialist community and policy workers represent an exception to this generalisation).

Basic to all social work that seeks to legitimise the voice of the marginalised is the notion of empowerment. The ideal of empowerment incorporates both the personal and the political, and it requires good interpersonal skills as much as it requires political and organisational skills. It involves understanding the real life experiences of the disadvantaged and the marginalised, validating those experiences, valuing the wisdom and expertise the marginalised have developed, and enabling that wisdom to be expressed by helping the disempowered to give expression to their visions and aspirations (Rees 1991). But social workers also have a role in interacting with other structures in order to create space for the marginalised to speak, and to promote a climate in which they can be heard. Working to empower the marginalised also involves working with the powerful; not in conveying the message of the marginalised themselves, but in helping to create a more receptive climate. This leads to the next challenge for social workers, which relates to their own role in oppositional politics.

Developing and supporting an oppositional politics

While it is important for social workers to help in legitimising the voices of the marginalised, and not to dominate by embracing an advocacy approach that only serves to disempower, there is also a role for social workers to be heard *as social workers*, and to act in a more specifically political way. It is clear that the existing social, economic and political order is not conducive to the achievement of social justice goals, and so it is important for social workers to be involved in mounting a credible critique of the existing order and helping to articulate alternatives.

Social workers, of course, are not the only people engaged in such a task, and it would be wrong for social workers to indulge in their characteristic delusions of omnipotence and try to do it all by themselves. This is a potential trap for social workers; one of the problems with earlier Marxist social work accounts was that they sometimes seemed to assume (or at least were read as assuming) that social work practice *by itself* could overthrow the capitalist system, and hence the survival and resurgence of capitalism implies that Marxist social work

183

must be counted as a failure. Social workers like to think of themselves as being able to achieve almost anything through social work practice—it is one of the consequences of a holistic perspective—and so set themselves up for failure when the system does not change as a result of their efforts.

The struggle to establish and support oppositional, or alternative, politics is therefore one that must not be seen as being for social workers alone, but rather one in which social workers need to work alongside others who are committed to similar ends. This includes others in the helping professions, but also trade unions, action groups, some political parties, social justice and human rights groups, and so on. Many social workers, indeed, are active participants in such groups, but there is room for much stronger alliances between social workers and other groups working for social and political change.

Of particular interest in this regard is the role of social movements, and social work's contribution to them. For some commentators, social movements represent the politics of the future (Burgmann 1993; Mendlovitz and Walker 1987; Pakulski 1991), with much more potential for genuine participation and the achievement of the humanist ideal than is the case with conventional party politics. The mainstream parties in most Western nations, including Australia, have reacted to the forces of globalisation and economic rationalism by moving closer together and giving the voter very little choice. The 'Tweedledum and Tweedledumber' approach to electoral politics in Australia, as in other countries, represents perhaps the ultimate form of disempowerment in a so-called democracy. By contrast, social movements such as the peace movement, the women's movement, the Green movement, the labour movement, the human rights movement, the gay and lesbian rights movement, the Aboriginal rights movement, and so on, represent an opportunity for genuinely participatory political action, and have been able to achieve significant progress in their respective areas, in terms of both policy decisions and public awareness. While electoral politics can still represent an important arena for political struggle, the activist social worker is likely to achieve more in terms of the promotion of social justice by participating in and contributing to activist social movements, than by active involvement in a mainstream political party. The relationship between political parties and social movements is a complex one, and some social movements have sought to become political parties, the most recent prominent example being the green movement. There are many in the green movement, however, who regard this as a waste of time and energy, and suggest that the green movement has better things to do than to become involved in the morally corrupt games of formal political power. This is perhaps too extreme a position—after all, the labour movement was dramatically successful in becoming a political party a century ago, and has achieved a great deal as a result, though many would question whether the current version of the ALP adequately represents the interests of labour.

While social workers do become involved in mainstream political parties, and will continue to do so and to see this as a legitimate location for radical practice, the potential for social workers to make a contribution to social movements is more interesting in terms of the discussion in previous chapters. Social movements can benefit from both the analysis and practice that social workers are able to bring. The danger for a single issue movement, which social movements usually are, is that concentration on a single issue leads to other structural factors being ignored. For example, in the green movement there is a real need for sound class, race and gender analyses to prevent green activists from seeking solutions to environmental problems that will only serve to entrench structural inequalities (Ife 1991, 1995). Similarly, many feminists have pointed to the need for feminism to incorporate class and race perspectives, and so on. Social workers, because of their holistic under-standing of the dimensions of oppression and disadvantage, are able to provide such an analysis within social movements, and can prevent a more comprehensive goal of social justice from being lost. Social workers can also make a significant contri-bution in terms of practice skills. Many social movements are seeking skills and expertise in mediation, group consensus decision-making, and a number of other areas where social workers have developed particular skills. Indeed, working in or with a social movement might be seen as a form of community work, and can draw on the skills of social workers who have developed experience in community development and change processes.

The development of oppositional politics, therefore, can extend outside the more narrow definitions of the 'political'. If one accepts both the need for fundamental change in the social, economic and political system, and the critique of the rationalist and modernist paradigm, then the development of an oppositional politics requires a move to 'new paradigm' thinking. This finds its expression in a number of different writers, from Capra to Derrida and from Freire to Foucault, and this new paradigm thinking is reflected in the various new social movements. This is a fertile ground for social work, in its attempts to develop a viable alternative future. New social movements have been established not only because of new paradigm thinking, however, but because they are forums through which marginalised groups (women, Aboriginal people, gays and lesbians, etc.) can find a voice. They therefore represent a location for social work that relates both to developing an oppositional politics and to legitimising the voices of the marginalised.

Indeed, these two agendas for social work are closely related. The critical approach outlined in Chapter 5 requires that they be seen as part of the same process. Legitimising the voices of the marginalised is indeed an important way, and perhaps the only legitimate way, to challenge existing structures and to create an oppositional politics that seeks to develop an alternative based on social justice. The corollary is that to attempt to establish an oppositional or alternative politics without including the voices of the marginalised is to further reinforce their marginalisation, and will not contribute to a more just society.

Beyond the welfare state: relocating social work

As pointed out in Chapter 1, social work has largely been located within welfare state structures, and has been defined in these terms. Yet the welfare state is clearly in decline, and to continue to define social work in this way will thus be to ensure the decline of social work (Ife 1989). It is therefore very important, whatever practice models are developed, for social work to look at ways it can be redefined and reconstructed so that it can survive the decline of the welfare state, and can address the problems and issues of the post-welfare state era. In order to do this, it is necessary first to consider the question of what will replace the welfare state.

Throughout Western history there have been different institutions that have at different times had responsibility for the meeting of human need, namely the *family*, the *church*, the *market* and the *state*. The era of the welfare *state* has largely coincided with the twentieth century, and it seems unlikely to outlast the century by very much, though just as there are still elements of family-based, church-based and market-based welfare, it is most unlikely that state welfare will disappear completely. The important thing to be noted, however, is that the welfare state has only been in existence for a relatively brief historical period, and has only served a relatively small proportion of the world's population. Just as we have done without the welfare state in the past, it is likely that we will have to do so in the future. Current policy trends are seeking to put back the clock, and revert to the family, the market and (through contracting out) the church as the main providers of welfare services. It can be suggested that just as these have proved to be inadequate in the past, they will do so again, and some other form of service provision will need to be found. Elsewhere (Ife 1993, 1995) I have discussed the potential for the community as the basis for the delivery of human services, and suggested that this provides the most promising ground for developing reasonable alternatives to economic rationalism and the welfare state. Without repeating these arguments here, this transition would only be possible or desirable under certain circumstances, because of the conservative aspects of much of what currently passes for a 'community-based' approach, and would need to be accompanied by a program of genuine community development in an attempt to reverse the assault on human community resulting from 200 years of capitalism. Such a possibility, however, is consistent with the direction of a number of social movements, which seem to be seeking some form of community-based alternative, and of course it is entirely compatible with the analysis of earlier chapters. The humanist/anarchist approach is fully consistent with such a direction, and in the terminology developed in Chapter 2 it was even referred to as the community-based discourse.

If indeed 'community' in some form represents the next viable form of human service provision, it also provides the location for social work seeking to redefine its position beyond the welfare state era. This would require social workers to think of ways in which they can be located in, and work for, community-based structures, seeking a community development approach to service delivery. This is an area where social work already has considerable skills and experience, though this now seems to be under-valued in the era of individualism and managerialism, where individual casework and measurable commodified 'services' are the norm. This suggests that the community work, or community development, aspects of social work could become the most important in the future, and may replace individualised professionalised service as the norm for social work activity. This is not to say that social work will no longer be concerned with the needs of individuals, but rather that it will work with them in a more developmental and community-based way.

Social workers as 'street-level intellectuals'

The role of the social worker can be seen as analogous to Gramsci's notion of the intellectual. Gramsci (1973) regards intellectuals not simply as people with high academic qualifications working in universities and writing books nobody can understand, or as the occasional publicly acknowledged intellectual who is regarded by the media as particularly wise and profound (for example, in the Australian context, Manning Clark, H. C. Coombs, Donald Horne, Patrick White or Dame Leonie Kramer). Rather, he identifies two types of intellectuals: the traditional intellectuals such as priests, teachers and professors, who continue to explore and communicate ideas and intellectual understandings in a relatively static and context-free way; and organic intellectuals who are more directly linked to the structures of power (defined by Gramsci in class terms), and who seek to exercise and increase power and control. In many instances organic intellectuals are identified with and linked to oppressive structures, examples being advertising and marketing consultants, management consultants and so on, who use their knowledge and skills to exercise control in the interests of the powerful (Said 1994). On the other hand, organic intellectuals may link themselves to oppressed groups and work alongside them—indeed will seek to belong to them and identify with them—in their struggle (Leonard 1993). This suggests that the role of the intellectual is not to develop ideas and knowledge in the abstract, but rather to develop *and use* those ideas in action, to link theory and practice, and to seek to change the world as well as to understand it.

If such work is clearly identified with the aspirations of oppressed groups, and so linked to their struggles for liberation or for justice, this fits with the understanding of practice (or praxis) arising from critical theory. Social workers, potentially, can be seen as such organic intellectuals, working in the interests of their clients and of disadvantaged individuals and groups. They are responsible, in terms of critical theory, for the use of their expertise to liberate and empower the disadvantaged, and to bring their special knowledge and skills to bear in such a way that they can form a genuine partnership with the disadvantaged in working for change.

Defining social workers as street-level intellectuals (rather than Lipsky's (1980) term of 'street-level bureaucrats'), has significant implications. Most social workers would not regard themselves as intellectuals, nor would they see their work as intellectual work; 'intellectual' social work would be seen as primarily located in university departments rather than in the 'real world' of the welfare agency. Defining social workers as intellectuals, however, emphasises the importance of intellectual endeavour, analysis, conceptualisation, thought, and reflection in forming a critical social work practice. Although intuitive application of 'practice wisdom' is important, and even essential, it is not sufficient. The anti-theory, and even anti-intellectual (Ife 1986) trends in social work are simply not acceptable if alternative, or critical practice, is to be effective.

The idea of critical theory, however, requires that this intellectual activity not be confined to the social worker alone, but that it be shared with the 'client' in a dialogical relationship that equally values the client's own expertise, wisdom and experience, and shares the insights of both. Hence the social worker must not only be able to engage in intellectual analysis, but also must be able to transfer that understanding to the client, by making it accessible and relevant to the client's immediate perceived needs and aspirations. Therefore the social work skill of reframing is, perhaps, the most important skill of all, if one defines the social worker as a *street-level* intellectual. Social work is therefore contextualised intellectual work that is accessible to the disadvantaged people, groups or communities with which a social worker is engaged. Social work is intellectual activity, but it is intellectual activity carried out in partnership with the disadvantaged.

The notion of social workers as intellectuals, however, has a further consequence. An alternative, more elitist, and more usual formulation to Gramsci's is that of Benda (see Said 1994), who sees intellectuals as a small and elite group who hold to their ideals and analysis even in the face of the sternest opposition, and who do not 'sell out' to the interests of the powerful. From Socrates and Jesus through to Vaclav Havel and Aung San Suu Kyi, this small number of exceptional individuals have been prepared to face up to the heaviest forms of state repression in the belief that their ideas and ideals are more powerful and important, and in doing so have inspired millions and have kept alive the human spirit. While this view of intellectuals is more elitist, and does not sit well with the understandings of critical theory, or with the reality of social work practice, it nevertheless holds an important implication for social workers. From this perspective the idea of the intellectual is linked to the notion of unswerving allegiance to ideals, to values, and to a view of the human spirit that transcends the attempts of state and other authorities to make one bend to the forces of authority, and to accept uncritically the status quo as somehow being 'natural' and 'right'. It also challenges the 'unquestionable' right of the government or the forces of global capital to determine and control the lives and destinies of people and communities. This loosens the control authorities have over intellectual activity, and explains why intellectuals (except for conservative organic intellectuals, in Gramsci's terms) have always been threats to established power. The intellectual (perhaps the modern equivalent is the professional) can claim a higher level justification for action or for non-compliance with the law, based on ethical, moral, religious or scientific grounds. To be an intellectual, in these terms, is to be (at least potentially) a radical, and this conception of social work is consistent with the view expressed earlier in this chapter of the inherent radicalism of social work practice.

Internationalism

If social work is to link the personal and the political in an effective and empowering way, it must have a strong internationalist orientation. In the era of globalisation of the economy, of communication, and of cultural hegemony, 'the political' is an international as well as a national and local phenomenon. Many decisions that affect people's lives, and impose and reinforce structures of disadvantage, are taken in the boardrooms of trans-national corporations, often on the other side of the world from the people most directly affected. Despite this, 'the political' is defined in popular debate primarily at a national, state or local level. This diverts attention from the important arena of globalisation, and results in most opposition to economic rationalism and managerialism being articulated in the national or state arenas. If it is to be effective, however, such opposition needs to incorporate an international analysis of power, and an international strategy for a politics of opposition.

Internationalism has been an important idea for the last century, when communication and travel opened up the world to more people, and the idea that 'we live in one world' has generated various themes of universal solidarity. While much of this internationalism has been coloured by an earlier (and in many ways enduring) colonialist agenda, at its finest it represents a great vision of the human spirit, and is the humanist vision of Chapter 4 cast in an international context. This internationalism has been seen in the establishment and on-going work of international organisations such as the Red Cross, aid and development agencies, Amnesty International, the Women's International League for Peace and Freedom, and many other organisations. It was the inspiration for the establishment of the United Nations and its various agencies such as UNESCO and UNICEF. It finds expression in many international treaties and agreements, most notably the Universal Declaration of Human Rights, and its various associated conventions and protocols.

In more recent times, however, this internationalism has been appropriated by the forces of economic rationalism, and has become redefined as 'globalisation'. In this process, the rhetoric and ideals of internationalism—'global village', 'we live in one world', etc.—have been used to justify the globalisation of the economy, free trade, the lowering of tariff protection, and so on. As is the case at national level, international interaction is seen primarily in terms of the global economy, with social and human rights issues relegated to the margins. It is simply a

191

case of economic rationalism defined at the global level. Indeed, social and human rights concerns are in retreat internationally, in the same way as in national politics, and are defined largely in terms of the health of the economy. The UN is under threat of withdrawal of funding, aid budgets are being cut (or being carefully diverted to other programs where they can be seen to be economically beneficial), and human rights and social development are being seen as of domestic rather than of international concern.

In such an environment, locating a political analysis of oppression at an international level can be readily disempowering. It appears to identify the problem on such a scale that the analysis or actions of an individual social worker, or of a single social agency, will have no impact. It becomes very tempting to say 'what is the point?' and retreat into a form of social work that engages in individual therapy or social control and leaves the problem for somebody else, reinforced by a postmodernist position that allows one to define such global analysis as a meaningless and pointless 'meta-narrative'. Yet the global agenda is increasingly dominant. National governments have largely lost their sovereignty in matters of economic policy and management. If those who are concerned for social justice are unable to address the issue of disadvantage at an international level, they are unlikely to achieve significant success.

Looked at in another way, however, the current climate of globalisation opens up some significant opportunities for social work action, or praxis, aimed at creating alternatives. A critical part of such praxis is, of course, the development of a good conceptual understanding and international awareness. This would require social workers to understand the links between their own practice, and indeed their own lives, and the global issues of poverty, environmental degradation, disease and political oppression. An internationalist understanding, that 'we live in one world', suggests that the lifestyles of people in 'developed' nations such as Australia are an integral part of the oppression of others. Our comfortable material lifestyle is maintained at the expense of others, conveniently located on the other side of the globe so that we can remain largely unaware of their suffering. The 'health of our economy' is maintained at the expense of other economies; if Australia is to be 'competitive' in world markets, who loses whenever we 'win' in the global market place? Human rights abuses in many 'developing' nations are not random acts of inhumanity; they are an important part of maintaining the control of the population which is required in order for those nations to continue to play their role in the global economy, namely to remain poor so that the affluent West can benefit. Our economic needs result in imprisonment, torture, disappearances and death squads, as well as starvation, disease, homelessness and squatter camps. There is not sufficient space to elaborate further on such an analysis, which has been more fully documented elsewhere (George 1992; Trainer 1985, 1989). The important point is that it is an analysis which must be part of the consciousness of every social worker, if social work practice is to make an effective connection between the personal and the political in the current practice environment.

One important form of practice is for social workers to become involved in organisations promoting an alternative form of internationalism. The International Federation of Social Workers (IFSW) has indeed taken significant initiatives in this regard, with its emphasis on human rights and the involvement of social workers in human rights discourse and action (Centre for Human Rights 1994; PAHRA 1995). Other opportunities exist through internationalist organisations, which are, more often than not, desperately seeking the kind of skills and commitment social workers can offer. They have a critically important role in keeping alive the older, humanist version of internationalism, in furthering internationalist understanding within Australian society, and in working towards change. Extending the notion of social workers and 'clients' working in partnership, it may well be possible for the individuals or communities with which social workers are engaged to become involved in such activities. An unemployed person who is lonely and seeking something to give meaning and purpose to life may well be interested in becoming a volunteer with Community Aid Abroad, a local community may decide to set up an Amnesty International group, and so on.

The international perspective, perhaps ironically, can be used to emphasise the importance of local action. As was pointed out in Chapter 6, while progressive change to social policy may not be possible at state and national levels because of the demands of global capitalism, small-scale alternatives created at a local level are not affected by such constraints. Establishing a local LETS scheme, for example (Dobson 1993), does not represent the same threat to the international order as would a national guaranteed minimum income or a significant increase in taxes to fund an adequate level of human services. Hence an important arena for social workers seeking alternatives is the local community, where there is much more room for innovation and creativity. An activist social worker may be able to affect directly the lives of the disadvantaged far more through local action than through investing large amounts of energy in lobbying, trying to achieve significant positions in the bureaucracy, or seeking to influence those 'in power'. While such positions may have the trappings of power, and those holding them have the illusion of power, this power is heavily circumscribed by global forces well beyond the reach of the activist social worker. Local community-based initiatives, however, if undertaken by enough people, in enough places, can generate a force for change far stronger than can social workers trying to influence state structures from within. This is not to deny the validity or the importance of the work for change done by social workers within the bureaucracy—it is important to be working on all fronts—but rather to emphasise the importance of grass-roots community level work as a critical way of bringing about change (Ekins 1992; Seabrook 1993a, 1993b).

This form of local activism is important, but if one is to work towards challenging the effects of globalisation (which directly affects the lives and life chances of one's clients) it is also necessary to seek a form of activism at the global level. The above paragraphs could be summarised in the famous green phrase, 'think globally, act locally', but the power of global forces is such that this is no longer sufficient. It is necessary also to *act globally*, that is, to find some way in which to have an impact at the international level in seeking to challenge the economic rationalism of globalisation.

Brecher and Costello (1994) have labelled the dominant form of globalisation as 'globalisation from above'. This is because it is globalisation exclusively in the interests of the powerful, and does not allow room for democratic participation, or adequate representation of the disadvantaged, in decision-making. It is, indeed, largely outside the control of democratically elected governments, and is able to operate without public accountability (an irony in an era where 'public accountability' is so popular, even though it is used principally as a justification for tighter hierarchical control). As a counter to globalisation from above, Brecher and Costello advocate *globalisation from below*, which is a form of globalisation involving ordinary people, grass-roots movements, and those concerned for the goals of social justice, human rights and environmental sustainability. Globalisation from above has been made possible by technological advances, and it is not surprising that the powerful have been in the best position to make use of new communication technologies, to speed the flow of capital around the world in the interests, largely, of speculative profit. It is surely possible, and indeed essential, for others to make use of this technology, in the pursuit of a rather different agenda. Just as it is now possible for the powerful to communicate and act more quickly and effectively, so it is possible for the disadvantaged. Exploring and realising these opportunities is an important task for social workers, who are working with disadvantaged groups, and who claim to allow the voices of those groups to be heard.

This involves seeking opportunities not only to link disadvantaged groups and individuals with others in the same immediate environment, but to find ways to put them in touch with others at an international level, with a view to seeking to develop some form of international action for change. One example of such grass-roots international action is the use of the internet by local environmental action groups to tap into international expertise as part of their local struggle. In this way local activists have been able to match the capacity of their transnational opponents to have access to information and technical skills from around the world. A second example is the way in which indigenous communities in different countries have been able to establish strong and effective communication links, at grass-roots level, to inform each other about their different, though related, struggles for justice, and to learn from each others' experiences. A third example is the way Amnesty International is able to mobilise over one million people world-wide to campaign against human rights abuses, as an international movement of solidarity with the victims, and as a voice of humanity that has been able to moderate (though unfortunately not eliminate) human rights abuses in many parts of the world.

These three very different examples point to the way in which it is possible to develop structures of globalisation from below. This represents one of the most fascinating challenges for social workers, and is a potential area for creative practice. Globalisation from below may take very different forms, as these examples show, but the attempt to form and encourage new grass roots level coalitions that extend beyond national boundaries is one of the most important areas for social workers seeking to practice within the critical paradigm developed in previous chapters. If the structures of oppression are now global, it is essential that the struggle to change or overthrow those structures also be conceptualised and carried out globally.

Macro and micro practice

It will have become clear from the previous discussion that the alternative approach to social work this book has sought to articulate does not incorporate a sharp distinction between macro and micro practice. Indeed, the separation between micro and macro, or casework and community work, has operated effectively to weaken the link between the personal and the political, which is at the heart of social work. It has allowed some social workers to be concerned primarily or even exclusively with the personal, leaving the political to their community-based colleagues, and similarly it has allowed other social workers to avoid confronting personal suffering or developing skills of inter-personal helping, leaving all that to the caseworkers. Such a split has been reinforced by the structures within which social workers are employed; most are mandated to provide personal services but not to engage in political or macro-level practice, while the smaller numbers who are engaged at the macro level tend not to see the provision of individual services as part of their mandate. Social workers need to challenge the artificiality of such organisational constraints, and to seek to define their work as being about the personal *and* the political wherever they are located.

This need not be undertaken in a confrontationist or opposi-tional way. The caseworker, after all, will always understand the 'client' in terms of the community and cultural context, and will be seeking solutions and supports at community level. A concern with community will therefore be present in the work of all social workers, and it is important that caseworkers make explicit, instead of keeping hidden, the community aspects of their work in the way they define and interpret their jobs to others (e.g., in the keeping of statistics, the drafting of position statements and job descriptions, the design of professional development programs, etc.). Similarly, a concern with the personal is very important for a community worker, who is, after all, working with individuals and their disempowerment. The skills of a community worker are in many respects the skills of the caseworker, though they may be labelled and contextualised differently. Community workers need considerable inter-personal skills, for example, and make use of them in a wide variety of circumstances. They use group work skills almost every day (as indeed do caseworkers in team meetings). Community workers also frequently meet people who are experiencing personal difficulty or crisis, and while they will often refer them to a specific service, they will in the process make use of interpersonal helping skills in building a relationship of trust, support, helping to identify and reframe a problem, and so on. In terms of skills, the difference between caseworkers and community workers is in reality much less than it might appear.

Because of this, the traditional split between macro and micro work must be seen as reflecting a political reality, or an ideological imperative, which is about separating the personal and the political, rather than reflecting the reality of good social work practice. It is therefore an essential part of the critical social work approach to question this separation. This is hardly a new notion, and many models of social work have attempted to do so through the various frameworks of genericism, unitary structures, and the like. Most social work courses, at least in theory, seek to teach a social work that does not make this distinct separation. The significant issue, then, is that despite these attempts, the distinction remains strong in the practice and vocabulary of social workers, and in the structures within which they work. This suggests that it is the result of a strong ideological message embedded in the structures and the discourse of power, namely the separation of the personal and the political. To challenge this, by changing the way in which social work is constructed and practised, can be one of the most important agendas for social workers.

Education

The approach to social work outlined in this book has significant implications for social work education programs.

As with social work itself, there are many practices in schools of social work that are already fully compatible with the critical approach, for example, the insistence on the integration of the macro and micro perspectives. In other ways, however, social work education practices fall well short of the critical ideal.

One of the most significant is the way in which social work education often fails to model critical practice in the way staff interact with students. To teach empowerment-based social work from within the disempowering structure of a contemporary university is a major contradiction, which has to be addressed as part of the educational task. Indeed, this can become the focus of an education which, in the Freire sense, is genuinely consciousness-raising, by requiring both students and teachers to reflect together on their organisational location and to seek genuinely liberatory forms of educational practice. This can become one of the most effective ways to 'teach' critical social work, as there are strong parallels between the educational and the social work tasks. A number of social work educators, indeed, seek to do this (e.g., de Maria 1993), but it is still too often seen as deviant not just within the university, but within the social work department itself. This marginalisation of empowerment-based education is similar to the marginalisation of radical, critical or alternative social work. If social work is to survive as an effective form of counter-oppressive practice in a hostile environment, such approaches will need to be incorporated at the centre rather than at the periphery of social work concerns, and this applies as much to social work education as it does to social work practice.

Because of the difficult political climate in which social workers are required to practice, the temptation for students to retreat into a safe, apparently 'apolitical' (there can in reality be no such thing) therapeutic social work, based entirely on interpersonal helping, is stronger than ever. It is important that schools of social work resist this tendency, by continuing to require students to confront the political nature of the social work task. This can be achieved by emphasising the point made earlier in this chapter, that 'radical' social work is not something different or marginal, but rather is an extension of the values and methods inherent in mainstream practice. It is in the reality of day-to-day social work practice that social workers can be radical. Students therefore need to be confronted with the political nature not just of the practice and educational contexts, but also of social work practice and education themselves, and helped to realise that 'apolitical social work' and 'apolitical education' are oxymorons.

There is still a tendency in many social work texts and articles to treat social work as ideologically neutral, rather than to define it as an essentially ideological activity, which is clearly the implication of critical practice. This can only be redressed by the publication of more material defining social work ideologically, and seeing social work practice essentially as 'political practice'. This then legitimises a significant literature from the social sciences, which has been concerned with political practice and its relationship to theory, as of central importance for all social work.

It is also important, from the point of view of critical social work, for the voices of the disadvantaged to have a central role in the education of social workers. Just as 'clients' must be involved in defining the social work task in partnership with social workers, so they must have a genuine role in defining the social work education task, so that the 'social work' to which students are introduced is not simply the construction of the teachers, the employers and the professional accrediting body, but is also the construction of the people or communities with which the students will be working. Again, there is some attempt to do this in most schools of social work, but what is required goes well beyond the occasional guest lecture by a consumer representative or the token Aboriginal representative on an advisory committee. Incorporating the voices of the disadvantaged in a significant way into both 'curriculum construction' and the actual educational experience, is a major challenge that must be met if students are to be prepared for truly critical practice.

A social work course based on a critical view of practice would seek to incorporate not only 'academic' knowledge in the conventional sense, but also wisdom that can be derived from other locations, as was discussed in Chapter 4. This includes theatre, poetry, art, music and other sources of both inspiration and understanding. The critical social worker must be a well-informed, broadly educated, critically reflective and sensitive person, and these qualities are gained from an educational experience that is significantly broader than simply attending lectures, reading, studying and writing essays, with the occasional break of a practice laboratory. Again, this perspective is not unknown in schools of social work, but is easily marginalised both by management and by students.

Fieldwork is perhaps the area of the social work curriculum where there is most scope for the development of critical practice, and where current educational practices largely ignore such opportunities. In many social work placements, the student learns a good deal about agency policy and procedures (which may be of little use if the student is going to work somewhere else), is able to demonstrate basic competence in interpersonal communication, is able to show that she/he can think systematically and analytically about a case, and is helped to feel comfortable in the role of a social worker. Not all placements, of course, are so limited or limiting, and in many instances students will learn rather more, both in terms of analysis and skills. However, the placements that genuinely utilise opportunities for learning critical practice are few, and tend to be limited to the small number of students who specifically request them (again, the marginalisation of critical practice), or those who are fortunate enough to have a supervisor who works from within this framework.

The point has been reiterated that critical social work is in many ways a simple extension of the commitments and practices of a good deal of mainstream social work. Hence placements offering critical social work opportunities need not be rare, but could be found almost anywhere social work is practised. The task is not necessarily to find new placements (though the critical approach does open up further locations in which social work can be legitimately located, e.g., social movements), but rather to develop curriculum expectations, liaison opportunities and, most importantly, awareness among supervisors, of the potential for critical practice and critical education. The nature of those opportunities will, of course, vary from one location to another, but it should in theory be possible to incorporate such an approach in at least one placement for every student in a social work course. Such a placement would take as its central theme the linking of the personal and the political, would require the student to conceptualise all 'cases' in this way, and would require practice at both personal and political levels in such a way that they were clearly linked. The student and the supervisor would seek to establish a dialogical and mutually empowering relationship, as discussed in Chapter 5, and the student would also have the opportunity to establish such relationships with some 'clients' or community groups. The link between education and social work would therefore be clearly made, and the student would be able to experience a model of empowerment-based practice. As a consequence of such a program, supervisors would have the opportunity to re-evaluate their own practice in the light of the critical perspective, as, like the entire social work course, it would be a mutually educative experience where the educator was learning from the encounter as much as the student. This, again, often happens in current practice where a supervisor is prepared to engage with a student in this way, but it is often coincidental rather than a specified requirement.

Such an approach to placements, however, is only a partial solution, because it incorporates the characteristically individual nature of student field-based learning by concentrating on the experience of 'the student' rather than 'students'. This in itself can be an inhibiting factor, as it serves to emphasise the dominant individualism within which the educational task is conceptualised. While social work education continues to be defined in individual terms, it will never reach its full potential as a preparation for critical practice. As with social work practice itself, social work education can increase its critical potential if it moves beyond such individualism to more collective understanding and action. Student placements need not be the largely individual learning experiences of current educational practice, and while most schools of social work also incorporate some group learning as part of the placement, there is undoubtedly potential for such group learning and consciousness-raising to be increased and enhanced within the agency context.

The critical approach, by emphasising the co-operative learning model, by incorporating the voices of the disadvantaged, and by emphasising the idea of praxis (learning by doing and doing by learning) can link the class and the field experiences of social work education much more closely. Fieldwork is thus not seen as somehow 'different' from classroom teaching, but the boundaries between them become inevitably blurred. Again, this already happens to some degree in most schools of social work, and is an aim of many social work educators, emphasising the compatibility between the critical approach and many aspects of current practice. As with social work itself, education within a critical paradigm represents an extension and development of current practices rather than something that needs to be conceptualised as a distinct separate activity.

Influencing the discourse

The strength of the discourse of economic rationalism has been a constant theme of this book. In Chapter 2, it was noted that the dominant debates in social and economic policy take place largely on the left hand side of Figure 2.2, where managerialism and the market predominate, and where the vision of humanity discussed in Chapter 4 is subordinated to the goal of economic prosperity. This economic rationalist discourse is clearly at odds with the values of social work, and the critical approach to social work developed in later chapters seeks to provide a stronger base from which economic rationalism can be challenged.

For this to happen, however, it is necessary for social workers to participate in the public debate about social and economic goals, and, even more importantly, to seek to have the voices of the disadvantaged also heard in such forums. This needs to be accomplished so that alternative views can be articulated, with a view to influencing the discourse of power.

Social workers will not be able to accomplish this alone; their numbers are too small and their political power too weak. But social workers are not alone in this struggle, and increasingly voices are being raised against the dominance of economic rationalism, even though they are often not validated by the mainstream media. Social workers, and the groups with whom they work, need to form more effective links with others who are working towards alternative systems, and to support their efforts. Indeed, as was pointed out in the discussion earlier in this chapter relating to social movements, social workers have some important insights and skills to contribute to such struggles.

Previous formulations of radical social work have tended to base themselves on either a Marxist or a feminist analysis (or sometimes both). This is hardly surprising, as it is in Marxism and feminism that the critique of the existing order has been most highly developed, and alternatives most clearly articulated. The danger, however, is that each has based its opposition to the existing order primarily around one form of oppression, and although each is critically important, a social work seeking to challenge economic rationalism on only one dimension of oppression is dangerously simplistic. These formulations have led to conclusions that social workers need to ally themselves closely with the struggles of either the labour movement or the women's movement; both are clearly important and indeed necessary if an effective challenge to oppression is to be maintained, but it is also necessary for social workers to look to other potential allies, and to join a more widely-based coalition of interests working towards social change. Such movements include the peace movement, the green movement, gay and lesbian movements, the human rights movement, Aboriginal communities, and those struggling for a better deal for people with disabilities, for the aged, for children, and for various ethnic and cultural minorities. Other professional, academic, occupational, political or sectoral groups are also potential allies, including the Doctors Reform Society, the Councils of Social Service, other helping professions, political parties (especially the Greens and the Democrats) and human rights groups. All these have an interest in developing the critique of economic rationalism and in articulating that critique in the public arena, and hence it is important for social workers to be seeking to work in close co-operation with them, and to build appropriate coalitions for that purpose.

The contradictions of economic rationalism are readily evident, and it is important to lose no opportunity to point them out in the public arena, for example, through media releases, statements, staged media events and the other opportunities social workers often have in the course of their work, such as talks to service clubs, school groups, community organisations, or whatever. This means that social workers must accept every opportunity to talk to the media, or to participate in public debate, either individually or as a profession (this is another way in which professional status can be useful). Social workers who are unable to make public comment, such as public servants, can often find ways to 'leak' information to others who can make use of it (is a code of ethics a help or a hindrance?), or can keep their colleagues informed about recent developments. Despite the dominance of economic rationalism in the mainstream media, one of the healthy characteristics of Australian society is its willingness to mistrust those in authority, to believe that the government has probably got it wrong, and to maintain a profound suspicion of the motives and the competence of political leaders. This provides fertile ground for exposing the contradictions and absurdities of current orthodoxies, and for suggesting that there might indeed be other ways of doing things.

In order to mount an effective opposition, it has already been suggested that social workers need to be economically and politically literate, and they need to help the disadvantaged to achieve similar levels of literacy. They also need to be able to articulate their position in such a way that it will be heard, rather than marginalised. Tactics of deliberate confrontation can sometimes be effective in raising consciousness, as the activist arms of the women's movement and the green movement have so clearly shown, but if that is all that is attempted it becomes easy for activists to be marginalised. The harder challenge is to develop one's alternative vision in such a way that people will accept its legitimacy, so that it emerges from their own felt needs and frustrations with the existing order, rather than from an idealised vision which a social worker seeks to impose on others. The alternative, therefore, must develop from the kind of critical practice discussed in Chapter 5. This is where social workers are in a uniquely strong position to help change the discourse of economic rationalism, because of their capacity to articulate the need for change at the political level in such a way that it relates directly to personal experience. The link between the personal and the political, which is the central concern of critical social work, is therefore of great significance. If social workers can indeed effectively link the personal and the political in their practice, if they can creatively articulate alternatives, and if they can be courageous and outspoken in their advocacy of humanity and social justice, they have the potential to be in the vanguard of progressive social change.

Grounds for hope

The challenges facing social workers, and indeed all those seeking a world based on principles of social justice and human rights, are indeed daunting. While this book has sought to provide a basis for understanding this struggle, and has suggested some possible directions for an alternative critical practice, there can be no easy answers, and social workers are faced with challenging and testing times. It is, of course, easy to become discouraged when considering the magnitude of the task, and it is therefore appropriate to conclude this book by considering some grounds for optimism that change may indeed be possible, and that social work can play a significant role in helping to achieve it. Some of these points have been made in previous chapters, but it may be useful to summarise them as a conclusion.

The existing social, economic and political order cannot last indefinitely, and all the signs are that its global dominance will be quite brief. The contradictions of capitalism, so clearly demonstrated by Marx, remain unresolved, and although Marx may have been wrong about the timing of the collapse of capitalism (for reasons explained by the strength of the hegemony of capitalist interests) the analysis remains strong. The contradictions of capitalism are further heightened by the ecological limits to growth and accumulation, which are becoming more apparent, and it is clear that before too long the whole system is likely to collapse under the weight of its own contradictions. The global economy only adds to this instability; throughout economic history, people have shown that they are unable to understand, let alone control, the workings of an economy, and every so often a national economy will collapse or run out of control as a result of mismanagement. This is bad enough when it happens to a regional or national economy, but the consequences when (as is only a matter of time) it happens to the complex and unstable global economy are potentially disastrous. For these reasons, it is quite wrong to assume that economic rationalism is here to stay. The only questions are firstly whether its demise will be in the near or the not-so near future, and secondly whether the transition to some other system will be accomplished as part of a process of rational change, or will be forced on us by a series of economic, ecological, political or social disasters. Social workers can play a role in advocating the former.

In either event, it appears certain that societies such as Australia are headed for a period of instability and crisis, as governments try to keep control of an increasingly un-controllable set of circumstances, and try to balance the essentially irreconcilable demands of a global economic system seeking accumulation and profit, and an electorate seeking the satisfaction of human needs and aspirations. Indeed it might be suggested that we are already entering such a period of crisis. Times of crisis, however, are also times of opportunity; they are the times when the unthinkable becomes thinkable, and when solutions that might have seemed totally unrealistic become possible. This opens up the potential for creative alternatives, and indeed it makes it important that social workers and others concerned with change explore, in the present context, possible different structures for delivering human services. It could be that the immediate future will again open a window of opportunity for significant change, and social workers need to be well prepared.

Indeed, many alternatives are already being put into practice. Increasing numbers of people, feeling that the mainstream economy or society no longer meets their needs, are seeking to develop their own alternative structures: LETS schemes, co-operatives, self-help groups, and so on. There is an important role for social workers to play in encouraging and supporting such community-based alternatives; their experience may be vital in building a future for humanity.

Social work has the very skills and understandings that will be not only useful but essential in a post-economic rationalist age. The capacity to link the personal and the political, the capacity to develop community-based structures, the insistence that the interests of the most vulnerable and disadvantaged be included in any alternative development, and that their voices be heard, the commitment to social justice and human rights, and the capacity to practice at both an individual and a community level, are all likely to be particularly important in the future, whether it is one of chaos and uncertainty, or one of conscious change towards a genuinely sustainable society where human values are given prominence.

In the more immediate context, it is worth noting the ecological perspective that nothing happens in isolation, or, in other words, that every action changes the world. The seemingly insignificant interchange with a client, a colleague, a manager or a friend can change the way that person views the world, their place in it, and their life, and this small change can lead to other changes as that person in turn interacts with others in different ways as a consequence. One of the strengths of the poststructuralist position is that it allows us to see reality and power as constantly being redefined, and hence one has the capacity to be affecting that redefinition in everything one does. It is not necessary to engage in the grand gesture or public action in order to change the world; social workers are changing the world all the time as a result of their practice. The consequences of good social work practice, based on a critical approach and a commitment to social justice, can be more far reaching than any social worker could ever imagine.

The fundamental source of hope for social workers is the vision of humanity, discussed in Chapter 4, which has survived the assaults of postmodernism, economic rationalism, and the other forces that have opposed it. This vision remains strong, and is capable of inspiring people to great achievements, and to the passionate pursuit of social justice, human rights, and a better world. Social work practice represents, in its own way, part of the continuing struggle for the triumph of the human spirit. Viewed in this light, social work practice has a critically important role to play, and is central to attempts to build a better world. Far from being marginalised, social workers have the opportunity to move to centre stage, and the coming decades promise to provide not only strong challenges for social workers, but remarkable opportunities for progressive change.

References

Alinsky, S., 1971, *Rules For Radicals: A Practical Primer for Realistic Radicals*, Random House, New York

Aung San Suu Kyi, 1995, *Freedom from Fear*, Penguin, London

Bates, E. and Linder-Pelz, S., 1990, *Health Care Issues*, 2nd ed., Allen & Unwin, St Leonards

Bailey, R. and Brake, M. (eds), 1975, *Radical Social Work*, Edward Arnold, London

Bamford, T., 1990, *The Future of Social Work*, Macmillan, London

Barber, J., 1991, *Beyond Casework*, Macmillan, London

Bauman, Z., 1991, *Postmodernity: Chance or Menace?* Centre for the Study of Cultural Values, Lancaster University, Lancaster

Beilharz, P., Considine, M. and Watts, R., 1992, *Arguing About the Welfare State: the Australian Experience*, Allen & Unwin, North Sydney

Benn, C., 1981, *Attacking Poverty Through Participation: A Community Approach*, PIT Publishing, Bundoora

Benn, C., 1991, 'Social Justice, Social Policy and Social Work' *Australian Social Work*, vol. 44, no. 4

Benn, T. (ed.), 1984, *Writings on the Wall: A Radical and Socialist Anthology 1215–1984*, Faber & Faber, London

Beresford, P. and Harding, T. (eds), 1993, *A Challenge to Change: Practical Experiences of Building User-led Services*, National Institute for Social Work, London

Bloom, M. and Fischer, J., 1982, *Evaluating Practice: Guidelines for the Accountable Professional*, Prentice-Hall, Englewood Cliffs, NJ

Brah, A., 1991, 'Questions of Difference and International Feminism' in Aaron, J. and Walley, S. (eds), *Out of the Margins: Women's Studies in the Nineties*, Falmer Press, London

Brecher, J. and Costello, T., 1994, *Global Village or Global Pillage: Economic Reconstruction from the Bottom Up*, South End Press, Boston

Bryson, L., 1992, *Welfare and the State*, Macmillan, London

Buchanan, J., 1995, 'Managing Labour in the 1990s' Rees, S. and Rodley, G. (eds), *The Human Costs of Managerialism: Advocating the Recovery of Humanity*, Pluto Press, Leichardt

Burgmann, V., 1993, *Power and Protest: Movements for Change in Australian Society*, Allen & Unwin, St Leonards, NSW

Burrell, G. and Morgan, G., 1979, *Sociological Paradigms and Organisational Analysis*, Heinemann, London

Calhoun, C., 1995, *Critical Social Theory*, Blackwell, Oxford

Camilleri, P., 1995, *Unravelling Social Work: Text, Talk and Gender as Practice*, PhD Thesis, Flinders University of South Australia

Capra, F., 1982, *The Turning Point—Science, Society and the Rising Culture*, Wildwood House, London

Carroll, J., 1993, *Humanism: the Wreck of Western Culture*, Fontana, London

Centre for Human Rights, 1994, *Human Rights and Social Work: A Manual for Schools of Social Work and the Social Work Profession*, United Nations, Professional Training Series no. 1, Geneva

Compton, B and Galaway, B., 1994, *Social Work Processes*, 5th ed., Brooks/Cole, Pacific Grove, Calif.

Coombs, H.C., 1981, *Trial Balance*, Macmillan, Melbourne

Coombs, H.C., 1990, *The Return of Scarcity: Strategies for an Economic Future*, Cambridge University Press, Melbourne

Coover, V., Deacon, E., Esser, C. and Moore, C., 1985, *Resource Manual for a Living Revolution*, New Society Publishers, Philadelphia

Corrigan, P. and Leonard, P., 1978, *Social Work Practice Under Capitalism: A Marxist Approach*, Macmillan, London

Dauncey, G., 1988, *After the Crash—the Emergence of the Rainbow Economy*, Green Print, Basingstoke

Davies, B., 1991, 'The Concept of Agency: A Feminist Poststructuralist Analysis', *Social Analysis*, vol. 30

de Maria, W., 1993, 'Critical Pedagogy and the Forgotten Social Work Student: The Return of Radical Practice' *Australian Social Work*, vol. 46, no. 1

Dillon, M., 1995, 'Sovereignty and Governmentality: From the Problematics of the "New World Order" to the Problematic of the World Order', *Alternatives*, vol. 20

Dingwall, R., Eekelaar, J. and Murray, T., 1995, *The Protection of Children: State Intervention in Family Life*, 2nd ed. Avebury, Aldershot

Dobson, R., 1993, *Bringing the Economy Home from the Market*, Black Rose, Montreal

Donnison, D., 1991, *A Radical Agenda: After the New Right and the Old Left*, Rivers Oram, London

Donovan, F. and Jackson, A., 1991, *Managing Human Service Organisations*, Prentice Hall, Sydney

Doyal, L. and Gough, I., 1991, *A Theory of Human Need*, Macmillan, London

Dryzek, J., 1995, 'Critical Theory as a Research Program' White, S., (ed.), *The Cambridge Companion to Habermas*, Cambridge University Press, Cambridge

Dworkin, J., 1990, 'Political, Economic and Social Aspects of Professional Authority', *Families in Society: Journal of Contemporary Human Services*, vol. 71, no. 9

Eckersley, R., 1992, *Environmentalism and Political Theory*, SUNY Press, New York

Ekins, P. 1992, *A New World Order: Grassroots Movements for Global Change*, Routledge, London

Ekins, P. and Max-Neef, M. (eds), 1992, *Real-Life Economics: Understanding Wealth Creation*, Routledge, London

England, H., 1986, *Social Work as Art: Making Sense For Good Practice*, Allen & Unwin, London

Farris, B., Murillo, G. and Hale, W., 1971, 'The Settlement House: Mediator for the Poor' in Schwartz, W. and Zalba, S. (eds), *The Practice of Groupwork*, Columbia University Press, New York

Fay, B., 1975, *Social Theory and Political Practice*, Allen & Unwin, London

Fay, B., 1987, *Critical Social Science*, Polity Press, Cambridge

Flynn, T., 1994, 'Foucault's Mapping of History' in Gutting, G. (ed.), *The Cambridge Companion to Foucault*, Cambridge University Press, Cambridge

Fook, J., 1993, *Radical Casework: A Theory of Practice*, Allen & Unwin, St Leonards, NSW

Fook, J., (ed.) 1996, *The Reflective Researcher: Social Workers' Theories of Practice Research*, Allen & Unwin, St Leonards NSW

Foucault, M., 1972, *The Archaeology of Knowledge*, Tavistock, London

Foucault, M., 1973, *Madness and Civilisation: A History of Insanity in an Age of Reason*, Vintage Books, New York

Foucault, M. 1975, *Discipline and Punish: The Birth of the Prison*, Vinage, New York

Fox, W., 1990, *Towards a Transpersonal Ecology: Developing New Foundations for Environmentalism*, Shambhala, Boston

Franklin, R., 1989, 'Wimps and Bullies: Press Reporting of Child Abuse' in Carter, P., Jeffs, T. and Smith, M. (eds) *Social Work and Social Welfare Yearbook*, Open University Press, Milton Keynes

Freire, P., 1972, *Pedagogy of the Oppressed*, Penguin, Harmondsworth

Frost, N. and Stein, M, 1989, 'What's Happening in Social Service Departments?' in Langan, M. and Lee, P. (eds), *Radical Social Work Today*, Unwin Hyman, London

Galtung, J., 1994, *Human Rights in Another Key*, Polity Press, Cambridge

Galper, J., 1975, *The Politics of Social Services*, Prentice-Hall, Englewood Cliffs, New Jersey

George, S., 1992, *The Debt Boomerang: How Third World Debt Harms Us All*, Westview Press, Boulder

George, V. and Wilding, P., 1984, *The Impact of Social Policy*, Routledge, London

George, V. and Wilding, P., 1985, *Ideology and Social Welfare*, 2nd ed., Routledge, London

Germain, C., 1991, *Human Behaviour in the Social Environment: An Ecological View*, Columbia University Press, New York

Geuss, R., 1981, *The Idea of a Critical Theory: Habermas and the Frankfurt School*, Cambridge University Press, Cambridge

Gibbs, L., 1991, *Scientific Reasoning for Social Workers: Bridging the Gap Between Research and Practice*, Macmillan, New York

Gough, I., 1979, *The Political Economy of the Welfare State*, Macmillan, London

Gramsci, A., 1973, *The Prison Notebooks: Selections*, trans. Q. Hoare and G. Nowell-Smith, Lawrence & Wishart, London

Graycar, A., 1990, 'Practice Under Pressure in the Changing Welfare State' *Australian Social Work*, vol. 43, no. 9

Gutting, G., (ed) 1994, *The Cambridge Companion to Foucault*, Cambridge University Press, Cambridge

Haber, H., 1994, *Beyond Postmodern Politics: Lyotard, Rorty, Foucault*, Routledge, New York

Habermas, J., 1987, *The Theory of Communicative Action*, trans. T. McCarthy, Beacon Press, Boston

Ham, C. and Hill, M., 1984, *The Policy Process in the Modern Capitalist State*, Wheatsheaf, Brighton

Hartman, A., 1991, 'Words Create Worlds' *Social Work*, vol. 36

Harvey, D., 1989, The *Condition of Postmodernity: An Enquiry into the Origins of Cultural Change*, Blackwell, Oxford

Havel, V., 1991. *Open Letters*, Faber & Faber, London

Havel, V., 1992, *Summer Meditations on Politics, Morality and Civility in a Time of Transition* Faber & Faber, London

Henderson, H., 1991, *Paradigms in Progress—Life Beyond Economics*, Knowledge Systems Inc., Indianapolis

Hooks, B., 1981, *Ain't I a Woman! Black Women and Feminism*, Pluto Press, London

Horne, D. (ed.) 1992, *The Trouble with Economic Rationalism*, Scribe, Newham, Vic.

Hough, G., 1994, 'Post-Industrial Work? The Use of Information Technology in the Restructuring of State Social Service Work' *Advances in Social Work and Welfare Education*, UWA, Perth

Hough, G., 1995, 'Dismantling Child Welfare' in Rees, S. and Rodley, G. (eds), *The Human Costs of Managerialism: Advocating the Recovery of Humanity*, Pluto Press, Leichardt

Howe, D., 1987, *An Introduction to Social Work Theory*, Aldershot, Gower

Howe, D., 1994, 'Modernity, Postmodernity and Social Work', *British Journal of Social Work*, vol. 24

Ife, J., 1980, 'The Determination of Social Need: A Model of Need Statements in Social Administration' *Australian Journal of Social Issues*, vol. 15, no. 2

Ife, J., 1986, 'Anti-Intellectualism and Social Work Education', *Advances in Social Work Education*, 1986

Ife, J., 1989, 'Can Social Work Survive the Decline of the Welfare State?' *Social Work in the Australian Context*, Proceedings of the 21st Biennial Conference of the Australian Association of Social Workers, Townsville

Ife, J., 1991, 'Social Policy and the Green Movement' *Australian Quarterly*, vol. 63, no. 3, pp. 336–346

Ife, J., 1993, 'Community-Based services: Opportunity or Con Trick?' in *Beyond Economic Rationalism: Alternative Futures for Social Policy*, P. Saunders and S. Graham (eds), Social Policy Research centre Reports and Proceedings, University of NSW, no. 105

Ife, J., 1995, *Community Development: Creating Community Alternatives—Vision, Analysis and Practice*, Longman, Melbourne

Illich, I., Zola, I., McKnight, J., Caplan, J. and Shaiken, S., 1977, *Disabling Professions*, Marion Boyars, London

Imre, R., 1990, 'Rationality with Feeling' *Families in Society*, vol. 71, no. 1

Jamrozik, A., 1991, *Class, Inequality and the State*, Macmillan, Melbourne

Jones, C., 1983, *State Social Work and the Working Class*, Macmillan, London

Jones, A. and May, J., 1992, *Working in Human Service Organisations*, Longman Cheshire, Melbourne

Jones, D. and Mayo, M. (eds) 1974, *Community Work One*, Routledge & Kegan Paul, London

Jones, D. and Mayo, M. (eds) 1975, *Community Work Two*, Routledge & Kegan Paul, London

Knapp., M., 1984, *The Economics of Social Care*, London, Macmillan

Kumar, K., 1995, *From Post-Industrial to Post-Modern Society: New Theories of the Contemporary World*, Blackwell, Oxford

Latting, J., 1995, 'Postmodern Feminist Theory and Social Work: A Deconstruction' *Social Work*, vol. 40, no. 6

Lechte, J., 1994, *Fifty Key Contemporary Thinkers: From Structuralism to Postmodernity*, Routledge, London

Lees, R. and Mayo, M., 1984, *Community Action for Change*, Routledge & Kegan Paul, London

Leonard, P. 1993, 'Critical Pedagogy and State Welfare: Intellectual Encounters with Freire and Gramsci, 1974–1986' McLaren, P. and Leonard, P., *Paulo Freire: A Critical Encounter*, Routledge, London

Leonard, P. 1995, 'Postmodernism, Socialism and Social Welfare' *Journal of Progressive Human Services*, vol. 6, no. 2

Leonard, S., 1990, *Critical Theory and Political Practice*, Princeton University Press, Princeton, NJ

Liffman, M., 1978, *Power for the Poor: The Family Centre Project, an Experiment in Self-Help*, Allen & Unwin, Hornsby, NSW

Lipsky, M., 1980, *Street -Level Bureaucracy: Dilemmas of the Individual in Public Services*, Russell Sage Foundation, New York

Lyotard, J.-F., 1984, *The Postmodern Condition: a Report on Knowledge*, Manchester University Press, Manchester

Mandela, N., 1994, *Long Walk to Freedom*, Abacus, London

Marchant, H. and Wearing, B., 1986, *Gender Reclaimed: Women and Social Work*, Hale & Iremonger, Sydney

Markiewicz, A,. 1994, 'How Social Workers Survive in Public Welfare: Training for Best Practice in a Declassified, Increasingly Narrowly-defined, Administrative Context', *Advances in Social Work and Welfare Education*, UWA, Perth

Marshall, P., 1992a, *Demanding the Impossible: A History of Anarchism*, Harper Collins, London

Marshall, P. 1992b, *Nature's Web: An Exploration of Ecological Thinking*, Simon & Schuster, London

Marshall, T.H., 1965, *Social Policy*, Hutchinson, London

Martin, B., 1993, *In the Public Interest? Privatisation and Public Sector Reform*, Zed Books, London

Marx, K., 1954, *Capital: A Critique of Political Economy, Volume 1: The Process of Production of Capital*, trans S. Moore and E. Aveling, Progress Publishers, Moscow

Maslow, A., 1970, *Motivation and Personality*, 2nd ed. Harper & Row, New York

McLaren, P. and Lankshear, C. (eds), 1994, *Politics of Liberation: Paths from Freire*, Routledge, London

McLaren, P. and Leonard, P. (eds), 1993, *Paulo Freire: A Critical Encounter*, Routledge, London

McIntyre, J., 1995 *Achieving Social Rights and Responsibility: Towards a Critical Humanist Approach to Community Development*, Community Quarterly, St Kilda

McKnight, J., 1977, 'The Professional Service Business' *Social Policy*, vol. 8, no. 3

Mellor, M., 1992, *Breaking the Boundaries: Towards a Feminist Green Socialism*, Virago, London

Mendlovitz, S. and Walker, R. (eds), 1987, *Towards a Just World Peace: Perspectives from Social Movements*, Butterworths, London

Mills, C.W., 1970, *The Sociological Imagination*, Penguin, Harmondsworth

Mishra, R., 1981, *Society and Social Policy: Theories and Practice of Social Welfare*, Macmillan, London

Mishra, R., 1984, *The Welfare State in Crisis*, Wheatsheaf, Brighton

Morrow, R. and Brown, D., 1994, *Critical Theory and Methodology*, Sage, London

Moxley, D., 1989, *The Practice of Case Management*, Sage, California

Mullaly, R., 1993, *Structural Social Work: Ideology, Theory and Practice*, McClelland & Stewart, Toronto

Ornstein, R. and Ehrlich, P., 1989, *New World, New Mind*, Touchstone, New York

Pakulski, J., 1991, *Social Movements: The Politics of Protest*, Longman Cheshire, Melbourne

Palmer, S., 1983, 'Authority: An Essential Part of Practice', *Social Work*, vol. 28, no. 2

Pardeck, J., Murphy, J. and Choi, J., 1994, 'Some Implications of Postmodernism for Social Work Practice' *Social Work*, vol. 39, no. 4

Pascall, G., 1986, *Social Policy: A Feminist Analysis*, Tavistock, London

Payne, M., 1991, *Modern Social Work Theory: A Critical Introduction*, Macmillan, London

Pease, R., 1990, 'Towards Collaborative Research on Socialist Theory and Practice in Social Work', Petruchenia, J. and Thorpe R. (eds), *Social Change and Social Welfare Practice*, Hale & Iremonger, Sydney.

Philippine Alliance of Human Rights Advocates (PAHRA), 1995, *Empowering People for Genuine Development Through Human Rights Education*, Proceedings of First Asia-Pacific Social

Workers' Consultation on Human Rights and Development, Quezon City, Philippines

Pierson, C., 1991, *Beyond the Welfare State?* Polity Press, Cambridge

Plumwood, V., 1993, *Feminism and the Mastery of Nature*, Routledge, London

Polsky, A., 1991, *The Rise of the Therapeutic State*, Princeton University Press, Princeton

Pusey, M., 1987, *Jürgen Habermas*, Routledge, London

Pusey, M., 1991, *Economic Rationalism in Canberra*, Cambridge University Press, Cambridge

Rabinow, P. (ed), 1984, *The Foucault Reader*, Penguin, London

Ragg, N., 1977, *People Not Cases: A Philosophical Approach to Social Work*, Routledge, London

Raif, N. and Shore, B., 1993, *Advanced Case Management: New Strategies for the Nineties*, Sage, California

Ray, L., 1993, *Rethinking Critical Theory: Emancipation in the Age of Global Social Movements*, Sage, London

Rees, S., 1991, *Achieving Power: Practice and Policy in Social Welfare*, Allen & Unwin, Sydney

Rees, S., 1994, 'Interpreting and Defining Humanity' *Advances in Social Work and Welfare Education*, UWA, Perth

Rees, S., 1995, 'Defining and Attaining Humanity' Rees, S. and Rodley, G. (eds), *The Human Costs of Managerialism: Advocating the Recovery of Humanity*, Pluto Press, Leichardt

Rees, S., Rodley, G. and Stilwell, F. (eds), 1993, *Beyond the Market: Alternatives to Economic Rationaism*, Pluto Press, Leichardt

Rees, S. and Rodley, G. (eds), 1995, The *Human Costs of Managerialism: Advocating the Recovery of Humanity*, Pluto Press, Leichardt

Reisman, B., 1986 'Management Theory and Agency Management: A New Compatibility', *Social Casework*, vol. 67, no. 4

Repo, M., 1977, 'Organising "The Poor"—Against the Working Class', Cowley, J., Kaye, A., Mayo, M. and Thompson, M. (eds), *Community or Class Struggle?*, Stage 1, London

Reynolds, B., 1942, *Learning and Teaching in the Practice of Social Work*, Russell & Russell, New York

Rojek, C., Peacock G. and Collins, S., 1988, *Social Work and Received Ideas*, Routledge, London

Rose, M., 1991, *The Post-Modern and the Post-Industrial: A Critical Analysis*, Cambridge University Press, Cambridge

Rose, S., 1992, *Case Management and Social Work Practice*, Longman, New York

Rosenau, P., 1992, *Post-Modernism and the Social Sciences*, Princeton University Press, Princeton

Rothfield, P., 1991, 'Alternative Epistemologies, Politics and Feminism', *Social Analysis*, vol. 30

Rouse, R., 1994, ' Power/Knowledge' in G. Gutting (ed), *The Cambridge Companion to Foucault*, Cambridge University Press, Cambridge

Said, E., 1994, *Representations of the Intellectual: the 1993 Reith Lectures*, Vintage, London

Sanzenbach, P., 1989, 'Religion and Social Work: It's Not That Simple' *Social Casework*, vol. 20, no. 9

Saunders, P., 1994, *Welfare and Inequality: National and International Perspectives on the Australian Welfare State*, Cambridge University Press, Melbourne

Schon, D., 1987, *Educating the Reflective Practitioner: Toward a New Design for Teaching and Learning in the Professions*, Jossey-Bass, San Francisco

Seabrook, J., 1993a, *Pioneers of Change: Experiments in Creating a Humane Society*, New Society Publishers, Philadelphia

Seabrook, J., 1993b, *Victims of Development: Resistance and Alternatives*, Verso, London

Seidman, S (ed.) 1994, *The Postmodern Turn: New Perspectives on Social Theory*, Cambridge University Press, Cambridge

Shields, K., 1991, *In the Tiger's Mouth: An Empowerment Guide for Social Action*, Millennium Books, Newtown, NSW

Simons, J., 1995, *Foucault and the Political*, Routledge, London

Skidmore, R., 1983, *Social Work Administration: Dynamic Management and Human Relationships*, Prentice-Hall, Englewood Cliffs, NJ

Solas, J., 1994, *The (De)Construction of Educational Practice in Social Work*, Avebury, Aldershot

Solondz, K, 1995, 'The Cost of Efficiency' Rees, S. and Rodley, G. (eds), *The Human Costs of Managerialism: Advocating the Recovery of Humanity*, Pluto Press, Leichardt

Stilwell, F., 1993, *Economic Inequality: Who Gets What in Australia?* Pluto Press, Leichardt

Stretton, H., 1987, *Political Essays*, Georgian House, Melbourne

Tawney, R.H., 1964, *Equality*, 5th ed., Unwin, London

Taylor-Gooby, P., 1993, *Postmodernism and Social Policy: A Great Leap Backwards?* Social Policy Research Centre Discussion Paper no. 45, University of NSW

Taylor-Gooby, P. and Dale, J., 1985, *Social Theory and Social Welfare*, Edward Arnold, London

Tesoriero, F. and Verity, F., 1993, 'Towards Citizen Control and Social Justice in a Disadvantaged Community' *Australian Social Work*, vol. 49, no. 1

Thompson, N., 1995, *Theory and Practice in Health and Social Welfare*, Open University Press, Buckingham

Throssell, H. (ed), 1975, *Social Work: Radical Essays*, University of Queensland Press, St Lucia

217

Titmuss, R., 1968, *Commitment to Welfare*, Allen & Unwin, London

Titmuss, R., 1974, *Social Policy: An Introduction*, Allen & Unwin, London

Titmuss, R., 1976, *Essays on the Welfare State*, 3rd ed., George Allen & Unwin, London

Tomlinson, J., 1977, *Is Band-aid Social Work Enough?*, Wobbly Press, Darwin

Towle, C., 1965, *Common Human Needs*, National Association of Social Workers, New York

Trainer, E., 1985, *Abandon Affluence*, Zed Books, London

Trainer, E., 1989, *Developed to Death: Rethinking World Development*, Green Print, London

Ward, C., 1988, *Anarchy in Action*, Freedom Press, London

Weeks, W., 1994, *Women Working Together: Lessons from Feminist Women's Services*, Longman, Melbourne

White, S., (ed) 1995, *The Cambridge Companion to Habermas*, Cambridge University Press, Cambridge

Wilding, P., 1982, *Professional Power and Social Welfare*, Routledge & Kegan Paul, London

Wilensky, H. and Lebeaux, C., 1965, *Industrial Society and Social Welfare*, 2nd ed. Free Press, New York

Wilkes, R. 1981, *Social Work With Undervalued Groups*, Tavistock, London

Woodroofe, K., 1962, *From Charity to Social Work in England and the United States*, University of Toronto Press, Toronto

Index

privatisation 14, 27, 32, 34, 53, 55,
58, 68, 82
problem posing and problem
solving 137, 179–180
production of welfare 49
productivity 14
professionalism 7–8, 49, 53, 55,
56–57, 71–74, 82–83, 142–146,
153–154, 156–157, 161–163,
169
promotion 42
psychoanalytic tradition 46
public sector 15, 65, 67, 159
purchase of service 14, 66, 70
Pusey, M. 15, 61, 65, 67, 134, 158

quality of life 14–15

Rabinow, P. 78, 128
race 41, 91, 95, 98, 106, 108, 117,
127, 165, 178
radical social work 4, 40, 60, 96,
98, 127–129, 132, 140, 175–
180, 190, 198, 202–203
Ragg, N. 46, 80, 100, 101, 117
Raif, N. 66
rationality 18–20, 23, 45, 63, 80, 165
Ray, L. 129
Red Cross 109, 191
reflexive practice 139
reframing 140, 180, 189
Rees, S. 2, 14, 15, 16, 31, 42, 44,
46, 55, 61, 64, 69, 72, 74, 91,
100, 155, 177, 182
Reisman, B. 67
relativism 117–121, 123, 132, 141
religion 10, 90, 101
Renaissance, the 101
Repo, M. 176
repression 31–34
restructuring 29
Reynolds, B. 176
Rodley, G. 2, 14, 15, 16, 31, 55,
61, 64, 69, 155

Rojek, C. 128
Rose, M. 85
Rose, S. 66
Rosenau, P. 88
Rothfield, P. 128
Rouse, R. 78
Rwanda 92, 108

Said, E. W. 188, 190
Sanzenbach, P. 9, 10
Saunders, P. 6, 13, 15
Schon, D. 139
Seabrook, J. 194
secular tradition 9–11
Seidman, S. 85
self-determination 63, 64, 65
self-help groups 167, 168, 206
services 4–5, 50, 149
settlement houses 3, 57
sexuality 95, 98
Shakespeare, William 115, 116
Shields, K. 96
Shore, B. 66
Shostakovich, Dmitri 115
Simons, J. 78, 103
single system design 45
Skidmore, R. 65
skills 11–12, 150, 168, 185
social action 33, 167
social justice 71, 72, 91, 92, 96,
99, 104, 106, 109, 118, 122,
128, 136
social movements 37, 57, 91, 96,
106, 184–185, 187, 203
social problems 5
social work and other professions
2, 34, 72, 155–156
social work education 8–9, 26, 60,
72, 155, 170–171, 197–202
socialism 40, 75, 96, 176
Solas, J. 85, 128, 177
Solondz, H. 63
South Africa 107
specialisation 8–9